*Praise for*

# waiting

"Ginsberg's book successfully weaves examples from her twenty years as a waitress with explorations of the sociopolitical implications of the American class structure. Her triumph, in this book, is that she shows us how the beautiful and the base coexist. That tension is what makes the job, and the book, so compelling."

—*Portland Oregonian*

"A lively and insightful look into restaurants. . . . Ginsberg is such a charming and talented writer."

—*San Francisco Chronicle*

"Ginsberg writes positively but not Pollyannaishly and has told an attractive story about coping with a life that has been different than what she expected."

—*New York Times Book Review*

"As this account shows, there's a lot of life in the waiting game."

—*Business Week*

"This book is more than a saga about workplace woes. The better story is the one in which Ginsberg relives her personal struggle, waiting for her life to 'happen.'"

—*Associated Press*

"Funny and ultimately satisfying."

—*Entertainment Weekly*

"[Ginsberg's] poignant, gently written stories of waitressing are metaphors for life."

— *Dallas Morning News*

"[Ginsberg] tells the story with enough honesty and wry humor to connect with other people—especially women—who've made their living dealing with the infamous public."

— *Detroit Free Press*

"A knowing memoir. . . . [Ginsberg] is great on dining room debacles she's endured."

— *Seattle Times*

"Hilarious . . . colorful."

— *Hartford Courant*

"A lively, often funny tale."

— *Newsday*

"This book may inspire bored office workers to get out from behind their desks and step up to the tables. . . . The appealing style never wavers. . . . Those unfamiliar with restaurant jobs are in for an eye-opening treat."

— *Booklist*

"Conveys the unpredictability and humanity of this humble but essential work. . . . Ginsberg's more personal segments . . . portray an intelligent single mom, fiercely committed to her son, with worries about her potential as a writer and her future . . . concluding that . . . there is beauty and simplicity in the small acts of her work."

— *Publishers Weekly*

"[Ginsberg] presents . . . the sounds, the smells, the panic, the steamy drama of a busy kitchen."

—*Kirkus Reviews*

"Every time I go to a restaurant now, I think of what must be happening behind the scenes. Ginsberg's stories really stay with you. A great read from start to finish."

—*Janet Fitch, author of White Oleander*

"Debra Ginsberg's great gift is the quiet way she's able to point up the truths that reside in the innocent setting of the restaurant, in the harmless summer job that becomes the lifelong career, in the transitory exchanges that oftentimes have lasting effects, and in the character that develops while pursuing the philosophically complex occupation of *waiting*. This book reminds the reader that the waitress taking your order is also, maybe, noting much more with her pen. This is a strong debut."

—*Antonya Nelson, author of Nobody's Girl*

"The debut of a new and compelling writer is always a cause for celebration. Debra Ginsberg culls from a lifetime of waiting a humor, insight, and compassion that places her in the tradition of fine old tale-spinners. We have here, perhaps for the first time in literature, a true portrait of the demanding art of waiting on tables, from which Ginsberg has fashioned a wise, page-turning commentary on the human condition."

—*Kim Chernin, author of In My Mother's House*

waiting

# waiting

### the true confessions of a waitress

## debra ginsberg

### Perennial

*An Imprint of HarperCollinsPublishers*

A hardcover edition of this book was published in 2000 by HarperCollins Publishers.

HarperCollins books may be purchased for educational, business, or sales promotional use. For information please write: Special Markets Department, HarperCollins Publishers Inc., 10 East 53rd Street, New York, NY 10022.

First Perennial edition published 2001.

*Designed by Lindgren/Fuller Design*

The Library of Congress has catalogued the hardcover edition as follows:

Ginsberg, Debra.
    Waiting: the true confessions of a waitress / Debra Ginsberg.—1st ed.
      p. cm.
    ISBN 0-06-019479-0
      1. Ginsberg, Debra. 2. Waitresses—United States—Biography.
    I. Title.
    TX910.5.G56 G56 2000
    647.95'092–dc21
    [B]                                   99–089033

ISBN 0-06-093281-3 (pbk.)

01 02 03 04 05 ❖/RRD 10 9 8 7 6 5 4 3 2

For these Ginsbergs:
Mel, Rosalind, Maya, Lavander,
Bodine, Déja, and Blaze—
with my love

# 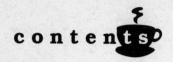contents

# acknowledgments

Although the act of writing is a solitary process, publishing a book is not. I had the invaluable support and help of many generous people both before and after *Waiting*, and I would like to offer my deep and heartfelt thanks to them now for all that was given:

My family for their love and support and for never letting me forget what is truly important.

The original champions of *Waiting*; my agent Amy Rennert who placed great faith in me from the outset and my editor Sally Kim, without whom I would surely still be waiting.

At HarperCollins, I would like to offer special thanks to the indefatigable Lisa Bullaro, who has an endless well of enthusiasm, and Marjorie Braman, who adopted *Waiting* after its hardcover publication and made good on her promise to love it as one of her own.

I am truly grateful for the overwhelming warmth and support I received from everyone in the San Diego literary community, especially Arthur Salm of the *San Diego Union-Tribune* and Carole Carden of Esmeralda Books who offered so much of both long before *Waiting* was even conceived.

Janell Cannon for regenerating the limbs.

All the servers I have known and continue to meet who have

shared their lives and their stories and who have become an indispensable part of *Waiting*.

Finally, belated but sincere thanks to Carl S. for taking all those tables and for always closing so that I could go home before it was too late.

# introduction

On a particularly hot and sticky night in August 1998, I stood in front of the display kitchen in the restaurant where I worked and waited for my food to appear. The cooks, sweating, frantic, and bad-tempered, shot me dirty looks.

"Table Five?" I questioned, smiling. "A lasagna and a spaghetti? Coming soon?" I shot a backward glance at Table Five. They were craning their necks as other waiters walked past their table with steaming plates. They were hungry, their water glasses were empty, and they were starting to get very foul looks on their faces. In the twenty minutes since I'd made their acquaintance, I'd learned that this particular couple were hashing out a divorce settlement and, for all intents and purposes, hated each other. I knew that if I didn't get them their food within five minutes, I was doomed. My tip would disappear. They'd ask to see the manager. There would be an ugly scene. Through no fault of my own, I would become another casualty of their divorce.

The cook muttered something bitter in Spanish. Although I didn't understand the exact meaning of the words, I hardly needed a translation to figure their intent. A recently hired coworker noticed my despair and shook his head.

"It's bad tonight," he said.

"Like every Saturday," I replied.

"Yeah?" he said. "How long have you been doing this?"

It took me a stunned moment to answer him. I took another look at Table Five. The soon-to-be-ex-husband made eye contact with me and raised his hands expectantly. I smiled and pointed to the kitchen. Turning back to my coworker, I said, "Twenty years. I've been doing this for exactly twenty years."

I watched his mouth drop open and wasn't sure which one of us was more horrified. My coworker, I realized, had not even been born by the summer of 1978 when I had my first job waiting on tables in a luncheonette.

"How old are you?" he asked, baffled.

"Does it matter?" I said, casting another desperate glance at the kitchen. "It's been twenty years and I'm still waiting."

The restaurant business has been part of my life since childhood. When I was a kid, both of my parents worked in the restaurants of several Catskill Mountain hotels in upstate New York, my father in the dining room and my mother in the bar. My mother's stint as a server didn't last very long at all. By all accounts, including her own, she was the worst cocktail waitress in the history of time. No matter who her customers were, my mother was never comfortable serving other people. Every time she approached a new table, she felt she should be sitting at it instead of waiting on it. Her service reached its nadir one night when a guest ordered a bottle of Pouilly-Fuissé. My mother placed the bottle and corkscrew on the table, asked the guest, "Can you open this?" and fled from the table. This was basically the end of her career as a waitress of any kind. My father, on the other hand, lasted considerably longer as a waiter.

Every night, he'd come home with stories of the various acts that still played the circuit of Brown's, The Concord, and Grossinger's. While most of these showpeople couldn't really be considered headliners any longer, I'd hear names I recognized and be moderately entertained.

Ever mindful of the sweet teeth in his family, my father also brought home treats. On Saturday nights, he'd arrive with a variety of confections wrapped in thick white napkins. We regularly sampled and fought over petits fours, chocolates, and gateaus, learning, in the process, how to tell apart the styles of different pastry chefs.

Far more intriguing than the sweets, however, were the stories my father told of the customers and the restaurant staff. After his shifts, he would sit at our big dining room table with my mother, drink coffee until late into the night, and discuss the denizens of this world while I listened avidly. There was Jerry, his demented busboy, who shouted, "Coffee? Coffee? Who wants coffee? Raise your hands." There was the chef who regularly threw ladles of mashed potatoes at upstart waiters. And there were a succession of elderly couples who shared every detail of their lives with my father. The most fascinating character was Carmen, a cocktail waitress gifted in the art of hair and makeup, who was casually drifting into the more lucrative business of prostitution.

My father's tales began to form a colorful quilt in my mind, each story its own square to be called up and viewed at will. Although I never visited any of the dining rooms my father worked in, I envisioned them and the minidramas that happened within them in great detail. My father's job was certainly a unique one in my peer group. My classmates all had fathers who disappeared into offices and performed nameless, faceless tasks. Not a single one of my friends had a parent who waited on tables for a living. None had heard any stories even remotely similar to the ones my father brought home.

Of course, there was also the money. My father came home with his pockets full of fives, tens, and twenties, which my mother would smooth out and pack away. Sometimes guests staying at the hotel for a week or longer would tip my father at the end of their stay. In those cases, he would bring home a stash of tiny manila envelopes and scatter them on our kitchen counter. Bulging with cash, these envelopes all had his first name carefully inscribed on the front, testimony to the level of familiarity between him and his customers. My father did quite well indeed. By 1978, he was supporting a family of five children quite comfortably on tips alone. This in itself was something I found quite impressive.

All in all, I viewed the whole concept of waiting tables as exciting, glamorous, and somewhat mysterious. It was a vision that would persist long into my own adulthood. And, although my father's stint as a waiter didn't last longer than a few years, he always maintained that it was "honest" work. And, hey, you couldn't beat the money for the hours you put in. Ultimately, every one of his four daughters would share this view. While my brother has always held table service in the same regard as my mother, my three sisters and I have all supported ourselves waiting tables for varying lengths of time (although I still hold the family record for duration).

When my parents rented a luncheonette the summer I turned sixteen, providing me with my first experience waiting tables, I was instantly hooked on the excitement, the hustle, and the money. The rest of the package—exhausted feet, customers bent on denigrating their waitress, sexist boneheaded managers, and occasional misanthropy—would come much later to form a love/hate relationship with what would ultimately become my living.

Perhaps if my father had been a fireman, car salesman, or lawyer, I would never have considered waiting on tables as a source of income, but I suspect I would have been drawn to it regardless. I have been a writer longer than I've been a waitress and, as such, a perpetual student of the human experience. My father's stories only confirmed what I'd already guessed: that I could only write what I knew and that I would know nothing without experiencing it directly. I wanted my own stories and saw no better way to collect them. This was a belief that has remained true for me even though the novelty of waiting has worn very thin. In fact, this notion is doubtless responsible for the fact that I've come back to waiting time and again for two decades.

Over those two decades, I have walked countless miles back and forth and have worn through enough shoes to stuff a landfill. I have met literally thousands of people, heard as many tales, and witnessed scenes of high drama and wild comedy. I have made many dear friends, men and women I couldn't have met at any other place but the table. I have even taken several nonwaitressing jobs offered by people I waited on. Through waiting, I met my son's father. It was again waiting that enabled me to support and raise my son as a single mother. In all these years of waiting, I have developed self-reliance, resilience, and the ability to manage high levels of stress, all of which have become invaluable life skills. Truly, there has never been a dull moment at the table. And the stories I have gathered there are colorful, passionate, absurd, and intimately human.

It is my turn, now, to share them.

But while all the events and tales in the following pages are absolutely true, my interpretation of them is entirely my own. And while I believe that many of my experiences will be familiar to any reader who has ever waited on tables or eaten in a restaurant, they are indelibly colored by my own opinions. Therefore, in order to protect the privacy of those who may not share my sensibilities, I have changed the names, identities, and (occasionally) locations of all who appear here save for myself and my immediate family. For those who find themselves here in some fashion, I can only say this: There are some experiences we all must share simply by virtue of being human. Waiting—in whatever form it takes—is one of them.

My coworker's innocent question on that Saturday night sparked a flood of memories. In sifting through them I realized that, while still relatively young, I have already lived a very interesting life, due in no small part to the job in question. In truth, I could not have predicted a better result when I first embarked on this journey.

And now, twenty years later, I am able to view the almost certain disaster of Table Five with a well-practiced trick.

I am, during these times, able to send myself into a brief fugue state. During this moment, the timpani of clattering plates and forks, the noise of conversation, yelled commands, espresso machines hissing, meats sizzling, frying, and roasting, and wineglasses clinking all fade almost to nothing. The restaurant takes on a strange out-of-focus glow and begins moving in slow motion. Time itself halts. Within this pocket, I am able to clear my mind of the fact that Table Six wants an olive, an onion, *and* a twist in his martini, that Table Seven wants the salad *after* the main course, and that I will have to apologize profusely to Table Five when and if their meals arrive. Instead, I know that I will soon be finished with this shift and I will go home with upward of one hundred dollars in cash. In less than two hours, I will be home and able to do whatever I please. As an invaluable bonus, I will also have another experience to add to a rich and varied store.

In the meantime, I'm just waiting.

# the luncheonette

**It's a very slow Friday night.** I've had precious few tables and the evening promises to be a bit of a wash. I check my watch for the tenth time. Only eight-thirty. Although the night drags interminably, I know better than to ask my manager to let me go home.

"You don't know," he'll say, "it could get busy. This is Friday night."

I know it won't get busy. The rush is over. Tomorrow he'll be complaining about skyrocketing labor costs. I fold napkins and wait. The hostess finally saunters over to one of my tables with another deuce. I've had nothing but couples sharing soup and salad tonight. My check average is going through the floor. When I cash out, my manager will complain about this too.

I approach the table and sense trouble immediately. Right off the bat, the drink order is problematic.

"I'll have the cabernet," she says.

"No, you don't want that," he says.

"Yes," she repeats firmly, "I do."

"You want the Chianti," he says, "it's very good here."

"I don't want the Chianti. You can have the Chianti."

"We'll have two cabernets," he says to me, smiling. He acts like he's trying to pacify her, and she looks pissed off already. Somehow, it's going to end up being my fault.

By the time I return with the wine, they're all geared up for a fight.

"I want the special linguini with extra mussels," she says.

"Instead of the shrimp?" I ask.

"No, I want the shrimp. But I also want extra mussels. Can you do that for me? I don't care, I'll pay extra. Whatever it costs." She's giving me a steely-eyed stare, just daring me to say no or even waver in my response.

"No problem," I tell her pointedly. "Would you care for a salad or appetizer?"

"I don't eat salad," she says. "Just the mussels. You're going to bring me the extra mussels, right?"

"Extra mussels," I repeat, "no problem." To convince her, I pull out my order pad and make a note. "What a bitch," I write and smile at her. I turn my attention to her date. "And for you, sir?"

"Let me tell you what I want," he says unctuously. This is a phrase that flags trouble as surely as a red cape in front of a bull. It means he's not even going to look at the menu and the dozens of entrees listed there. No, he's got something in his mind and he means for me to get it for him, whatever it is. Especially if it's not on the menu and we don't have it. Whether this is to impress his date, generally act like a big shot, or just to be a pest, I can't tell. He is, however, offering a challenge and setting up a dynamic between the three of us that will last for the duration of his meal. The game has begun and we're off and running.

"I want a shrimp scampi. You got anything like that?"

"You mean the large prawns?"

"Yes."

"Garlic and butter?"

"Yes."

"No," I tell him, "we don't have that. We only have the small shrimp. Sorry." I've picked up the gauntlet. Why should I make this easy? He's certainly not going to.

"Tell the chef to make something for me, then. Something like a shrimp scampi."

"Well, we really don't have any—"

"Just tell him." He smiles again and this time the smile says, "If you don't do what I say, I'm going to call the manager over and make a really big scene."

I take inventory of the situation. His date is pouting smugly. She's really enjoying this. He is a bit of a parody, wearing a gold pinkie ring, a heavy gold bracelet, and enough gold neck chains to choke a horse. When he speaks, he sounds like a bad imitation of Billy Crystal doing Fernando Lamas. He's got Witness Protection Program written all over him. She has a very pretty face, which is spoiled by an inch-thick layer of makeup. She's wearing very little jewelry and often clutches at her purse, which she's kept within reaching distance as if she might need to bolt at any second. Her body-hugging pantsuit is understated but looks expensive. The thought of getting into it with these two is suddenly exhausting. I just don't have the stomach for it tonight. And in the split second I stand there contemplating my next move, I change my mind about my entire plan. Why not give them what they want? It's not as if I don't have the time to go the extra mile for them. I decide I'll even go talk to the chef, despite possible risks to my own mental health. Their date is obviously not going that well. Perhaps, I think, I can help to make this a better evening for them.

"Just a second," I tell them, "I'll be right back."

I approach the chef, who is so bored on this slow night that he's removing the bones from a sea bass at tableside. Normally, he's not overly fond of appearing in front of customers.

"I need you," I whisper to him.

"Oh really?" he says, raising his eyebrows suggestively.

"Yes, really."

As soon as the sea bass has been sufficiently ripped to flaky shreds, the chef follows me to the table. My couple seems quite surprised to see him there.

"I've brought the chef out personally to speak to you," I tell them.

"Oh, this is wonderful," Mr. Gold Chains says. The chef is totally ingratiating, although I can tell he is barely containing his inherently sarcastic streak.

"I just want some shrimp scampi," Gold Chains says.

"Well, I don't have the large prawns," the chef says. "I have only the smaller ones, but I can make a plate with those if you want."

"Fantastic," Gold Chains says.

"So I make a plate with the shrimp and a little olive oil and garlic?"

"Maybe a little pasta."

"You want pasta as well?"

"I don't know. You decide. Yes, OK, pasta."

"You've got to give me a little more information," the chef says. "I can make it for you, but you have to tell me what you like."

They hash out the details a little longer while I watch. Finally the chef departs.

"He seems very nice," Gold Chains tells me.

"Tonight," I respond.

"Oh really, ha ha, he isn't like that all the time?"

"I'm just kidding," I say, smiling.

"Thank you for bringing him over," Gold Chains says.

"Yes," his date says acidly, "thank you."

They've gotten what they wanted. Everybody's happy. Life is wonderful.

"We'll have another glass of cabernet," Gold Chains tells me. The date shakes her head no and he overrides her again.

I have to wonder what the story is between these two. Their body language offers a few clues. They're sitting on the same side of the table, but she holds herself back from him, unconsciously shielding her prominent breasts with crossed arms. He leans toward her as she inches back, his arm slung over the back of her chair. There is a palpable tension between them. Judging from the proprietary tone he takes with her, this can't be their first date. Nor are they married. For one thing, her left fourth finger is bare. For another, married couples very rarely sit on the same side of the table. So, I'd guess third or fourth date. He seems to want to get her drunk. Another sign. Maybe they met through the personals.

Their dinners arrive shortly and I have to chuckle as I walk the plates over to them. For Gold Chains, the chef has prepared a barely modified version of a dish we already have on the menu. If the customer had bothered to look at said menu, he could have easily ordered this meal himself.

"Looks wonderful," Gold Chains says. Something has shifted in the relationship between Gold Chains and his date since I was last at the table. They seem to have come to some sort of tacit agreement. Her posture is more relaxed. He orders another glass of wine for himself after finishing hers.

"Tell the chef that this is wonderful," Gold Chains says. "Tell him I want to buy him a drink. Go, go tell him."

I leave dutifully and head to the kitchen, where the chef is busy poking his finger into several pounds of uncooked calamari.

"He loves it," I tell the chef.

"Of course he loves it," the chef says.

"He wants to buy you a drink."

"You know I don't drink," the chef tells me.

"He insists."

"Then order a bottle of Dom Pérignon and I'll share it with you after work."

"I don't think that's what he had in mind."

"Then charge him for the most expensive glass of wine we have and tell the bartender not to pour it."

"I can't do that, it's unethical."

The chef shrugs. "What do you want me to do? Tell him thank you, but no thank you."

"That works for me," I tell the chef.

For all their demands, Gold Chains and his date eat hardly any food. After a bite or two of her dinner, the date disappears into the ladies' room. I take the opportunity to check back with Gold Chains and make sure that his specially designed meal is satisfactory.

"Yes, it's wonderful," he says, "but let me tell you something." He beckons me to come closer, to lean over to him. "This is not the first time a chef comes over to my table," he says, blasting my face with his garlic breath. I stifle an involuntary gag reflex.

"They always come over and they always make me what I want," Gold Chains continues. "It's not such a big deal for the chef to come over. They can always do it for me. You should remember that."

"Right. Terrific," I tell him, "I'm glad it worked out for you." I hightail it away from the table. I'm thinking I should have taken the chef's advice. I should have charged this guy extra for everything. I should have added the glass of wine. There's no respect here. With one garlicky blast, Gold Chains has managed to defeat any altruistic intent I had toward him. He doesn't care that I'm going the extra mile for him. As far as he's concerned, the extra mile is included with the price of the meal. I probably don't even rate as a person.

I'm tired of trying to relate to people on a human level. A familiar feeling washes over me. Waiting on tables, I think, is surely a bizarre way to make a living. I remember a scene from *Deconstructing Harry,* the Woody Allen film I saw several months ago. Woody Allen's character is with a prostitute and he asks her how she manages to do the kind of work she does. The prostitute responds that it's better than waitressing. Woody Allen's character then goes on for a while about how every prostitute he's asked about the trade has had this response. Given this, he concludes that waitressing has to be the worst job in the world. I saw the film with two other waitresses. At first we laughed when we heard this interchange. Then we applauded. Woody makes an interesting point. Waitressing may not be the worst job in the world, but prostitution does seem to have more inherent honesty about it. My mother, queen of euphemistic phrases, defined *hooker* for me this way when I was about twelve years old: "A hooker is a woman who is nice to men for money." Really, I think to myself, is that so different from what I'm doing at this very moment?

Gold Chains motions for me to clear the plates. They'll think about dessert, he informs me. Maybe later they'll have some coffee. He snuggles up close to his date and begins whispering in her ear. I am no longer needed or wanted at the table. I suspect it's going to be a while before these two leave. I watch them from afar as I fold napkins and wait for a sign that they want something else. As I do, I reflect again on the strangeness of my job.

I was a teenager when I had my first waitressing job. Had anyone told me then that I'd still be hustling plates at the end of the millennium, I would have thought they were crazy. I can barely believe it now. There must be a reason, I tell myself, that I still show up for these shifts. A reason why I still play the kind of game I've played with Gold Chains, several times on a nightly basis.

As I stack the napkins beside me, I disengage myself from the chatter and hum of the restaurant. I begin a process of sorting and sifting through my memories that I've perfected over these years of waiting on tables. I flip through the colors and sounds of my past until I come to the scene I'm looking for. I stop there, on this particular frame of memory, and allow myself to experience it once more.

I turned sixteen in 1978. *Grease* was released for the first time. While none of my girlfriends would admit it, they all wanted to look like Olivia Newton-John after she put on those skinny black clothes. I was the only one I knew who thought Stockard Channing was sexier. At the very least, the character she played was much more interesting. But these were unpopular opinions and I kept them to myself.

I began hassling my father in the spring, telling him I wanted to get a job and work in the summer like all my friends. His response was predictable: "Why do you want to get a job?" he said. "You've got your whole life to work. Why don't you enjoy your freedom while you can?"

I didn't find my father's logic comforting. The thought of spending another sticky summer at the poolside of the Jewish Community Center, lacing my hair with lemon juice and Sun-In in order to achieve a perfect shade of blond, was beyond depressing. The previous year had been bad enough. Serial killer Son of Sam had been on the loose until August and I'd listened to anxious matrons hypothesizing about where he might strike next—"The last one was in Yonkers, you know, it's only a matter of time before he makes it up here. He could be here now." The reflected sunlight from their tanning panels was blinding (nobody gave a thought to skin cancer at that point), but it beat the sight of their pudgy fourteen-year-old sons doing cannonballs into the pool. Foreigner's "Cold As Ice" blared from the sound system several times daily. It was altogether an unpleasant memory.

Besides all of this, I was sadly behind all of my friends in valuable life experiences. Tenth grade had been very eventful for many of my peers. Valerie Grossman, for example, had conducted a forbidden affair with a Puerto Rican boyfriend and had actually gone all the way (several times). Christmas vacation found her trotting off to Planned Parenthood for a diaphragm after a much-whispered-about pregnancy scare. The boy I'd spent the whole year pining over was graduating and going into the army. I had a sense of life passing me by as I stood on the sidelines and watched. I needed to catch up. I needed some excitement. I needed a job.

After more nudging, my father struck a sort of compromise. "You want a job?" he said finally. "Well, I've got one for you. You can work in the luncheonette."

The luncheonette he spoke of was located in the middle of Maxman's Cottages, a bungalow colony. Along with hotels such as The Concord, Grossinger's, and Kutscher's, the bungalow colony was something of an institution in our city of Monticello in upstate New York. Most of the summer tenants made the two-hour drive up from the city en famille right after school let out, and settled in. The fathers usually went back down to the city to work during the week and left the wife and kids until the weekend. Some bungalow colonies actually had themes: vegetarian, for example, or Hassidic. Maxman's (which had seemed to have the sole theme of making as much money as possible from its renters) housed a diner, game room, "casino," two pools, and a grocery. After Labor Day, the whole thing shut down. The owners of Maxman's rented the bungalows and the diner out for the summer and stored enough nuts to last them through the frosty winter months. Many of the tenants had been coming up for years, effectively transporting their own neighborhoods upstate. While these makeshift communities enjoyed their peak in the 1950s and '60s, there were still hundreds throughout the Catskills in the late '70s.

Looking for a change of pace and wanting eventually to open their own restaurant, my parents had decided to rent the luncheonette for the summer. It wasn't quite a "real" job, I reckoned, since I'd be working for my parents, but it was close enough. The promise of adventure loomed large.

My father was very creative when it came to the menu. He devised daily $1.99 lunch specials for the kids who attended day camp in the community. One day it was a burger, fries, and a soda, another day it was grilled cheese sandwiches and pickles. After a few weeks, he tried new twists on old themes. After breakfast one morning, he instructed me to make a sign saying, "Today's Special: Las Vegas Hot Dogs." What would those be? we all wanted to know. As my father dumped the dogs into the deep fryer instead of cooking them on the flat grill, he proclaimed, "There you go, Las Vegas Hot Dogs. Come and get 'em."

The luncheonette had a beautiful old soda fountain that reminded my father of his childhood days in Brooklyn diners, so he taught me and my sister to make lime rickeys and egg creams (which contain neither eggs nor cream). We had an ancient milkshake machine in which my father made malteds. We served coffee and brewed Sanka. After a couple of weeks of trial and error, our basic menu was complete.

It took very little time to become acquainted with the denizens, most of whom were quite friendly and liked the idea of a family running the luncheonette. For me, the local color was made considerably brighter by the addition of a large group of teens around my own age. The girls were primarily a catty bunch, concerned mostly with their hair and their tans (with the possible exception of fifteen-year-old Lori Zucker, who gave impromptu seminars on the art of fellatio from one of the luncheonette's corner booths. "You should really learn how to do it," she would say, "you won't believe how much the boy likes it").

The boys, however, were a different story. To me, they all seemed like incredibly cool guys from the city who knew much more about life than I did. (My main source of information regarding love and romance at that point was *The Thorn Birds*, a book I'd read so many times it fell apart at the spine.) The first few weeks of summer saw old romances reignite and new ones form. I was a totally fresh face in the crowd and was, to my pleasure, immediately sized up as a potential girlfriend.

My burgeoning popularity with the lads at Maxman's didn't mean that their parents were any less demanding when it came to their meals. As one of the luncheonette's two waitresses (my sister Maya, thirteen at the time, was the other), I was the canary in the coal mine. My father preferred to remain behind the counter or in the kitchen. Nobody, he reckoned, was going to beat up on an innocent little sixteen-year-old. He was mistaken. For me, the luncheonette was a radical introduction into the vagaries of human nature as it pertained to service. Everybody who ate at the luncheonette was a regular. Everybody liked their meals just so and none were afraid to voice their opinions.

There was Mr. Grubman, for example, who loudly informed the community at large that he had a bypassed intestine. Mr. Grubman ate as if trying to find a spot in the *Guinness Book of Records*, yet the hefty Mr. Grubman could eat only certain items. Whole meat platters disappeared down his gullet, followed by whole cheese platters. "I need my protein," Mr. Grubman said. "You got any more of this?" My father was rarely able to keep up with Mr. Grubman's appetite.

Then there was little Ricky Scalini. Most mornings, Ricky hoisted himself atop a counter stool and, with the worldliness and inflections of a Scorsese character, demanded, "Gimme a bagel and coffee. Cream cheese." Ricky was four years old. Ricky's mother, Baby, sometimes accompanied her son. She chain-smoked and drank Tab. My father was anxious to please her because, he confided, they'd gone to the same high school. "She was a hitter," my father said.

By far the scariest character, however, was Sophie Zucker, grandmother of the sexually precocious Lori. The mountainous Mrs. Zucker ate in the luncheonette almost every day, but she really hit her stride on the weekends.

Saturday nights were our busiest. We worked until three o'clock Sunday morning. The owners of Maxman's booked fourth-rate Catskill comedians who showed up and gave incredibly weak sets. On Saturday nights, the last set ended well after midnight. We served food throughout the night, and after the show ended on a Saturday night, the luncheonette would fill up with a ravenous crowd who ate their way into the wee hours.

Since we were serving dinner while the shows were going on, we got to see the acts only in bits and pieces. One popular joke involved the comedian holding out his hand, fingers splayed. "Pick a finger," he told an audience member. "Wait," he continued, shaking his hand vigorously, "let me mix 'em up." The locals roared with laughter and ate our hamburgers, roast pork on garlic bread (a favorite among Jewish patrons interested in flaunting the laws of kashruth), chickens baked from my mother's memories, and submarine sandwiches. We served mostly in plastic baskets, but sometimes, on Saturday nights, we used real china.

Sophie Zucker was usually first in line for the roast pork on garlic bread, and every time she ate it, without fail, she called me over. I always approached her table with a sense of dread.

"Duhlink," she said in heavily accented English, "ask your fuhdder to put a little more meat on the samvich. Please, duhlink, look at dis." She held the sandwich open. It always seemed as if there was more than enough meat on the sandwich and on the towering Mrs. Zucker to feed a small country of starving children. Yet, somehow, there was never enough meat for Mrs. Zucker.

The first time this happened, I'd carried the sandwich back to my father in the kitchen, where he was sweating over Mr. Grubman's platters, and told him that the sandwich didn't meet Mrs. Zucker's needs.

"Bullshit," my father replied, "there's half a pig on that bread." He rearranged the sandwich with slightly more pork and sent it back out.

"No, no, duhlink," Mrs. Zucker said, raising her voice. She went off on a minitirade about how people should get their money's worth, how she wasn't going to pay for such a measly sandwich, how she wasn't going to be taken advantage of. The whole thing became very personal. "You should tell your fuhdder," she shouted. "Tell him!"

Mrs. Zucker terrified me and I had no doubt she could snap me in half like a twig had she wanted to. I had more trepidation, however, about facing my father with the sandwich again. But my father knew where his garlic bread was buttered. Mrs. Zucker got more meat on her sandwich that night. But every Saturday night until Labor Day, no matter what the sandwich, Mrs. Zucker demanded still more meat.

Serving in the luncheonette was much harder than I'd imagined. Pleasing my father was even more difficult. Although I would hesitate to call him a taskmaster, he was a perfectionist. And of course, he was much more exacting with his daughters than he would have been with a nonrelative. There was his attitude toward cantaloupes, for example. When he discovered that I'd wrapped a halved cantaloupe and stored it without removing the seeds, he gave me a fifteen-minute lecture on why the seeds should be removed as opposed to simply instructing me to take them out.

"Doesn't it make sense to take them out?" he asked. "Can't you see that this melon will rot faster if you leave these seeds in there?"

"I guess," I said.

"You guess? I don't think you understand this and I want to know why not, because if you don't understand, you're going to put another melon in the fridge with the seeds in and it's going to go bad and I'm going to be very upset about that because it's just a waste of good fruit."

For my father, the luncheonette was not an opportunity to have some summer fun and he wanted to make sure that I knew it was *work*. He wouldn't tolerate sloppiness of any kind and whatever we prepared had to go out looking as good as possible, cantaloupes included. My father also hated idle hands. It had taken us two weeks to scour the previous tenant's dirt from the interior of the luncheonette and shine it up the way my father wanted before we served that first cup of Sanka. After we opened for business, I spent hours polishing the counter and the soda fountain.

We all came home bone weary every night. Our dinner rushes on Friday and Saturday nights were exercises in endurance. My sister wasn't quite as adept at dealing with the long hours and constant running as my father and I. In fact, we could set our watches by her tearful interludes on Saturday nights. She'd start looking weepy, commence sniffing, and finally hit the wall and burst into tears and we'd know it was 11 P.M. I didn't mind the late hours, and the running produced an endorphin rush that would later become singularly addictive. It was the tough customers, the ones who sent back my father's meals and made my sister cry, who bothered the hell out out of me. Late at night, in the privacy of my room, I complained to my journal. It was too hard, I wrote, and I hated being bitched at and treated like an idiot.

I took complaints very personally, as if they were barbs directed specifically at me and my family. I couldn't understand why basic civilities seemed to be all but abandoned when people sat down to eat. Between my father's glowering looks when things weren't going smoothly and the lack of respect on the part of our customers, I began to think the summer was going to become more like an extended punishment than the adventure I had hoped for.

There was, however, a single factor that, by the middle of July, changed my entire attitude and made working at the luncheonette not only bearable but irresistible. That factor was Steve, the boldest and best looking of Maxman's eligible boys. I first noticed him when he walked by the luncheonette's windows, tossing his long hair and a handful of quarters in the air. He sat in a corner booth with a group of other boys, playing cards, plotting strategies to obtain beer, and shooting sidelong glances my way. At first, I was too shy to talk to him and merely smiled when he insisted his hamburgers be very well done and his french fries be "burnt." When he leaned over the counter and took my hand in his one afternoon, my heart began a crazy flutter.

Of all the strapping youths looking for a summer romance at Maxman's, Steve was the one who persisted the longest and most insistently in seeking my attention. He sat at the counter at the luncheonette every day, drinking Coke, eating his burnt fries, and cracking wise, until I agreed to take a swim with him on my break. He was a self-proclaimed "bad boy" from Long Island who dazzled me with tales of selling joints on the subway for pocket change. His reputation was only enhanced by Lori Zucker, who informed me, once Steve and I had become an item, "I don't know how far you go with boys, but let me tell you, if it's not very far you can forget about Steve." He had a dimpled chin and wore thick braided gold chains and shirts open to his waist. Like everyone else in the summer of 1978, his hair was feathered and he spent at least a half hour drying and styling it.

"You're so cute, it's unreal," he told me and I was hooked.

We made out in the indoor swimming pool and drew initialed hearts pierced with arrows over the game-room jukebox.

Like every other teenage couple that summer, we had our own song. Steve cared very little about this detail, so I chose G4, "You Belong to Me." Since I was on call for all three meals in the luncheonette, Steve spent a lot of time waiting for me to take breaks. He rose late and drank coffee in the mornings and played pinball through lunch. He'd stay up with me on Saturday nights as I worked, stealing me away for frequent make-out breaks on the paddleball courts. Sometimes he'd come in with his friends for dinner and they'd tease me when I came over to their table. No matter what meal I was serving, though, he was always there, smiling admiringly and whispering vaguely obscene comments as I passed by serving fruit plates and wiping down tables. Although I served breakfast and worked into lunch, my day didn't really begin until I glimpsed the sight of Steve walking through the door, tossing his quarters, and heard him say, "Morning, babe. When are you getting out of here today?"

Steve's mother, a flaming redhead with a Brenda Vaccaro voice, thought I was "adorable" and took several Polaroids of the two us posing, *Grease* style, at the pool. My father was definitely not as enamored with Steve. He kept a constant watchful eye on me, his eldest daughter, and grimaced every time he saw us flirting. To avoid confrontations with my father, Steve and I would hold hands under newspapers on the counter and sneak short kisses behind the soda fountain. Every time my father disappeared into the kitchen, we'd hurry to brush past each other to touch, however briefly. But one afternoon, my father came back to the luncheonette early after picking up some produce and found me sitting at a table next to Steve, who had his hand resting on my naked knee. I knew I was in for it when my father's gaze shot immediately to my leg. Steve yanked his hand back as if he'd been burned and I jumped up at the same time, but it was too late. My father was absolutely horrified and demanded that I "cool it with that boy" immediately. Of course, his disapproval added an element of the forbidden to the whole thing and made it infinitely more appealing.

As the summer progressed, I got better at the tableside parrying that was so integral to the job. I learned to carry more than one item at a time (although it would be many years before I could balance three plates on one arm while I carried a fourth in the other) and I learned to anticipate what our customers would order. I began receiving tips. Even Sophie Zucker left some crumpled dollar bills on her table after a meal.

(I also became aware of a fact that continues to be true. New Yorkers tip well. To this day, when I find a New Yorker seated at my table, I breathe a sigh of relief. No matter what the demands or how blunt the comments, I know there will be a nice reward waiting for me at the end.)

My liaison with Steve heated up as July moved into August. After one particularly late Saturday night, my family decided to spend the night at Maxman's instead of driving home. I snuck out with Steve and two other couples and we spent the hours until dawn sitting on a cliff overhanging the freeway. This kind of make-out party was old hat for Steve and his buddies, but for me it was the most daring and exciting thing I'd ever done. I watched the sun rise in slow streaks of gold on the horizon as Steve dozed on my shoulder and knew I'd be in deep trouble for staying out all night, but I couldn't have cared less at the moment. What I was doing just seemed so daring. The taste of that riskiness and its attendant freedom was truly sweet.

When I strolled into the luncheonette a few hours later (alone—I insisted that Steve not accompany me out of fear for *him*), my father was practically apoplectic. We had a tremendous fight over where I had been and what I had done, which ended with me tearfully shouting, "But I didn't do anything wrong!" My father didn't exactly forbid me to see Steve any longer, but disappearing with my boyfriend was no longer possible. My father and

I didn't speak to each other for two weeks, which made working together in the heat of the luncheonette quite unpleasant. (To my father's credit, he never confronted Steve about his misgivings, preferring to keep it strictly within the family, saving me from what would have been a supremely embarrassing scene.)

Naturally, this family feud only helped to make the relationship more intense, and as September crept into view, Steve accelerated his efforts to take it one step further. Although I dreaded to think where she'd gotten her information, it appeared that Lori Zucker's predictions were coming to pass. Tired of rounding the same two bases after six weeks, Steve sought creative arguments to entice me into going all the way. We'd soon be separated, he told me. He loved me, he said, didn't I love him, too? Finally, he added, he'd be gentle. Despite a healthy curiosity on my part, I took the lesson of Valerie Grossman to heart and remained clothed from the waist down. Steve persisted. This struggle reached a feverish pitch over the Labor Day weekend. Aware that Steve and I would shortly be torn asunder, my father (he wasn't heartless, after all) let me take Saturday night off so that I could spend it with Steve. While his parents enjoyed the last show of the season in the casino, Steve and I huddled together in his darkened bungalow. After an hour of endearments, persuasions, and passionate petting, I finally yielded.

"OK," I told Steve, "let's do it."

"You mean it?"

"I mean it," I said, wondering if I did.

Over the years, I've often wondered what happened to Steve in that moment because what he said next truly surprised me.

"No, I don't think so."

"What?"

"You're not ready," Steve said, "and I don't want your first time to be a bad experience. I can wait. I want to wait until you're ready."

Could he really be this sensitive, I wondered, or had his body been temporarily overtaken by an alien being? At any rate, I was astonished, amazed, and, from that moment forward, completely in love. I burst into tears of joy. Steve, too, was moved by his own gallantry and shed one or two of his own. We declared passionate and undying love for each other and then stumbled out into the brightness of the luncheonette, arms wrapped around each other. My father looked relieved that we'd emerged so early, and I helped close down dinner with a complacency that must have totally confused him.

In the last twenty years, I have rarely experienced moments such as the one I did that night in 1978. I had a devoted boyfriend who had just demonstrated his love for me in the most touching way I could have hoped for. My father was smiling at me, totally contented with my behavior for the first time all summer. Even my sister seemed unusually energetic and lively. I had everything I wanted and I was so happy I began weeping all over again. I felt I would live forever. Perhaps when one is sixteen this feeling is not such a difficult one to come by, but there have been precious few times since then when all seemed so right with the world and the future felt so full of life and promise. The color and bustle of the luncheonette were an integral part of all this, and it became, in my memory, forever fused with danger and delight, first love and triumph.

Over the next few days, we packed up the luncheonette and watched our regulars drift back to the city. My sister and I both received unexpected bonuses: many of our customers gave us chunks of cash for our devoted service throughout the summer. Sophie Zucker was among them.

School, when I returned the following week, seemed gray, uninviting, and terribly quiet. I missed the excitement horribly and spent the evenings writing down every moment of the previous two months in my journal. I also wrote Steve a series of long letters filled with yearning and declarations of love. When he proved to be a less than reliable correspondent, I turned my letters into short stories and folded them into notebooks at school, where they could be viewed over and over again.

My parents had quite a different reaction. My father spoke of going on a spiritual retreat after his experience running the luncheonette. In fact, he did something similar; nine months later we all moved to Oregon, a state considered so rural my friends couldn't even pronounce it properly. And after sweating over roast pork and chicken all summer, all seven members of my family became vegetarian.

Although Steve and I had sworn to remain close, we drifted out of touch within a few months. I've never seen him again and so he remains forever the cute boy in tight white pants, smiling into the lens of a Polaroid camera. As for Maxman's, it no longer exists. We had come into the luncheonette at the tail end of an era. Almost all of the bungalow colonies shut down and faded away shortly after.

I am jolted out of my reverie now by Gold Chains and his date, who are frantically waving me over to their table. Beside me is a stack of folded napkins a foot high. I've drifted far afield remembering the luncheonette. But I know once again why I am still here. There is the same underlying thrill of excitement and movement to this job now as when I was sixteen. To be sure, I have changed and the landscape is considerably different. I no longer feel I will live forever. Yet I can still remember what it felt like when every night was a new adventure. Gold Chains and his date are as much a part of these feelings as Sophie Zucker or even Steve. In the end, my relationships with all of these people (however short) are what have kept me coming back for more. There is still the thrill of a good challenge for me here. More important, perhaps, there is a certain romance inherent in making human connections.

As I head over to Gold Chains and his date, my attitude toward them shifts once again. They are my last table, and cashing them out will finally allow me to go home. When Gold Chains asks for the check (they are now in a tremendous hurry to leave), I am actually grateful. I don't even care what or if they tip. I've already written them off and moved on.

The tip, in fact, will be the last piece of this adventure. Will I be rewarded for my efforts? I suspect not. The check is fifty-four dollars and change. Gold Chains pays with a hundred-dollar bill (somehow I'm not surprised—he just doesn't look like the credit card type). I make change at the bar, which consists of a five-dollar bill and two twenties. I don't bother breaking the twenties down. As far as I'm concerned, the smart bet is on a five-dollar tip. So be it. From a distance, I watch Gold Chains take some money out of the check cover and push the remainder toward the edge of the table. It's my cue to come pick it up. After waiting a decent interval, I do just that.

"Thanks again," Gold Chains tells me.

"Thank *you*," I respond.

I wait until I'm out of view to open the check cover and look at the tip. Nestled there safely is one crisp twenty-dollar bill.

# tipping
# (it's not a city in china)

**My last year of high school** was an exercise in homogenized boredom. In the spring of my junior year, my family moved from upstate New York to a suburban area outside Portland, Oregon. It was pretty and it was green, but I found absolutely nothing to connect with in my new school or my new classmates. I'd gone from a scrappy, decidedly multicultural environment to one that very closely resembled Ira Levin's Stepford. Everyone at my new school, it seemed, was given a car for his or her seventeenth birthday. The highest social achievement for boys was a spot on the football team. For girls, it was the pep squad. When, inexplicably, the Drama Department decided to stage *Fiddler on the Roof* as their musical, the cast was made up of blond, blue-eyed cheerleaders and football players who had tremendous trouble pronouncing the names of the characters. My sister, who played the actual fiddler, was the sole Jewish cast member.

I felt extremely out of place in this environment and made no lasting friends. I felt I was in a state of suspended animation

for much of my last year in high school. In my journal, which
had become my best and closest confidant, I ended almost every
entry by whining that I was waiting, eternally it seemed, for my
life to really begin.

Instead of participating in after-school activities (not that
there were any for me), I decided to find a job. Since the luncheonette, my father had changed his tune about not wanting
me to work. He now thought it might be quite a good idea for
me to save money for college, where we all agreed I would be
going as soon as I graduated.

I spread several applications around the town we lived in
and received a few job offers. The one I decided to take was at
Petit Morsel: An Eatery, which was a new family-owned restaurant near my house. My first clue to the trouble that lay ahead
should have been the fact that the restaurant chose to advertise
itself as "an eatery." Any restaurant that feels the need to
instruct patrons that they are actually supposed to eat there is a
little frightening. *Eatery* also implies that the restaurant has
absolutely no idea what category their menu falls into. (Come
and eat here—we don't know what we're doing, but we know
you're supposed to put it in your face. Hey, it's an eatery, right?)
But, of course, I didn't know any of this at the time. I was just
happy to have a job.

Petit Morsel was very dark, in terms of both its design and
the mood of its owners, a young couple who took turns cooking,
cleaning, and managing. The tables were made of varnished tree
stumps, and the counter area, where guests ordered their food,
was framed by a series of heavy wooden beams. The ambience,
complemented by rough-hewn candles on the tables, was cave-
like. The menu followed along similar lines. Most of the dishes
contained either tofu, millet, or sprouts. Vegetarian fast food
was still considered fairly revolutionary in those days and had
none of the flair or lightness of the current "spa cuisine." And

so, despite their meatlessness, those plates weighed a ton once they were piled with this "healthy" fare.

The owners of Petit Morsel hired me grudgingly. They didn't really want to spend extra money on labor, but it was impossible for the two of them to do everything. I was interviewed by the wife, who made the job seem as unappealing as possible. "You'll have to do a lot of cleaning up," she said. "You'll be responsible for keeping all the tables wiped down and you'll have to carry lots of dishes." When I told her that this wouldn't be a problem, she sighed. "OK," she said, "then I guess you can start at the end of the week."

My job was to take orders at the counter and then deliver the food to the table when it came out. Because I went to school during the day, I could work only the dinner shift, which usually began at 5 P.M. and ended by 8 or 9 P.M. I rarely worked with the husband. Most often I worked alone with the wife. On those nights, she prepped and cooked all the meals and then washed all the dishes. Although I could see that she worked very hard, I found her to be an absolute misery. She was worse when her husband was around, bitching almost constantly about how horrible everything was. At least when he was absent, she frowned in silence.

After my second or third shift I became aware that Petit Morsel had a totally inadequate ventilation system. When I left the restaurant, the smell of fried tofu clung to me like white on rice. Fried food, I learned, is singularly smelly when its odors linger in the air or on an individual. I smelled so bad after my three or four hours there that my father, who usually picked me up from work, had serious qualms about even letting me sit in the car. He would hold his nose and complain the entire way home, saying things like "Don't they notice how it stinks in there? It's almost unnatural." My mother complained even louder when I walked in the door. She couldn't stand it, she claimed, and I was going to have to do something about it or quit the job. The compromise, such as it was, involved me shedding my clothes in the garage before I had a chance to pollute the house. I was treated like a walking biohazard, and while I can't exactly blame my family, their attitude didn't contribute to the rapidly dwindling appeal of my job.

Ultimately, though, it wasn't the bad ventilation or the debatable food that finally made me throw in the towel. It was, rather, the tipping situation. When I first started working at the restaurant, the owners informed me that the tips would most likely be nonexistent. They had placed a jar on the counter for patrons to toss in the odd dollar or change when they saw fit, but since there was no regular table service, they reckoned there would be no regular tips. The guests, however—at least the ones I waited on—had other ideas. The flow of cash was light when I first started working at Petit Morsel, but soon I started receiving rather generous tips, left on the table instead of in the tip jar. The first time I saw a five-dollar bill left under a plate, I actually thought the customer had made a mistake and left his change on the table. I've often speculated on the reasons why this happened. Perhaps the customers felt sorry for me. When the restaurant was busy, I ran around like a headless chicken, managing up to ten tables at a time. It was obvious that I got no support from my surly bosses, neither of whom could ever be accused of cracking a smile. Perhaps, too, the many families who came in to eat liked the way I treated their children. I've never been one of those waitresses who hated having kids at her tables. Even before I had a child of my own, I've always felt that kids are a little more interesting than adults and, as the eldest of five, understood that taking a passel of kids out to a restaurant wasn't always the easiest situation to handle. A final possibility was that I simply gave good service to these people and they sought to reward me for it (this option, so many years later, is still my favorite). Whatever the reason, after a week or two I was regularly stuffing bills into my apron pocket as I cleared and wiped down the tree stumps.

My joy in this newfound wealth, however, was short-lived.

My boss called me aside after my shift one evening and spoke to me as she chopped vegetables for the next day.

"It's come to our attention that you've been getting tips," she said sourly.

"Yes," I answered perkily, "people have been great. They must love the food."

"Well, anyway," she continued, "you're not supposed to be keeping those tips for yourself."

"I'm not?"

"We don't really have tipping at the table here. If you get a tip, you need to put it in the tip jar"—she gestured to the counter with her butcher knife—"and it will get divided up amongst all of us the next day. That way it's fair for everybody."

The "all of us" she referred to consisted of her (the owner), her husband (the owner), the day waitress (her sister), and myself. I had real difficulty conceiving how splitting my tips four ways with that group could be considered fair.

"But I think they mean for me to have those tips," I said weakly.

"Well, that's not the way we do it here," she said. "Since you didn't seem to understand that, you can keep what you collected tonight, but starting tomorrow, you need to put everything extra you get into the jar. Good night."

I was stunned. Everything I knew about truth, justice, and the American Way dictated that I should keep my tips. Had I fallen into a parallel universe where this was no longer the way things were done? When my father arrived to pick me up, I told him what had happened. He laughed the kind of mirthless but explosive laugh I'd come to know meant he thought a situation was particularly ridiculous.

"What, is she *insane?*" he said. "She wants you—a little
girl—to give your tips to her—the owner? Ha ha ha. That's
beyond absurd. Ha ha ha. I think she must have been kidding."
He rolled down the window to breathe in some fresh air since I
was starting to stink up the car. "You're not actually going to do
it, are you?" he asked.

My boss had put me in an awkward position. I was faced
with a couple of grim options. I could continue to keep my tips
as I received them, risk the wrath of my bosses, and possibly get
fired. If I did this, I'd have to watch over my shoulder constantly
and feel like a fugitive. The other option was to tow the line and
dump all of my earnings into the tip jar. Somehow I couldn't
even visualize this scenario. The situation did seem, as my father
had put it, absurd. Although I'd had very little direct experience
working in restaurants at that point, I knew instinctively that
there was almost no point in donning an apron and schlepping
plates without the promise of a tip.

Waiters and waitresses come into the business for a variety
of reasons. How long they stay in it is also determined by a number of factors. But I can almost guarantee that all of them would
agree that while they are there, their major motivator is the tip.
Tips are not just a side perk. They are not an added bonus. For a
waiter or waitress, tipping is the raison d'être of a restaurant,
considered an absolute right by those on the receiving end. Thou
shalt not fuck with the tip. The tip is everything.

Tipping has a long and colorful history in this country. Although
the exact origins of tipping are lost to the distant past, there are
a couple of different theories on how it all began. The most commonly accepted tale is that tipping began in England hundreds of
years ago. In order to provide some motivation for faster service,
the story goes, coin-filled boxes were placed on the tables of

eighteenth-century coffeehouses (some say sixteenth century, but who's counting?) and marked with the words "to insure promptness" (or promptitude). Thus, the acronym TIP. There is some quibbling over the details of this particular theory. For one, acronyms themselves didn't exist until the twentieth century. For another, English etymology tells us that the the word *tip* was actually a medieval term meaning "give it to me" (although it sounds crass, this theory seems to hold the most weight, for me at least). Still others (who have time to think about these kinds of things) claim that tipping began in the Roman Empire—*stips* being Latin for "gift."

Regardless of which theory, if any, is the true one, the custom of tipping obviously found its way to the United States and remains, for better or worse, a firmly established social ritual. Public misunderstanding of exactly why, how much, or whether to tip leads to some very interesting interactions between patron and server. On a small scale, the customer literally holds the server's fate in his pocket. This imbues the customer with a certain amount of power as soon as he sits down at the table. And power, as the saying goes, corrupts. In a way, the server is immediately placed on the defensive. Her livelihood is not determined so much by whether or not she takes an order correctly, brings the food on time, or smiles often. Rather, she must gauge a customer's mood, pick up cues as to his background, and based on all of this, anticipate his needs and wants. The server is, effectively, the customer's private dancer for the two hours he sits at her table.

Food servers depend on tips for their living more than those in any other tipped profession. The reason for this is simple: waiters and waitresses are the only employees who can be exempt from the minimum wage. Although this varies from state to state, it is rare to find a restaurant that pays its servers *more* than the minimum wage. The theory for this is that servers will more than make up the difference with their tips. This win-win equation is further emphasized by the notion that should employers pay their servers adequately (and this would have to be a pretty penny to convince servers to put up with the vagaries of the business), they would have to raise the prices of their menu items to make up the cost, making dining out much less affordable. Tipping is still optional, after all. Unless a preset tip is worked into the bill (usually for large parties or banquets), the amount of extra cash a patron leaves at the end of a meal is up to him and based, supposedly, on the quality of service rendered. Sounds reasonable. However, there are many variables that inter-rupt a seamless implementation of this fairly simple notion.

One such variable is the tip-out policy. Almost every restau-rant I've worked in has required that servers tip out a certain per-centage of their tips to other workers. The tip-out where I work now is as follows: 15 percent to the busboy, 8 percent to the bar-tender, 5 percent to the hostess, 5 percent to the food expediter, and 2 percent to the extremely underpaid wretch who makes cof-fee drinks. The math is easy to do. In order to walk out the door with $100 in tips, I have to earn $155 (and when I do tip out, I am sure to have detractors, my busboy chief among them, who will claim they did all kinds of work for me that they didn't get paid for and curse me on the way out). On some nights my bus-boy, who services three waiters at a time, will actually make more than me (and this after he tells me, "Listen, I take care of you tonight, make all your tables happy. Twenny percen' tonight, *chap-parita*, OK?"). The bartender makes more than me every night.

The tip-out doesn't really end there. Because as we all know, one of the two sure things in this life is taxes—and we do pay them. Servers are required by law to report all their tips. Before the use of credit cards exploded (and I am actually old enough to remember such a time), waiters and waitresses barely declared anything. Sometime during the Bush administration, the IRS decided to crack down on these scofflaws (after all, everybody knows waiters make six-figure incomes, right?). I know several waiters who got busted for back taxes this way. Regardless of whether or not a server declares all of her tips, the government knows how much she has sold during the course of the year because her restaurant is required to report it. In the old days, 8 percent of what you'd sold was considered taxable income. That figure has since gone up. The last time I tried to calculate, it was hovering between 10 and 15 percent, but these days I prefer to give all my paperwork to an accountant and let *him* figure it out.

To illustrate how this all plays out, I'll offer an example. Say on a given night I sell $1,000 in food and beverages. Say it's been an average night and I've netted $150 in tips. After I tip out, I have $97 left in my pocket. But shortly I will owe more of that $97 to the IRS, and that will be subtracted from my hourly wage. In fact, the more I sell, the more I will owe, regardless of whether I've made any set percentage or not. If I am not tipped, or tipped badly, I will still owe a percentage of my sales. Guests who don't tip, therefore, are effectively *costing* their server money.

I am sure most diners are not aware of these complexities, nor should they be. Their responsibility is not to calculate how well their waitress is doing financially but rather to realize that tipping is a fact of dining (at least in this country) and deal with it accordingly. There are certain agreed-upon percentages at this point. On the East Coast 20 percent has become the norm but is still considered a good tip; less than 15 percent of the total bill implies that your service was lacking in some way (not liking the waitress's hairdo or eye makeup shouldn't really be a factor); 10 percent or less is just insulting and implies that you have been grievously wronged by your server. I have heard many servers say that they'd rather get nothing than a 5 or 10 percent tip. At least that way, they can lull themselves into believing that the diner just forgot.

There are some who steadfastly maintain that tipping is a form of extortion and refuse to do it on principle. In 1905, a large group of traveling salesmen revolted against the policy of tipping. Calling themselves the Anti-Tipping Society of America, this group actually managed to eliminate tipping in several states until anti-tipping laws were declared unconstitutional in 1919. Currently, there are a couple of national organizations that have selected tipping as their focus. Tippers International, founded in the late 1960s, is one such group. It seeks to educate members on how much to tip based on the particulars of the service. Those who join receive report cards they can leave at the table, grading the server's job performance and explaining the amount of the tip left. While this ratings system is probably preferable to a message of displeasure scrawled across a credit card slip, where the manager and owner can view it later and possibly discipline or fire the waiter, most servers still take umbrage at being told how to do their jobs by someone outside the business.

WANT (Wages And Not Tips) is a much more extreme group whose members leave business cards with their checks stating that they don't believe in tipping. According to this group, employers should pay their employees fairly and spare the customer the agony of trying to calculate and then fork over a tip. Get a life, I say. And watch your back on the way out of the restaurant because those who don't tip can expect unique repercussions from those they stiff.

I've had some bad tips in my career as a waitress. I have occasionally been left with several pennies on the table (the universal symbol for "We hated you") as well as being left with nothing at all. There isn't much one can do in the face of this kind of disaster. Part of the problem is that it all seems so personal (and often it is). In the places I've worked, management rarely backs up the waitstaff, nor does the waitstaff expect such support very often. In most restaurants, middle managers, drunk with what little power they have, make a lower annual salary than the waiters they police and really couldn't care less if a waiter gets stiffed. Usually, the recipient of a particularly bad tip can expect a gathering of his coworkers wherein everybody mourns the state of the world and curses the exiting diners.

In my restaurant, servers are expressly forbidden to demand a tip or even question the discretion of the guest. I have therefore witnessed some very colorful curses from my waiter friends upon the discovery of a bad tip. One particularly awful night, a waiter launched into a five-minute spiel in Italian, complete with hand gestures, which he punctuated by spitting on the ground. When I asked him what he had said, he told me he had wished a curse on the customer that involved the guest getting into his car, becoming lost and disoriented in the fog, and then plunging off a cliff into the ocean. He also wanted the customer to die a long, slow, extremely painful death and if, by chance, the customer had any children, they too should meet a similar fate. It was so detailed and so vehement, I actually got chills. Why would anyone risk this kind of vitriol? I asked myself. Could it really be worth saving a couple of dollars?

Occasionally, a waiter driven insane by his job will follow a customer out of the restaurant and demand justice. I watched a waitress do this once. It had been a very busy night and she'd been waiting on a group of ostentatiously wealthy young women who seemed determined to give her a hard time. The check was high and the waitress really worked hard. In the end, however, the women fled without tipping, taking the credit card receipt with them. The waitress followed them outside and began a heated debate. My coworkers and I watched from the bar, which had a large picture window facing out on the patio where they stood. We stood, bemused, until we saw one of the customers actually attack the waitress, pulling her hair and punching her.

"Hmm, catfight," mused the bartender, who disliked the waitress and refused to get involved. Finally, the managers pulled the waitress and the customer off each other. The end result? The lovely ladies got their dinner for free and the waitress sued (and lost) for assault and battery.

There is, too, the case of recurring bad tippers. Regulars who tip badly don't usually last very long. For one thing, one waiter after another refuses to wait on these people until they run through the entire staff. A couple who fits this profile comes into my restaurant now. Waiters scurry like rats off a sinking ship as soon as their faces appear at the door. Lately, these two have been forced to order from the chef while whatever sorry wretch has been assigned to them grudgingly fetches their bread basket. Tip-challenged customers who frequent the same spot get not only the worst service but leftover bread, dirty glasses, and plates that have been prodded at and sometimes eaten off. When a regular is high maintenance *and* a bad tipper, servers really lose it. And yes, I have seen servers spit in food and drinks. Occasionally, some kind soul will straighten the bad-tipping regular out as a public service and then adopt the customer as his own. The customer, believe it or not, is usually grateful and will reward that server (but only that server) accordingly.

My favorite bad-tipping memory, however, comes from Marcello, a waiter I worked with several years ago. Marcello claimed to be an Italian (although other Italians claimed that the way he spoke their language was barely intelligible) who grew up in Switzerland (there was very little proof of this) and had made his living largely through "import/export" (slang for just about anything illegal). Nobody could tell a joke worse than Marcello, and his punch lines were often so mangled that the humor would be in how badly he screwed them up. Well into the 1990s, Marcello showed up for employee meetings dressed like an extra from *GoodFellas,* wearing white jeans, shirts open to his waist, and white patent leather shoes. He was built like a very squat brick house and plowed through the dining room arms akimbo, mowing down just about everybody in sight. Marcello once slammed into me as I was carrying two mixed salads. He hit me so hard that the salads went flying, smashing on the tile in an explosion of glass, lettuce, and tomatoes, and knocked the wind out of me so completely it took ten minutes for me to catch my breath. At the time of Marcello's fall from grace in the restaurant, he claimed to be studying law at a school nobody had ever heard of. We assumed it was some sort of mail-order scam that would be exposed, sooner or later, on a weekly TV newsmagazine.

Marcello had been developing something of a bad attitude over a period of a few months. He was getting burned out and venting his frustration on whoever happened to be in his path. He started stealing desserts that other waiters had ordered and giving them to his tables in order to enhance his tips. He pretended to make mistakes on his drink orders at the bar and imbibed the results. He became very aggressive at the table and began getting complaints from the few customers who weren't afraid of him.

One night Marcello went through his usual drill, free desserts and the like, for a large party. He was counting on a fat tip, but he was out of luck and received something way below his expectations. Marcello proceeded to chase the customer out to the front of the restaurant and then, in full view of several patrons, loudly berated said customer for his penurious persuasion.

"I didn't tip on purpose," the customer shouted back. "You were rude and awful. You're an asshole, frankly."

"*Va fa'n culo!*" Marcello yelled. He then made the universal "up yours" gesture with his arm and fist and stalked off, muttering under his breath, "Call me an asshole? I'll kill you, motherfucker!"

The customer Marcello yelled at was a regular at the restaurant and was singularly unhappy. He, too, ended up getting his dinner on the house. Marcello was fired. Law student that he was, however, Marcello applied for unemployment benefits, claiming that he had been unjustly terminated. The case actually wound up in front of a judge, who told Marcello that telling a customer to fuck off was certainly grounds for termination. Marcello claimed that he never told the customer anything of the kind. *"Va fa'n culo,"* he claimed, was a form of greeting in Italy similar to, say, "Shalom." The judge turned to the general manager (also an Italian) who had fired Marcello and asked him if this was true. The GM replied, "Not in the part of Italy I come from. Where I come from it means 'fuck you.'" Marcello never received unemployment. Last we heard of him, he was doing "contract work" in Las Vegas.

Admittedly, I have never had an experience that rivals Marcello's. Generally, fear of losing my job keeps me from making any kind of fuss over a bad tip. Ultimately, I've found, it evens out. One table may leave me a lousy tip, but the one after it probably won't. There are other factors to take into consideration as well. Perhaps a particular table didn't anticipate the high prices and has come up short. Perhaps they're too drunk or confused to figure the correct percentage.

I waited on a three-generation family once who seemed to really be enjoying themselves. They had several dietary restrictions, so I ordered special dishes for them and recommended a couple of different wines. They took an interest in me and so I shared some details from my personal life with them. They were pleasant to wait on and they were very complimentary about the service. When I picked up the bill, however, I saw that they had written in a fifteen-dollar tip on a two-hundred-dollar tab. I was actually saddened more than upset over the low tip because I thought they'd really liked me. I spent the rest of the evening trying to figure out what I'd done wrong. A full week later, I was standing at the bar when I felt a tap on my shoulder. Turning around, I saw a woman from this same party.

"I'm so glad I found you," she said. "I'm very sorry about the tip we gave you last week. I didn't realize until we left how low it was. My husband told me to 'add fifteen' to the bill and I thought he meant fifteen dollars instead of fifteen percent. It's been bothering me all week because you were so nice to us. I wanted to give you this." She handed me a twenty-dollar bill and smiled.

While this type of scenario serves to reinforce one's faith in the human race, it is regrettably rare.

I have had two experiences that stand out as polar opposites on the tipping spectrum. Both occurred in the same restaurant. Viewed together, the two illustrate perfectly the peculiarity of the tipping system and its inherent contradictions.

The first involves a man who has since become a regular customer in my restaurant. On one of his first visits, however, he sat down with three other men in my section. They seemed a crusty lot and were fairly demanding, but I'd decided to try to make the most of it and chatted with them while I was at the table. Mr. X had an accent I recognized as coming from the country of my mother's birth. I asked him what city he was from and he confirmed that he'd grown up very near my mother's family. As the evening progressed, I learned that he was actually a boyhood chum of my uncle's. By dessert, we had discussed our families, traded stories, and marveled at how small the world was that we could end up meeting in such a way. When I presented the bill, I was confident that I'd be receiving quite a nice tip. In fact, they left nothing at all. Since I was sure there had been some mistake and because I felt I'd formed such a bond with Mr. X, I approached the table and asked them if their meal had been satisfactory and if they felt they received good service. They assured me that everything had been just fine.

"Well, you didn't leave me a tip," I said. "And I'm just wondering why."

"No, there's no tip," Mr. X barked. "Your prices are outrageous."

"I'm sorry, but they're not *my* prices," I said. "I don't have anything to do with that."

"Doesn't matter," Mr. X frowned. "There's no tip."

Several months later, I found myself working the cocktail area of the same restaurant. It had been a very quiet shift until a pro football player with the San Diego Chargers came in with a date. He ordered a bottle of Cristal, which was the highest ticket item on the menu. I chilled a couple of glasses for the two of them and set an ice bucket next to their table. We exchanged a few pleasantries while I opened the champagne and poured out two glasses. I asked if there was anything else I could do for them, and he told me that they were going to have dinner shortly so I could just cash him out. The bill came to about a hundred and fifty dollars. He paid with a credit card and wrote in a hundred-dollar tip. I thanked him profusely, but he waved me off, grinning broadly, and told me it was his pleasure.

I'm not sure that there is a way to adequately explain these types of extremes except to say that tipping itself creates a bizarre psychology. Consider these examples, if you will.

After assuring me throughout his dinner that everything was perfectly fine, a customer of mine once left me a very low tip. He also left me a note explaining why. I am including it here in all its glory (which is to say with all its unintelligible language and spelling errors intact).

*This 10% tip was given due to the servis was good but not up to stades. The plates should have been taken by the busboy. The crumbs cleaned at the end of the meal and small things like a 'marrow fork' given with the Osobouco. Thank you for your attention to this items and your tip will be 18–22% of the Bill. I hope this helps.*

It helped, all right. I've rarely had such a good laugh. This note, which I have kept for many years, completely made up for the lack of tip. In spades.

Going from the ridiculous to the sublime, there is the tale of my friend Lucy. One night, in her exclusive high-end restaurant, Lucy waited on a man who told her, "I'll give you fifty dollars right now if you can tell me which song this line comes from: 'Say, can I have some of your purple berries.'" Lucy knew immediately and told her customer, who responded by jumping up with joy. She was the first waitress who had known, he claimed, and he'd asked every server who had ever waited on him. It was, he said, an absolute triumph. Did he give Lucy the fifty dollars? Indeed he did, plus an additional fifteen as a "regular" tip.

Scientific studies on tipping (and there have been several) say that servers can increase their tips by touching a patron lightly on the shoulder, writing "thank you" on the check, or introducing themselves by name. But anyone who has waited tables longer than a few months knows that a controlled study of something as wildly variable as tipping has little validity. Every diner is different. Some are impossible to please and would leave a lousy tip even if their waitress offered them a full body massage, never mind a light touch on the shoulder. Others will tip high if their server just leaves them alone and remains invisible. The fact that there is no way of telling which way it's going to go with a particular table is part of the challenge and excitement of waiting. Natural disasters and lazy busboys notwithstanding, how I fare on a particular table, night, or week is entirely up to me and my ability to mold myself to the customer.

Servers dislike being punished, certainly, but they also feel uneasy being rewarded unjustly. I can recall plenty of instances where waitresses receiving exorbitant tips have approached customers and asked if they really meant to leave so much money. It's a way of getting affirmation (because hardly anyone errs on the side of too much) for a job well done. And perhaps because financial success at this job does require living by one's wits, waiters (even those who swear that they're quitting at the end of the shift) want and need to take pride in what they do.

Unfortunately, this very philosophy leads to the formation of certain prejudices on the part of waiters and waitresses everywhere. The same radar that allows a seasoned waiter to know what a particular customer needs also cues him to anticipate the amount of a tip based on a patron's gender, age, profession, and nationality.

For several years I've worked in a city that thrives on a healthy tourist trade. The restaurants here regularly serve people from all over the world as well as a large group of (mostly moneyed) locals. Ask any waiter in my restaurant to describe his ideal table and he'll tell you "four businessmen in suits." Preferably stockbrokers from New York. The worst? Probably a party of Frenchwomen with children in tow. For better or worse, customers are instantly categorized as soon as the waiter approaches the table (sometimes even earlier). Every waiter and waitress I've worked beside agrees that almost everyone from the East Coast can be counted on for a good tip. They also agree that Europeans are the very worst tippers. I've actually seen fights break out over which country, France or Germany, has the cheapest diners.

(Of course, in Europe, the service is included in the bill, so the argument can be made that these guests are unaware that they are supposed to tip in this country. However, the level of sophistication among our European patrons implies that they are, in fact, aware of this American custom and simply choose to feign ignorance.)

As far as gender goes, there are some unwritten rules that almost always apply. Men (unfortunately this really is true) usually tip better than women. And men tip pretty waitresses best of all. This is probably due to complex psychological reasons best not gotten into here. There is one customer in particular, a regular diner in my restaurant, who becomes enraged if he sees a male waiter at his table. "Get me a girl," he always says. "I want a girl to wait on me." Women (at least in my experience) tip lightly in general, but tip waitresses worse than waiters. I have given away countless tables to my male coworkers upon encountering unbridled hostility the minute I approached a table of women. The younger the women, the tougher they are to wait on and the lower the tip at the end of the meal. I swear I have actually heard hissing at some of these tables when my back was turned. Frankly, I can do without these women, who threaten my fragile belief in universal sisterhood. I'd much rather give up the table and let them torture a waiter for two hours. Incidentally, I am not alone in my observations of gender-based tipping policies. Those silly studies, already mentioned, back me up completely.

Finally, there is one type of customer who transcends all boundaries of gender, age, and nationality. That customer is a fellow server. When waiters and waitresses dine out, they can always expect exemplary service. Who but a fellow waiter can understand better that the kitchen is slow and that the specials have run out at 7:30 P.M.? Who else can relate to the fact that you've got an obnoxious party of six bent on making you work like a slave for every penny of the tip they might not leave? In our restaurant, coworkers receive better service than celebrities. In addition, they can count on getting the straight dope on what dishes are of debatable quality that evening and what looks good. Often, the server will convince the manager to buy dessert or the chef to make up a plate of appetizers. Waiters from other restaurants also get plenty of attention and often commiserate on the state of the business. An extremely generous tip at the end of such a meal goes beyond professional courtesy, it reflects a deep emotional bond. This expectation does generate a certain amount of pressure, for as any server will attest, waiters who stiff other waiters have a special spot in hell marked just for them.

I have been on the receiving end of waiter prejudice several times and I don't enjoy the feeling. I have a friend I visit several times a year and we always pick a new restaurant in which to eat. Both of us look younger than we are and both of us tend to dress casually. My friend is an eccentric genius type who is very successful in his field. Having been forced to wear vests and wingtips in the early part of his career, he now actively dresses down. I never identify myself as a waitress when we go out and I've been amazed at how many times our server checks us out and frowns disapprovingly. Sometimes we get service that can only be described as spotty, and I know it's based on this initial impression. My favorite part of this game is when the check comes and my friend pulls out his Platinum American Express card and lays it on the table. There is invariably a look of shock and dismay on the server's face when he realizes his misjudgment. If we've been treated really badly, my friend will hand me the check and say, "You decide what to tip." Then he'll turn to the server, gesture to me, and say, "She's a waitress." Naturally, neither my friend nor I ever leave less than a 20 percent tip. That would be to needlessly tempt fate.

These experiences have taught me that pigeonholing any customer before the end of the meal is a dangerous game. Even if the past dictates that a party of Australian surfers will probably leave a handful of change on the table, you just never know. There is a lottery aspect to the whole thing. Again, this is part of the job's challenge and one of its joys as well as one of its pitfalls. This is also why so many waiters and waitresses dislike preset tips, despite the fact that such tips remove a certain anxiety from the process. Not only is there no incentive to excel when the tip has already been determined but there is no possibility of receiving a bonanza at the end. In short, the thrill is gone.

When my boss at Petit Morsel instructed me to surrender my tips to the common pool, I knew nothing of percentages, Tippers International, or the history of the gratuity. I knew only that those I waited on were thanking me, specifically, for taking care of them, and by doing so, they were acting in accordance with natural laws that had been in place long before my teenage existence. Really, after so long, not much has changed in my understanding of this very basic philosophy.

I continued working at Petit Morsel for a couple of weeks after my boss's ultimatum. During those shifts, I kept almost all of my tips, saving only a couple of dollars for the jar. I resented having to duck and hide my tips, especially when I felt it was so unjustified, and left the restaurant angry every night. Finally I quit in disgust. My family was extremely relieved. The whole experience left a bad taste in my mouth, which persisted until I left for college several months later.

A recent check confirmed that Petit Morsel is still in operation. Since it's been almost twenty years since I worked there, I am very curious about what the menu looks like now and how the staff functions. Is there still a community tip jar, I wonder, or do the servers get their due? When I decide to take a tour of my old stomping grounds, Petit Morsel will certainly be on the list. I plan to go prepared, ready to press a big fat tip into my waitress's hand.

# the back of the house

**In May of 1982,** I found myself disembarking from a Greyhound bus in the northwest corner of Wyoming. My clothes provided pitifully inadequate insulation against the blast of cold air that assaulted me. I looked at the place that was to be my home for the next three months. It was singularly uninviting. There was a foot of fresh snow on the ground. My very first thought was that I had made a terrible mistake. "What am I doing here?" I asked myself softly. Not surprisingly, there was nobody there to answer.

Several months earlier, I'd filled out an application for summer employment at Yellowstone National Park. Although this was the first I'd heard of it, many of the national parks advertised for employees through colleges and universities around the country. The draw was that in addition to getting paid to work in one of the most beautiful places in the country, room and board was thrown in and there was ample opportunity to explore the surroundings. In truth, the only reason I'd applied at all was because Ray, my boyfriend at the time, thought it would be a great idea for the two of us to work side by side in the great outdoors away from the pressures and rigors of school. A year ahead of me, he was getting ready to write his senior thesis and graduate in the spring of 1983. It was a last hurrah for him, a chance to revel in youth before entering the "real" world. Besides all of this, he considered himself something of an outdoorsman, an expert when it came to backpacking, rock climbing, or any activity that required some sort of convergence with nature. I couldn't have been more opposite in my thinking, but I wanted to get away as much as he did and, at the time, I wanted to be with him as well.

Ray prepped me for disappointment as we filled out our applications together. It was entirely possible, he claimed, that he would be accepted and I would be rejected. He had much better experience, he said, and the national parks probably had quotas on how many students they could hire from individual schools. There were spots on the application that allowed us to state our preferences as to where we would work. Ray listed the ranger station as his first pick. As I filled in the spot marked "Waitress, Dining Room," I realized he was probably right. I wouldn't get hired and he'd be off on a big adventure for the summer. I began to plan an alternative course of action.

By the time we heard back from Yellowstone, the spring term was almost over. Ray and I had gone through the sort of rapid relationship change inherent in youthful romances. In fact, we were in the process of an ugly, drawn-out breakup. His letter arrived first, a thin missive thanking him for applying but stating that they were unable to hire him. His keen disappointment deepened a few days later when I received a thick packet from Yellowstone welcoming me to the summer team and listing my assignment. "Kitchen Prep," it said.

"Well, maybe I won't go," I told Ray. "I don't really want to work in a kitchen."

"You have to go," he said bitterly. "Why would you pass up such a great opportunity? And it's not like you want to be with *me.*"

He wasn't entirely incorrect. Truth be told, part of the reason (well, actually most of the reason) that Ray and I were breaking up was because I had fallen hard for one of his best friends earlier in the year. In turn, the friend had rejected *me* in a most painful fashion while still allowing for just enough possibility that something might happen between the two of us in the future to drive me mad with longing. Ray and I had gone through rather an intense few months hashing all of this out, our confused feelings for each other further complicated by stringent academic demands. By the end of the semester, I found that despite having deep feelings for Ray, I was still in love with his friend. It was an impossible situation. I needed desperately to get away and sort out my muddled emotions. I wanted to be in a place where nobody knew me and where I would have to rely entirely on myself. Kitchen or no, Yellowstone seemed like the perfect place to do this.

I decided to take the job.

In the weeks before I left, as we divided up our pots, pans, and pathetic collection of furniture, all I heard from Ray was how he couldn't believe they hired me instead of him. He wasn't convinced our relationship was over and he believed he knew what was best for me. "You'll never make it there," he warned me. "You don't like hiking and you hate snow!"

"This job has nothing to do with snow" was my response.

My parents thought that working in Yellowstone was a great idea. They felt I'd grown entirely too dependent on Ray (they'd never gotten over the fact that I'd moved in with him against their express commands) and too immersed in the cloistered environment of school. I had been the first child to leave the house and go away to school (although school was only a half hour away, I didn't live at home and visited only on holidays), and the growing pains as I attempted to separate from my family had been particularly intense for my mother and father.

With all this psychological baggage packed securely along with several sticks of incense, a thick notepad, and some warm socks, I boarded a bus to Wyoming. The bus took a convoluted route to Yellowstone, driving first to Tacoma, through Montana, and down into "Big Sky" country. It took two days to get there. In Tacoma, I was befriended by a trucker on his way to Bozeman.

"Why don't I take you out for a sandwich when we get to Spokane?" he asked. "I know the city really well."

"OK," I agreed, although I sensed I probably shouldn't. But after all, I wondered, what could really happen? We were both captive on the bus, and he would be getting off before me. He didn't seem like the type to kidnap me and force me into slavery. This was to be the first of several leaps of faith I made on my journey.

At first it seemed as if overriding my instincts was the right thing to do. My trucker was personable and acted like a benevolent uncle. He bought me a grilled cheese sandwich in Spokane (we ate very near the bus station at my request—I wasn't a total idiot, after all) and told me about his life on the road, an ex-wife in Idaho, and a ten-year-old son he adored but didn't get to see very often. I drank coffee and he ordered beers for himself. By the time we reboarded the bus, I felt he was an old pal and something of a protector.

Deep into Montana, in the dark of night, my trucker decided to become more than a friend. I sat next to the window and he sat in the seat next to me. Gradually he edged closer and closer, until I was wedged against the glass. Since I was obviously not taking any of his hints to get cozy, he finally began pawing at me in earnest, sliding his hands along my legs first and then progressing up. When he made a move for my breast, I slapped his hand off and said, "Please don't do that."

"Aw, come on, honey," he said. "It's real dark. Nobody will see."

"No," I said and contemplated bursting into tears. I felt he'd let me down, somehow, and now I was going to have to hate him for the rest of the trip. Mostly, though, I just felt incredibly stupid for not anticipating this scenario. Because I felt totally responsible for getting myself, literally, into such a tight spot and because I was more than a little scared, I didn't move. I opted instead to continue fighting the trucker off in silence, moving his hands constantly and occasionally slapping him. He drifted off, finally, and fell across me. It took all the strength I had to shove him back to his side of the seat.

We pulled into Butte at dawn and the trucker woke up, yawned, and smiled over at me as if we'd shared a particularly pleasant and intimate night together.

"Buy you a cup of coffee?" he asked.

"No thanks," I said crisply and disembarked, losing myself in the diner where we stopped. When the bus pulled out forty minutes later, I changed my seat, opting to sit next to a very large woman who ate from a seemingly bottomless box of pastries. I watched the trucker get back on the bus, scan around for me, shrug, and sit down in his old seat. When he finally left the bus in Bozeman, I felt I was exhaling for the first time in hours.

There were a series of tour buses waiting at the Wyoming Greyhound station to take tourists into Yellowstone. In contrast to the bleak misery of the Greyhound, the driver of the next bus was relentlessly perky, pointing out areas of interest in a countryside that seemed so foreign to me it might as well have been on the moon. I paid little attention to the spiel until we passed an area that was carpeted with animal bones.

"Winter kill," explained the bus driver. "This is where they come to die."

Somehow, I couldn't help feeling that this was a bad omen.

By the time I arrived in the village of Lakeshore, I was tired, ratty, and overcome by the high altitude, which was making me light-headed. I checked into the main office and was processed like a piece of salmon caught in a net. The dormitories assigned to employees were small, gray, and depressing. When I hauled my belongings into my new room and laid them down on the creaking bed, I finally allowed myself a few tears of self-pity. I had the sinking feeling that Yellowstone was not going to be the haven I'd anticipated. I felt I'd started what was supposed to be an enriching experience on a sour note (I was having a little trouble banishing the trucker from my thoughts) and I wasn't sure I could bounce back in such forbidding territory. Moreover, instead of feeling wildly independent, I just felt unbearable lonely.

But again it occurred to me that my situation was a direct result of my own actions. Nobody had forced me to come to this land of summer snow and bleached bones. If it seemed grim, I had nobody to blame but myself. And of course, I had only just gotten there. I still didn't know what was behind Door Number Three. And so I donned a sweater and headed down to the hotel bar.

Employee dorms were single sex by floor, two to a room. My roommate, Susie, was a year older than me and from a very wealthy family in Virginia. Her parents, she said, were totally opposed to her coming to Wyoming. They considered it slumming of the highest order. She was engaged to a politician whom she claimed not to like very much but whose diamond engagement ring she displayed proudly on her left fourth finger. She needed to get away from him for a while, she said, and from the suffocating atmosphere of her home. She had been hired as a clerk at the front desk, a coveted position. I wondered who, exactly, determined the placement for all these summer employees and what kind of bizarre system was used to determine roommates. Not that it mattered, because my roommate and I got along pretty well, but the whole thing did seem fairly arbitrary.

There were a couple of days of orientation before we took our positions, and we were provided with a sheaf of rules and warnings to absorb. Hiking through the park was encouraged, but we were to watch for fresh bear droppings (it was bear season, after all), never keep food in our tents, and follow established and maintained trails. We were not to fraternize with tourists. Lights out at 11 P.M. We were forbidden to become physically involved with each other (I later discovered that this was one rule employees took particular pleasure in flaunting). Should we decide to leave the park before our allotted time was up, there were several forms to fill out and a lengthy exit interview. In short, it was a little like being in a work release program.

The pervasive sense of uneasiness I felt turned to despair on my first day at work. The kitchen was enormous, a cold masterwork of white tile and steel. My section, the pantry, was larger than most entire restaurant kitchens. Sound echoed off the walls and bounced off the floors. All the utensils, bowls, and pots were oversized jumbo appliances that dwarfed the humans using them. My first look around the kitchen convinced me that I was in some sort of surrealist nightmare. What struck me more than the physical surroundings of the kitchen, however, were the hierarchy and delicate balance of power within it. Before coming to Yellowstone, I'd worked in small family-owned restaurants of a decidedly casual nature. This was an entirely different story. There were literally dozens of employees in the kitchen and dining room, and each had a specific role to fulfill in these minisocieties. The kitchen was to be a very different kind of learning environment than the one I'd just left, but no less important in the long run. Although I was too busy contemplating my own fate at the time, observing and understanding the complicated structures of the kitchen and dining room would later prove to be valuable lessons indeed.

My introduction to the actual work involved being lined up with the other hapless pantry hires in front of our supervisor, an ageless giantess wielding a huge whisk. Smiling, she pulled a shrimp from a vast trough in front of her and stripped its back vein.

"Y'all gotta clean out this black stuff in the back," she said, "and y'all gotta do it right." She demonstrated the process on a few more shrimp. "Now we do a lot of shrimp down here, so y'all gotta be fast, too." Several of my coworkers were starting to look a little green around the gills. "Now I know I say 'y'all' a lot, but I'm tellin' y'all, I'm from Mississippi, and I'm gonna have y'all sayin' 'y'all' before I'm done with y'all."

Shrimp wasn't the only fleshy item we were responsible for in the pantry. We had to slice and prepare the vast storehouse of meat needed for all three meals. The meat slicer looked like a marginally updated version of the guillotine. No matter how hard I tried, I could not picture myself using it.

"Now y'all gotta be real careful usin' this baby," our supervisor said, stroking the killing steel surface. "I don't want none a y'all losin' no fingers while I'm here. Ain't nothin' uglier than a bloody fingertip in some poor guest's food."

"Um, excuse me," I piped in timidly. "I don't think I'll be able to use the slicer. I think I'm too, uh, short to reach it." I blushed crimson while my skyscraper of a supervisor looked me up and down.

"OK, then," she said disdainfully, "Little Bit here don't use the slicer." Then she turned to me and said, "You're gonna be on salads every day, then."

"Sure," I said, immeasurably relieved that I wouldn't have to touch the deadly meat machine. It was even worth the embarrassment of being called Little Bit by everyone in the kitchen from that moment on.

The salads, however, presented a problem all on their own. We were instructed on how to soak the lettuce in a preservative to keep it fresh throughout the day. The preservative came in a cannister marked with the caution that it should not be inhaled directly. I could feel my lungs shredding as I poured these granules into a vat of water. The lettuce was terrified into crispness after immersion in this chemical bath and was then fashioned into either a garden salad (with the addition of a sad wedge of tomato), a Cobb salad (with the addition of large slabs of processed cold meats and cheese), or a shrimp cocktail (complete with deveined shrimp, which seemed to regularly leap off the salad glasses in postmortem protest). Naturally, the salads required dressings. A perennial favorite was Thousand Island dressing, which we made by the tub. I have never been able to understand the appeal of Thousand Island dressing. A hideous combination of mayonnaise, ketchup, and pickle relish, this thick sauce has an unnaturally pinkish hue and a noxious odor to match. The addition of this dressing to any salad more or less ensures total obliteration of any natural flavors. I developed an allergy to ketchup then that persists to this day. Vegetable or no, I can't even smell it without my stomach turning.

Then there were the desserts. My favorites among the confections were the napoleons. Made with yard-long sheets of pastry dough layered with chocolate and vanilla pudding, these culinary miracles required the use of a mixer that was large enough to contain my entire body. I had to stand on a chair to reach into the mixer and had a coworker hold on to my legs so that I didn't fall in. Once all these items were prepared, they had to be stacked in individual dishes and placed on huge trays where the waiters and waitresses could grab them as they flew through the kitchen.

I was never tempted by any of the food I helped to prepare. Once I'd eliminated what would either kill me or alter my genetic structure, I was left with mashed potatoes (made from a powder, of course) and chocolate pudding. The employee meals, exercises in fat and starch, were even worse. By the time I left Yellowstone, I'd lost ten pounds.

Learning the basic tasks of my job took very little time. Soaking lettuce and mixing vats of pudding requires only so much skill. Once these things started becoming routine, I began noticing what else was going on around me in the kitchen (the "back of the house") and in the dining room (the "front of the house"). This kitchen had a hierarchy I would see repeated in every subsequent restaurant.

Allow me to illustrate.

Dishwashers are on the very bottom rung of the ladder, clinging, tenuously, for their lives. The dishwashing area in this particular kitchen was far removed from all other forms of life. Nobody ever saw the dishwashers, they were considered unclean, the untouchables, slaves of their own misfortune. As a result, they hardly ever spoke (at least not to anyone who wasn't also a dishwasher) and kept themselves as anonymous as possible. The irony, of course, comes in the fact that a restaurant simply cannot function without efficient dishwashers. Years later, I worked in a restaurant in which the dishwashers occasionally revolted and left their stations to go drink themselves into oblivion. Dirty dishes, glasses, and silverware stacked up until a large portion of the kitchen had been transformed into a miniature toxic waste dump. And then everything came to a complete standstill until the chef could convince some sorry knave to start scraping and rinsing.

In the Yellowstone kitchen, pantry workers were considered only one step up from dishwashers. Since pantry wasn't responsible for any "real" cooking, it didn't command very much respect. We didn't sweat over a hot line and turn out fifty plates at a time. We did not keep our faces in the fire. We were not real men, we were merely girls. In the kitchens I saw later, pantry workers were similarly denied respect, even when they were responsible for more than just preparation.

The chefs (or cooks—a not-so-subtle difference), at the top of the ladder, had their own pyramid of power. Line cooks (most often those with less experience, who got paid the least, never got to do any menu design, and were forced to prepare eggs every morning) were at the bottom, followed by sous chefs (who were just below executive chefs, got to do some menu planning, and were allowed to boss line cooks and other kitchen workers around), and then executive chefs (responsible for menu planning, design, ordering, and kitchen personnel). In contrast to the rest of the kitchen employees, all the cooks had previous experience preparing food. Some had been employed by the park for several years.

Chefs and cooks are an interesting breed. They work in a controlled frenzy, often producing mass quantities of food with individual specifications for each dish. They have a small space and a limited time frame in which to operate. They are responsible for producing food that is not merely edible but tantalizing and attractive. And they do all of this, literally, in the fire. I have worked with very few real chefs who didn't consider what they did an art form and who weren't truly disturbed if they turned out plates that were obviously below par. But most chefs receive very few accolades. They can't stroll around gathering compliments from the guests who eat their art. Instead, a chef has only the server as a link between him (or, rarely, her) and his "public." Unfortunately, servers are often too busy with their own problems (usually that their food is coming out too late) to care about the chef's efforts. In many cases, the chef is correct in assuming he is underappreciated. More often than not, I've seen a chef place a particularly beautiful dish on the line only to have the waitress cart it off without so much as a smile to acknowledge his efforts. Clashes between the chef and his crew and the waitstaff are therefore routine.

So it was no surprise that while there were some internecine wars among the cooks, they were united on one point: they hated the waitstaff. Waiters and waitresses were considered money-grubbing scum who had no clue to how hard the kitchen worked for them. In my long career as a waitress, I have seen variations on this theme but have never experienced its absence, whether the chef was a talented and experienced artist or a third-rate cook. At any rate, the cook's level of expertise matters not; if he wants to, he will make a waitress's life hell and no amount of skill on her part will save her. On the flip side, a waitress who gets on the cook's good side will invariably experience less stress and make a lot more money. I saw ample evidence of this at Yellowstone and have never forgotten it.

For as depressed as I was over my own job, I felt a deep, unmitigated pity for the waiters and waitresses, many of whom had no prior experience in a dining room. From my vantage point in the pantry, I watched them slam through the kitchen doors, frantic and sweating:

"Where's my oatmeal?"

"No, no, I wanted over easy, not scrambled!"

"Anybody seen my toast!?"

"I can't find the Thousand Island dressing!"

Full trays of food were dropped regularly. Many waitresses broke into tears on a daily basis.

As befitting our lowly station, we kept pretty quiet in the pantry, but the cooks were relentless, torturing the waitstaff at any opportunity. They were generally a scary lot, hardened by their service at the hotel. Singularly unfriendly and crude beyond anyone's expectations, these men made a game out of ignoring the waiters and harassing the waitresses. One popular trick (a crowd pleaser to this day) involved putting up a thermonuclear plate on the line and waiting for the waiter to touch it bare-handed. Invariably, after the waiter shrieked in pain, the cook would smile and say, "Careful, it's hot."

The cooks called the servers by number as the dishes came up, often delaying delivery of a particular order until the frenzied waitress gave up waiting for her food to come up and headed out to the dining room to apologize for the lateness of a meal. The moment her back reached the door, the cooks called her number and then berated her for not arriving at the line sooner. Server number nine, a lissome beauty from Tennessee and a particularly slow waitress, experienced this maneuver several times. In the middle of the lunch rush one day, her orders began stacking up and dying slowly in the window.

"Number Nine, pick up," a cook called. After a few minutes, he repeated the call. "Anyone seen number nine?" As if they'd preplanned it, all the cooks (and there were several behind the line) launched into a version of the Beatles' "Revolution Number 9," repeating, "Number Nine, Number Nine, Number Nine. . . ."

Number Nine never picked up her food. She had left the dining room, the park, and the state—the first of many to flee.

Of course, the cooks were not immune to the call of nature and many of them were wolfishly on the make. More than once, I walked into the cavernous cold storage unit and found a cook rubbing pelvises with a waitress. This, too, was a scenario I would see duplicated in various forms in the years to come.

The waitress-cook combination, however, is one of the few that allows the front of the house to fraternize freely with the back of the house. The waitstaff are part of their own unique power structure, one that resembles the feudal pyramids of medieval times. At the bottom of this pyramid are the busboys. Busboys have a symbiotic relationship with their servers. In a full-service restaurant, a waitress cannot perform her job without her handy slave cleaning her tables, delivering bread, and refilling water glasses. On the other hand, the busboy cannot make any kind of decent night's wage if his waitress's tables tip badly due to slow or inattentive service.

Hosts and hostesses are a cut above busboys. In some restaurants, the host or hostess is given a considerable amount of power by virtue of the fact that he or she controls the reservation book, the holy grail of the dining room. The hostess is the first person to greet the guest and the first to make an impression. A hostess can "get you in" at the table you want at the time you want. A hostess can also present a waiter with a section full of deuces or a section full of large parties. Sometimes, power corrupts. Although this was not the case at Yellowstone, I would work at a restaurant many years later that was almost controlled by a cartel of cash-hungry hostesses. These lovely ladies took tips at the door from guests wanting specific tables and actual kickbacks from waiters desiring profitable parties. I'd spent years listening to my father complain about kickbacks in the hotel restaurants where he worked, and I refused to knuckle under. As a result, for several months I received whatever was left over after the prime tables had been seated. No amount of complaining or accusing helped my situation, even though there were plenty of other servers in the same position. The hostesses denied everything up and down, and management backed them up (management, it turned out, was actually having affairs with the hostesses, but that's another story).

Servers are in the middle of the dining room pyramid and take up most of it. Often, they are the only connection between the guest and his food. Therefore, they alone deal simultaneously with the front and back of the house. Servers, too, are responsible for controlling the wild variables everywhere in between: disgruntled busboys, rapacious hostesses, hungry guests, surly chefs, and profit-minded managers, just to name a few.

Managers and owners make up the top of the dining room power structure. As I've already pointed out, salaried middle managers often make less money than the servers they police, leading to resentment and abuses of their power. It's very easy for a manager to impose punitive measures on a server without ever being held accountable. The schedule is key. Failing to comply with a particular manager's sense of subordination can guarantee a week of lunch shifts or, worse, brunch. A week of such shifts can easily cut a server's income in half. Regardless of whether the manager is also the owner or just one of many supervisors, however, he or she is likely to have an eye on cash flow. Customer service is always important but must lead to financial gain for the restaurant. The last thing on a manager's mind is how well the server is doing, monetarily or otherwise.

This may all seem self-explanatory or, possibly, irrelevant to the average diner. But consider the following scenario. You arrive in a restaurant and are seated immediately. Right next to the rest room. Your waitress arrives at the table promptly to take your drink order, but you wait an interminable time for your bread and water. Your salads arrive quickly, but you grow old waiting for your entrees, which, when they arrive, are only lukewarm. You complain to a manager you see walking by your table and he apologizes profusely. Your waitress is replaced by a waiter who brings a you a free dessert but seems harried and overburdened. Your dining experience is ultimately not a good one. Here are some of the possible reasons why.

The hostess who seated you is saving a better table for a guest who has already slipped her a twenty-dollar bill for the privilege. Your waitress is at odds with her busboy, who feels she stiffed him the last time they worked together, so he's not bending over backward to help any of her tables. Stressed out by this fact, your waitress complains in the kitchen that everything takes too long. The chef responds by holding up her tickets or neglecting to tell her when her food is ready. The manager hears your complaints and fears you'll never be back to sink more money into the restaurant, so he removes the offensive waitress from your table and substitutes a waiter who already has too many tables because he kicked back to the hostess earlier and she's seated his entire section with parties of six. This waiter can't be bothered with you and your free dessert. In fact, the manager has told him how unhappy you are and he's *sure* you won't be tipping well.

The structure has slipped. The network has become unbalanced. Everybody suffers.

Despite my intentions to make the best of it, I hated everything about Yellowstone. My work in the pantry could only be described as drudgery. I worked from 5 A.M. until 2 P.M. five days a week and loathed every minute of it, shrimp and all. As waiters and waitresses dropped out (the high attrition rate was something the orientation packet didn't mention), I learned that I could move "up" and join their ranks, but I opted to stay in my designated area. If possible, the waitstaff was even more miserable than I was. What's more, since they didn't exactly rake in the cash, they were worse off financially.

I was moved out of the kitchen occasionally to serve breakfast from behind a hot buffet. One Sunday morning, I watched a large group of foreign tourists file into the dining room with cameras. Before they brought their plates up to be served, they all stood and took several photos of me and my pantry mate as we stood behind steaming trays of hash browns and scrambled eggs. My pantry mate turned to me as the flashbulbs snapped and shook her head in disbelief. "Oh. My. God," she said.

"Oh, honey," a waitress said, walking by, "this happens all the time in here."

Aside from Susie, whom I rarely saw, I made no friends. Despite the fact that Yellowstone was the ultimate melting pot, employing people from every state in the union, it seemed like a sociology experiment gone horribly wrong. Employees formed into cliques, seeking out others from their home state. A class structure in miniature appeared within weeks of the summer season, based on geographic region, race, and level of education. There was absolutely no sense of commonality aside from the fact that nobody seemed to be having a good time.

I called home whenever possible and complained bitterly. My parents were unsympathetic. Stick it out, they told me. I had several long conversations with Ray, who was now looking a lot better than he had a few weeks earlier. In fact, I was starting to wonder what had possessed me to leave him in the first place. After smugly reminding me that he knew I was too soft to make it at Yellowstone, he told me that he was planning to drive from Oregon to Massachusetts, where his parents lived, and he'd be happy to come pick me up along the way. I was very tempted and began weighing my options.

To pass the time when I wasn't working, I did what everybody else did to fill the hours—I drank. Because of the altitude, it was easy to get drunk with very little effort, so I drank silly cocktails such as Amaretto Sours and, since I was so often hungry, lingered over the garnish. To balance my lack of machismo, I bought a cowboy hat and wore it into the hotel bar. Most of the time, I sat at the bar by myself and talked to whatever bartender happened to be on shift. Sometimes, though, I just sat and watched the tourists, who seemed to have come from points other than Earth.

Any notion I might have had of visiting anywhere as a tourist perished at Yellowstone. As if big Hawaiian shirts combined with cowboy hats weren't bad enough, visitors felt compelled to call attention to themselves in an astonishing variety of ways. Like employees, guests were cautioned to respect the free-roaming wildlife around the park. Respect, however, was last on the list of some of the idiots I saw. I watched with horror one day as a woman actually kicked a bison to get it to stand up and fit into a photo her husband was taking. Still another tourist crammed his camera into the face of a moose who, it turned out, was guarding her young. Extremely unhappy with the intrusion, the moose charged the tourist right out of the village. In the dining room, waiters regularly got requests for elk burgers or bison steak.

"Doncha have any of that? What kind of a place is this?"

"Oh, mama," one waitress sang, "don't let yer babies grow up to be tourists . . . "

During my tenure there, I left the confines of Lakeshore exactly twice. Once was to go to dinner with Susie and her politician fiancé, who had flown in from Washington, D.C., to make sure she was all right. Susie insisted that I come with the two of them to a restaurant he claimed was "the best in Montana." Thus, we drove for hours in his rented car to Pray, Montana (a town so named for the plethora of clasped hands adorning just about everything), and ate chocolate-covered strawberries in a chalet-style restaurant with tuxedo service. We were literally blinded by a furious blizzard on the way back to the park. It was early June.

"What kind of godforsaken wilderness is this, anyway?" Susie's fiancé demanded.

"I didn't ask you to come here," Susie snapped.

"I wouldn't have had to come here if you hadn't run away," he retorted, his knuckles white on the steering wheel.

The two of them then commenced arguing about their relationship while I pictured myself as a statistic. Summer kill, perhaps.

The second outing came after I'd more or less made up my mind to leave Yellowstone as soon as possible. I decided I needed to take at least one hike through the wilderness, since it was certainly the last time I'd ever have the opportunity. One of my pantry mates and I, along with her roommate and a guy who was looking to be anybody's boyfriend, set out on what was supposed to be a day hike through some of the prettiest country in the park. Like everything else at Yellowstone, the hike turned into the type of disaster one usually refers to later as "a learning experience." The boyfriend wannabe had decided to take control of our direction, stating that he was an experienced hiker and, well, a man, after all. Foolishly, we let him lead us way off our designated course. On the way to nowhere, we passed yet another boneyard. This time I knelt down and touched a skull on the ground.

"Can you tell what animal this comes from?" I asked Boyfriend, who examined it carefully.

"It seems to have the specific markings of a Lakeshore kitchen worker," he said, deadpan.

Bones soon gave way to animal prints in the earth.

"Do you think these are fresh?" my pantry mate asked tentatively. As we looked at each other, trying to decide whether the droppings we were standing in came from bears or bison, a powerful thunderstorm broke over our heads. As rain pelted down on us we realized that our metal-frame packs were the highest points around. If we managed to escape the bears, Boyfriend pointed out, we would most likely be electrocuted. The four of us then squeezed into a two-man tent and proceeded to drink the three bottles of wine that my pantry mate had the foresight to bring, reckoning that if we were going to perish in the wilderness, we were going down with smiles on our faces. In the tent, Boyfriend got assigned to me by default as my pantry mate and her roommate soon started making out with each other on their twelve inches of space. Shrugging at fate and giggling hopelessly after the last wine bottle was emptied, Boyfriend and I fell asleep wrapped in a damp embrace.

The next morning, still alive but extremely hung over, we became hopelessly lost hiking out and managed to walk an extra fifteen miles through bear country before we reached the main road at sunset. All four of us bent down and kissed the macadam.

Ray arrived in Yellowstone three days later, in the middle of the night. I worked my scheduled shift until 2 P.M. the next day and then walked into the office. A woman behind a gray metal desk looked up from a stack of ancient-looking files and exhaled a lungful of menthol cigarette smoke in my direction. She was wearing a cowboy hat. The plastic shingle on her desk advertised not her name but her department: Personnel.

"Help you?" she said.

"I've decided to leave the park," I replied.

"That's too bad." It was quite obvious that she'd said these same words many, many times. "When were you thinking of going?"

"Now," I told her.

When I got back to my room, Ray was rested and ready to go. "Are you sure you want to come?" he asked, knowing full well what my answer would be.

"Just drive me out of here," I said.

I had lasted four weeks at Yellowstone and come away with two hundred dollars, a cowboy hat, and a strong desire never to see the inside of another bar as long as I lived. As we left the park behind and I watched the Grand Tetons come into view, I felt exhilarated, as if I'd pulled off an amazing escape. I also felt strangely guilty.

My journey across the country with Ray took almost four days. It was a trip punctuated by truck stop waitresses and hallucinations. Sometimes the two were interchangeable.

It was my job to plan our route with the aid of several maps that Ray had brought along. This is how I learned my United States geography. Wyoming led into Colorado, which led into

Kansas and then to Missouri, Illinois, Indiana, Ohio. . . . Until we got to Missouri, all I could talk about was my Yellowstone experience, attempting to process it in my own mind before it became forever distorted by memory. Ray was still smarting over the fact that he hadn't been hired and was uninterested in my tales. He had one question: "Did you sleep with anyone while you were there?" and once that was answered to his satisfaction, he stopped listening, preferring instead to dwell on the state of our relationship and whether or not it was going to last into the following year.

I celebrated my twentieth birthday in the endless state of Kansas under a blistering June sun. The car Ray was driving had no tape deck and received only AM radio stations. For hours, all we heard were songs by Toto (appropriately enough), which drove Ray nearly insane. To this day, I can't hear "Rosanna" without having an instant vision of the parched grasses and endless highway running through Kansas. By the time Missouri came into view, I had been without sleep for three days and my hallucinations were interfering with my ability to read the map or even sustain a conversation. I looked up at one point and saw an entire chorus line of prunes in martini glasses dancing across the shimmering horizon.

When Ray and I crossed the state line into New York two days later, we had run out of things to say to each other that wouldn't lead to an immediate argument. Somewhere in Pennsylvania, he had descended into knight-in-shining-armor mode and was convinced that he'd saved me from a fate worse than death. I was, in his mind, totally ungrateful for all his efforts. What's more, he had taken to grilling me about my feelings for his friend, a topic that even in my altered state I was totally unwilling to discuss. It was probably mean-spirited on my part, but I felt he was overwhelmed by thoughts of his own significance in the grand scheme of things.

As a way of centering myself and deflecting the conversation away from the two of us, I asked Ray to drive into my old hometown of Monticello. I wanted to drive by my old high school and my old house. I wanted to swing by Maxman's and see if the luncheonette was still there. Ray had always been a bit of a sucker for nostalgia, so he consulted the map and fearlessly drove into my past. I was surprised to see that so much of the terrain was unchanged. My old house was still exactly where we'd left it, the only difference being that there was a stranger in front of it mowing the lawn instead of my father. Ray kept uncharacteristically quiet while I looked at the house and let myself drown in memories. We were less successful when we looked for the luncheonette. Whether we were on the wrong road or it really was gone I wasn't sure, but Maxman's seemed to have vanished, Brigadoon-like, into the mists of time. Although I thanked Ray for taking the time to visit, I found the whole detour a bit depressing, as if too much of my life was impermanent and subject to the illusion of memory.

As we headed to Massachusetts and Ray began his transformation into the role of prodigal son, I was sure of almost nothing. I didn't know then that I would find his family pleasant but extremely strange. Nor did I have the foresight to predict that within days I would become so suddenly homesick and fearful of becoming beholden to this family that I would take the last of my money and board yet another bus back to Portland. I couldn't know that I would spend five days on this bus, during which I would have plenty of time to consider the mistakes I had made in the previous weeks and weigh the damages against the rewards.

I did, however, come to a realization that had been building since I first set foot in the Yellowstone kitchen. I felt that at twenty years old, I still knew nothing and had experienced very little of what I considered real life. I hadn't been able to rely on myself long enough to stick out my job at Yellowstone. I saw my inability to turn the experience into a successful adventure as something of a failure. Therefore, I reckoned, *I* was something of a failure. It was a difficult conclusion to come to at an age when the state of one's self is usually of paramount importance. Now more than ever, it seemed, my future consisted of a series of tales waiting to be told. And as was usual for me, I was in a terrific hurry to get on with it. Certainly one of the supreme ironies in my life has been my lack of patience. And although I didn't fully understand it at the time, learning to wait gracefully was a lesson that, for me, had only just begun.

# working the fantasy

**There are many questions** I am able to answer with ease. "What do you recommend this evening?" for example, or "Which one of your chardonnays is the most buttery?" (as if even 1 percent of those asking know what *buttery* means in any context other than toast). I can even come up with quick responses to other, more complicated questions such as "What is the meaning of life?" (which is what customers *always* say when I ask them if they have any questions and neglect to add "about the menu"). There is one question, however, that still gives me trouble: "What do you do?"

Sometimes this question is asked by a customer who follows it with "I mean, when you're not here," as if serving them is not really "doing" anything. Strangely enough, most of the waiters and waitresses I've worked with share this point of view. Most of them feel that it's not quite socially acceptable to say "I'm a waiter." Usually the response is more like "Well, I'm an actor/artist/model/ teacher/musician. . . ." They never seem able to admit that waiting is actually their *profession*. It's a temporary living at best.

In my experience, those who have never waited tables sometimes express a strange sort of fascination when I tell them that

I work in a restaurant. Comments have ranged from "I'll bet you meet lots of rich single men doing that" to "How can you stand to have people order you around?" It's not that much of a stretch to assume that this job isn't considered one to aspire to.

Perhaps this is why "a real job" is commonly accepted restaurant slang for anything other than waiting tables.

I have fallen prey to the same sort of social shiftiness in my career as a waitress. When I enrolled my son in school for the first time, for example, I was required to fill out an emergency information card that asked for my occupation. I debated long before I finally admitted to being a "food server." I was convinced that my son's teachers would have a rather low opinion of a single mother who worked as a waitress, especially since his school district was rather a tony one. I was actually waiting on most of the parents of his peers on a regular basis.

Lately, though, I've been able to get around this quandary. These days, although it's still the most profitable, waitressing is just one of many jobs I hold. Others include reviewing books for my local newspaper, freelance editing, and working in a special program for preschool-age children. In conversation, I usually list these others as what I "do" and then add "and I also work in a restaurant." My hope is that by the time I get to the end of this list, whoever I'm talking to will be so dazzled by the myriad of other more socially acceptable jobs I have that they won't even notice the waitressing angle.

On the other hand, I sometimes throw the waitressing out first just to see what kind of reaction I get. After twenty years serving the public, I've developed a sixth sense about the social standards of various people. I know that some of the people I encounter in my neighborhood, through my son's school, or even wait on consider restaurant work low class—something that immediately places me in a different social stratum. On the flip side, there are people who automatically feel more comfortable with me as one of the working class when they learn that I'm a waitress. My years of waiting tables are solely responsible for my ability to tell who is who.

Aside from the social repercussions, there are several reasons why table service isn't uppermost on the list of desirable prospective jobs. For one, there are rarely medical or retirement benefits. For another, it gets more difficult to cope with the physical demands of the job after a certain number of years. And depending on the restaurant, there is always the chance you will be replaced by a younger, firmer version of yourself. There is no possibility of advancement, either, unless one is trying to get into management (and few restaurant managers make more than waiters in good restaurants). For all these reasons, waiters and waitresses are primarily a transient bunch, and in my experience I've found that with few exceptions they are not only waiting on tables but waiting to get out of the business. They are putting themselves through school or making a few extra bucks on the side. They are in the arts or trying to open their own businesses. Occasionally, they are waiting to be "discovered." Even the elite few who do consider themselves professional waiters or waitresses (called "lifers" in the business) usually have something else on the side that they're waiting for, such as the dream of opening their own restaurant.

Although I'd waited tables at Maxman's, worked at Yellowstone, and even made a few sandwiches in the campus coffee shop, I didn't begin what I considered an adult version of this waiting game until after I graduated from college. My sense of accomplishment at having attained a diploma was tempered by the knowledge that I would shortly have to start paying off four years of student loans and the sneaking suspicion that, after what I considered a grueling term of study, I had very little in the way of marketable skills. Somehow, I couldn't see that my degree was going to open any doors I'd care to walk through.

I should explain.

I had graduated with a B.A. in English literature, one of those majors that, in my mind, guaranteed that I could either hold my own at a cocktail party or go on to graduate school. Most of my classmates were going the latter route, having considered themselves pre-law, pre-med, or pre-education. For me, a life of academia was never in the cards. I'd always thought of my college education as being pre–real life. Over the course of four years, I'd been able to cover my tuition with a complicated combination of scholarships, grants, and loans. Nevertheless, I had been completely responsible for my own upkeep throughout and took full advantage of every work-study program that was thrown my way. Almost all of my classmates came from families that could afford to send their kids to this exclusive and pricey college. Yet, for whatever reason, most of my peers attempted to disguise the fact that they were covered financially if for some reason they couldn't scrape enough money together to buy books one semester or purchase new skis or throw a party with five kegs of beer. This was an attitude that bothered me in a subtle but insistent way. It seemed to me inherently dishonest and a little spoiled. The thought of racking up more loans and spending more years in this type of rarefied atmosphere was a bit repugnant.

Besides all of this, I had just finished writing my first novel. As far as I was concerned, I was officially a writer. Not only was I sure of this, but I wanted to write what *I* wanted to write—an attitude that had already caused some consternation among my professors. Being a writer came with certain responsibilities, to my mind. For one, I was under the impression (in an only vaguely conscious way) that suffering was a key element in the development of a decent writer. I figured I wasn't going to experience any true suffering (at least the kind I considered valuable) in graduate school. Nor, I figured, was I going to find it in an office job, which seemed like the logical next step.

I had spent the previous two months working for a temporary agency, moving from one office to another, and I considered the life of an office drone a fate worse than death. My days were spent crossing and uncrossing my legs, digging papers out of files, calling strangers on the phone who didn't want to speak to me, waiting for lunch breaks, coffee breaks, any break from the stifling routine. And the office gossip was the most deadening of all: petty sniping, humorless jokes, and grade school–style flirtations. I was offered a couple of permanent positions at entry-level wages, but I ran from them as fast as I could. My plan was to get lucky and sell my novel. At some point, I would be discovered for the big talent I knew I was. In the meantime, I had to have heat, electricity, and a phone (there were limits to the amount of suffering I felt I needed). To finance this life I'd designed for myself, I would most certainly have to work somewhere.

Waitressing still had the same glitzy appeal for me then as it had when I was sixteen. Only this time I wasn't going to settle for a coffee shop or a Petit Morsel. I would go for the big time, I reckoned, and make a lot of money.

There were other considerations as well. I wanted to meet people who were living real lives. Up to that point in time, I'd always felt like an observer of my own life. It was as if I were just moving my piece around a game board. The outcome had already been determined and I was just watching—and waiting—to see how it turned out. Waiting tables was a way to become part of what I'd always seen as the outside world. And, of course, it would only be temporary.

With all of this in mind, I put my diploma away and applied for a job I saw advertised in the paper. The Dining Room of a Prestigious Club, the ad said, needed Waitresses with at least Two Years of Fine Dining Experience. I felt absolutely no qualms bluffing about my experience. None of the restaurants I had worked in could be remotely considered fine dining. But I had a college degree, after all. I figured I didn't have to know brain surgery to open a bottle of wine (and, actually, one *doesn't* have to know brain surgery to open a bottle of wine, but, as I soon learned, one really does have to know how to open a bottle of wine in order to get that cork out with anything resembling grace).

I was called in for an interview with Carol, the overbearing matriarch who ran the Dining Room. I could tell immediately that Carol hated me on sight. Moreover, I suspected she knew that my résumé was mostly fakery. Nevertheless, she brought the food and beverage manager over to complete the interview. The F and B man was Hans, a strange Swiss import, brought in recently (I later found out) to improve the Dining Room's bottom line. Hans interviewed my breasts, apparently finding them quite qualified. I was hired.

I had the great good fortune to be assigned to a waiter named Deane on my first training shift. Although Deane was less than pleased to have a new waitress follow him around (almost every waiter hates training new hires, as it is nearly impossible to maintain the type of internal rhythm necessary to get through a shift when you have to stop and explain everything to another person who is usually hanging about like a spare part), he was happy to provide me with a quick dossier on everyone on the waitstaff. There was a group of older waitresses, he told me, who had been working at the club for years and had a steady stream of regulars. These women would never accept me, Deane went on, as they were generally unwilling to deal with any kind of change in the landscape of their work. They had names from another era (Thelma, Agnes, Ethel) and hairstyles to match. Most of them worked breakfast and lunch, Deane told me, but a few held the coveted dinner shifts, which were very difficult to get. (In any restaurant, dinners are the money shifts, with Friday and Saturday nights being the best among them. Waiters who are unable or unwilling to move from lunches—the purgatorial training shifts—to dinners are considered inept or simply insane.)

For the rest, Deane explained, there were a coterie of older waiters (most of whom, he claimed, were gay like himself) mixed with younger women like myself who had been hired by Hans. I began to get a sense of what Hans felt was a better "bottom line."

Deane also took it upon himself to warn me that the diners I would wait on were all members of the club and that there was "a reason they are called *members,* if you know what I mean." They were very wealthy, old (sometimes ancient, Deane stressed), bitter, racist, sexist, and generally in ill health. So many of them had dentures, he said, that they were forced to gum their steaks to death. "Tapioca," Deane said, "is a very popular item here." Because I was so new to the job and eager to make a good impression, I purposely disregarded this bit of information, storing it for later use should I need it.

Finally, Deane showed me around the labyrinthine corridors and rooms that made up the club's dining facilities. The main dining room was made up of two vast rooms decorated in muted institutional beiges and olives and separated by a shortened wall. The bus stations (where coffee, trays, dishes, silverware, and frantic food servers were kept) were hidden from the diner's view behind similar walls. Two ballroom-size banquet rooms were located just off the main dining room on one side. On the other side, a short passage led to the Men's Bar, a darkly paneled atavism containing leather chairs and plenty of ashtrays. Although women were allowed in the Men's Bar, they were forbidden to enter its subdivision, the Card Room. Cocktail waitresses were the only females permitted to grace the Card Room, where relics of another age (the Civil War, maybe) smoked, drank highballs, played poker, and feebly grabbed at the backsides of said cocktail waitresses. Oddly, there was actually a set of waitresses, I learned, who *preferred* to work the Card Room.

The kitchen, which serviced all these areas, was very clean, very white, and large enough to get lost in. All the chefs were meticulously attired and all boasted formal training. (A couple of them, I noticed, were quite good-looking and one of them was a dead ringer for Bruce Springsteen. Deane informed me that "Bruce" was in the middle of a hot affair with a married banquet waitress and that this was the scandal du jour.) Obeying the usual rule of thumb, however, the chefs more or less detested the waitstaff with few exceptions.

Contributing to the whole *Upstairs, Downstairs* feel of the club were the stringent rules that all food and beverage employees were required to follow. We had regulation uniforms and shoes (which were hideous in every way), which we were to wear only in the Dining Room. We had to enter the club not only by a separate entrance but by a separate street, following a long corridor connecting two buildings. We were not to be seen in street clothes anywhere near the dining rooms. Thus, we were all assigned a space in a locker room to change. There were specifications for hair length (above the shoulder or tied back for women, very short for men), nail polish (forbidden), facial hair (moustaches only for men), and earrings (posts only). We were provided with one meal per shift, but it had to be eaten near the locker rooms, in a staff dining area far away from the Dining Room. We were not permitted to enter the club for any reason other than work.

I began to feel that I was in over my head very soon after I was hired. This was fine dining, after all. The salad fork had to be placed exactly thirteen inches from the teaspoon on the place setting. Carol walked around doing random inspections with a tape measure to make sure this rule was followed. The napkins had to be folded with exactly the right number of creases. We were required to serve from the right and remove plates from the left. We used tray service in the Dining Room and so each server was required to lift and balance large trays holding a maximum of six full-sized dinner plates with covers. I had never lifted a tray that size in my life and I wasn't sure I could do it.

The menu in the Dining Room came from the same Jurassic time period as the members who ate there. Cholesterol was an unknown enemy, and more was always better. Breakfast items featured tapioca (actually, tapioca was a staple with all three meals), sausages, bacon, pancakes, and eggs tortured in every imaginable way. These meals were a kind of upscale version of breakfast specials in truck stop diners across the country. Shrimp was a very big item for lunch. There were shrimp cocktails, shrimp salads, and grilled shrimp platters. There were also a variety of salads (the Cobb presented nightmarish flashbacks to Yellowstone) and sandwiches, including the ultimate in fatty excess, the Reuben. Most of the members couldn't finish half of what they ordered and most of them demanded that the unfinished portions be wrapped. Those who didn't usually put their cigarettes out in their half-eaten sandwiches, signaling a rather unpleasant end to their meal.

The dinner menu was a grateful nod to the traditions of old-style steak houses. There was filet mignon, prime rib, rack of veal, rack of lamb, and ad infinitum. A regular offering, "Surf and Turf," was extremely popular. Having never seen it before, I was baffled and asked Deane what it meant.

"Oh, you must know," he said, rolling his eyes. "Surf, where the fish swim . . . "—he made swimming motions with his arms. "Turf, where the cows graze . . ."—he made hoof-stomping motions with his foot. "Oh, Lord, what's the matter with you, girl?" he said, exasperated. "Steak and seafood. I can't *believe* you've never heard of this."

"Perhaps," I told him, "it's a bit before my time."

The pièce de résistance, however, was the flaming Steak Diane, prepared tableside by Tracy, the inappropriately named linebacker who was our maitre d'. Poor Tracy was a tortured soul (also a writer, he confessed to me) who felt he was destined for much grander things than service in the Dining Room. He'd recently dragged himself through college with no help from his alcoholic, abusive parents and had promptly married Lisa, a pretty young waitress who worked beside him in the Dining Room. Lisa wanted to start a family right away and Tracy wanted to wait as long as possible. This was already the source of frequent quarrels between the two. The stress was often evident on Tracy's face as he wheeled the stainless steel cart over to a table and set a steak on fire.

Dinner shifts were added to my schedule soon after I was hired. I suspect that this honor had less to do with the fact that I was a good waitress and more to do with the fact that I was young and willing to work up to five split shifts a week.

The split shift in a restaurant is a grueling one, fitting in eight hours of floor time over a ten-hour period. Add the time it takes to get dressed and commute to and from work, and the amount of hours involved in one day's work can easily add up to twelve. Besides this, split shifts can sometimes be less profitable than single shifts since, to avoid paying overtime wages, managers phase out waiters working splits first, truncating tips. Other restaurants I worked in allowed waiters to work splits off the clock and stay as long as they wanted, but the Dining Room was fastidious about obeying certain labor laws.

I felt entirely unequipped to handle dinner shifts in the Dining Room. There were many more details to attend to, for one thing. Table settings were expanded to include soup spoons, glasses for white wine, and goblets for red. The napkins for dinner had to be folded into a standing fan as opposed to the flat fold for lunch. Dinners went at a much more leisurely pace as well, so that there was more time, in Carol's words, for "a higher quality of service." None of this bothered me. What did frighten me was the fact that sooner or later I'd have to open a bottle of wine, and I was absolutely clueless as to how to go about it. I was also going to have to haul a giant tray on my own, a feat I'd managed to avoid up to that point. But by far the most terrifying prospect for me was the thought of deboning a whole fish at the table. I resolved that I would find a way to weasel out of that one forever. For my first few dinner shifts, I struggled with the tray. It was sheer adrenaline and terror that allowed me to get my dishes to the table without dropping any of them. Still, I received some rather puzzled stares from my customers as I awkwardly set the tray down on a kickstand, which the busboy had grudgingly found for me. Wine was another story. I enlisted Tracy's help at the table, claiming that I was too busy or that he knew more about the type of wine the customer was ordering. Tracy was willing to help when he could, but I started running out of ruses. Finally, my moment of truth arrived in the form of an order for a bottle of pinot noir. Tracy was busy incinerating a steak at another table, and despite his friendliness I couldn't ask Deane for help. I was, after all, supposed to know how to do this.

As I stood trembling with the bottle in my hand, I received help from an unexpected quarter. Belinda, who was about my age and had been hired a week before me, saw my trepidation and took the bottle from me.

"Want me to do that for you?" she asked.

"Would you mind?" I asked. Belinda didn't need further prompting, flounced over to my table with the wine, and opened it expertly without ever putting the bottle down. When she returned, she said, "You don't know how to open wine, do you?" I admitted that I didn't but told her to keep mum since it would

surely be my job if anyone found out. Belinda, who had been
waiting tables solidly since her teens, took it upon herself at that
moment to teach me everything I needed to know. We began a
friendship that day that would last through three years and as
many restaurants.

Belinda came over to my apartment with a bottle of wine the
following night and had me practice opening it over and over while
we drank its contents. I would use what she showed me that
night to great effect and profit in every subsequent restaurant.

A brief note about wine: I found that, like many things, successfully recommending and serving wine is as much about acting as
if you know what you're talking about as actually having any real
knowledge. The reason for this is that most of my customers
over the years have known much less about wine than they'd
ever admit. Most people know that they prefer either red or
white and then select wines based on what they've heard about
chardonnay, cabernet, Chianti, merlot, or Riesling. There is certainly a difference between good wines and bad wines, which
even the most uneducated palate can discern. Beyond this, however, much of what appeals in a wine is entirely subjective for
the average diner. People have been trained to ask for white wine
with fish and red wine with meat, and some of my customers
have actually become visibly disturbed when I recommended
switching colors with these dishes. The only way to know what
you really like is to experiment with different wines and then
order accordingly. It's pointless to order a wine based on price or
what somebody else thinks you should be drinking.

I saw a perfect example of this type of wine blindness a few
years later in an Italian restaurant with a fairly diverse wine list. A
fellow waiter who claimed to be something of an expert had recommended and served an expensive bottle of Tignanello, which is

an Italian blend of several different grapes made in very limited quantities. He had been so enthusiastic about the wine that his table had left him a quarter of the bottle for his own consumption. The waiter foolishly left the bottle in the kitchen, where it was promptly drained by a couple of his coworkers. Upon discovering the absence of the bottle, the waiter ranted, raved, and accused everybody of being thieving scum. Another waiter, sick of hearing the complaints, rescued the empty bottle from the trash and replaced the Tignanello with the same amount of house red, a hideous blend not even worthy of being called jug wine. The injured waiter retracted his earlier slanderous comments and invited the second waiter to join him in a glass. The two then sat at the counter at the end of the shift and drank.

"Ah," said the injured waiter, savoring his glass, "this is really the stuff, isn't it?"

"Mmm," struggled the second waiter, who was choking on uncontrollable laughter. Although he tried to contain himself, the second waiter came perilously close to giving himself and the ruse away by literally falling off his bar stool with convulsive hysteria.

Chances are, then, that unless you have an expert or sommelier at your table, your waiter or waitress is recommending only what he or she likes personally or what the restaurant has instructed him or her to push. I can always tell if my customers know what they're talking about when it comes to wine or if they're merely trying to impress someone else at the table by ordering something expensive or sending back a bottle that is clearly fine. Mispronunciation is also a clue. Those who add the *t* on the end of *cabernet*, for example, are usually in the same league as those who ask for "a cup of chino" when they want that ubiquitous coffee drink commonly known as a cappuccino.

As for the cork, you can tell if the wine is spoiled only by looking at it. If the cork is crumbling or moldy, chances are that the wine has been improperly stored and is turning. But one can tell absolutely nothing by *smelling* the thing. A cork will always smell like a cork. In fact, proper protocol says that the waitress should remove the cork from the table altogether once the customer has had a chance to inspect it.

Champagne, or sparkling wine, is a bit of a different story. No matter how many bottles of champagne I open, I'm still terrified of being hit by a cork. It takes only one shot to the head or any other part of the body with one of these projectiles to know that it's an experience not worth repeating. I open champagne now taking great care to hold the bottle at a forty-five-degree angle, cover the cork with a napkin, and twist the bottle slowly to remove the cork. Opened this way, the cork gives a more muted pop than when forced out with two thumbs, but you also lose much less wine in the ensuing spray. I once opened a particularly bubbly bottle of Cristal and watched it foam over the top of the bottle into the wine bucket.

"Hey, hey," the customer said, "you just spilled about fifteen bucks worth there!"

♪ ♪ ♪

Belinda didn't stop her instruction with opening wine. She also showed me how to position a tray with my shoulder, distribute the weight evenly, and set it down without pulling every muscle in my back. She even demonstrated how to flip open a kickstand with one hand while the other balanced the tray. After two glasses of wine, I was convinced that Belinda was some kind of crazy acrobat waitress who could defy the laws of gravity. There seemed to be no aspect of table service that she hadn't seen or done herself. She even had beauty tips designed specifically for waitressing.

"Do you know why my eyes look so bright?" she asked me. I shook my head, noticing for the first time just how bright her eyes seemed.

"Clown White," she said triumphantly and pulled a tube of actual clown makeup out of her purse. "A little bit under the eyes," she said, spreading some on my face, "really makes them bright. That really helps, especially when you're working in a dark dining room."

Belinda was also the only waitress I've ever met who was content to make a career out of waiting tables. In her teens, she'd won a few local beauty pageants and had thought her calling was on the runway, but that promise had never materialized and she'd taken a job at Denny's during high school to save some money. Her tips at Denny's had afforded her the ability to move away from an oppressive rural family life and she'd never looked back, upgrading restaurants every few months, always looking for the biggest payoff. Belinda's long-term plan was to find and marry a rich man. In the meantime, she was having as much fun and making as much cash as possible.

Physically, Belinda was everything I was not. She was tall and had short, curly black hair, dark eyes, and pale skin. As we became friendlier and started giggling over the small absurdities of the Dining Room, Deane took to calling us Betty and Veronica. Though I wasn't sure of the reason, Deane never really liked Belinda and so my friendship with him developed on a separate path. Belinda, being much more of a professional (and also much pushier) than I, got moved to dinners immediately. She was even given the coveted "Fish Fantasy" shift mere weeks after being hired.

The Fish Fantasy (nicknamed "Neptune's Nightmare" by Deane) was the Dining Room's biggest event. On the first Friday night of every month, the club pulled out all the stops and put on a culinary show that would terrify the most stalwart of ocean dwellers. Every manner of Pacific crustacean, fish, and mammal was featured boiled, steamed, filleted, and surrounded by exotic garnishes and steaming lemon-scented towels. But the fun didn't stop there; also included in the price were elaborately carved ice sculptures of mermaids, dolphins, and Poseidon, sparkling fishing nets, and a variety of banners suggesting the deep sea. Attendance was very high on Fantasy nights and the waiters made good money.

As I had only recently learned to open a bottle of wine and still felt unsteady on my feet, I reckoned it would be quite a while before I was scheduled for a Fantasy. In the meantime, I spent my afternoons with Deane (we often worked split shifts together and so had two useless hours to kill in the middle of the day), running around downtown Portland, drinking espresso, and searching for the Edith Piaf records he collected. Sometimes he came over to my apartment and we sat around chain-smoking and sharing stories. Deane's tales were much more exciting than mine. Very matter-of-factly, he told me of his past promiscuity and of the fate of most of his exes. Almost everyone in Deane's circle of friends had either full-blown AIDS or ARC. He was just beginning to attend the funerals of friends and lovers. After getting to know him a little, I could tell that while he was cavalier about his past, Deane had real fear about his own future. I came upon him in the bus station one morning, scrutinizing a blemish on his face with a hand mirror. "Can you look at this for me?" he asked. "Do you think it's Kaposi's?"

Deane had been living with his current lover, Bill, for a couple of years and told me that they were very much in love. He had met Bill at an AA meeting and they shared a passion for collectibles of all kinds. He told me that his goal was to be able to save enough money to open his own shop with Bill.

Like Belinda, Deane also felt the need to educate me. When I asked him one afternoon why he had never felt the urge to at least *try* having sex with a woman, he laughed at me and blew coy smoke rings in my direction. "Are you volunteering?" he asked, and when he saw my expression, he added, "Oh, *honey,* there's something you've really got to see." The next day he took me on a tour of Portland's gay bars, complete with annotated descriptions of what went on in them. There was absolutely no tale that was too extreme for Deane, no conversational boundary that couldn't be crossed. Deane was possessed of an extraordinarily generous spirit and a cunning insight into the motivations of most of the people he met. Both of these qualities overrode his slightly neurotic and often bitchy behaviors. In all of these ways, he was an ideal friend. We developed a genuine affection for each other.

When we were "on the floor," however, Deane kept to himself. Helping out wasn't his strong suit. So I was on my own the night Hans came in for dinner and sat down at my table with a couple of executives from the upstairs offices. I was petrified to be waiting on him and sure I would make some sort of fatal mistake in my service. Naturally, I did. I served from the left instead of the right and removed the plates in the reverse order. And of course, Hans pointed it out at the end of the meal. As he went to sign off on his check, Hans said, "Your service was good, but I noticed that you served me from the left. Are you aware of that?"

I looked at Hans, sensing the end of my career in the Dining Room, and saw that he was staring back me, pen held poised in his left hand.

"Well, yes, sir," I answered him, "but I'd heard that you were left-handed and so I thought you'd be more comfortable if I served you from that direction." And then I smiled as broadly as I could. "I'm left-handed myself," I added, "so I can understand the difficulty of living in a world where everything is designed for right-handed people."

"Oh," was all Hans said, but there was an equally broad smile on his face and the acknowledgment that I had scored quite a few points.

Unfortunately, I was unable to score the same kinds of points with Carol, who attempted to make my schedule as unappealing as possible. Occasionally, she'd even schedule me in the Card Room. I needed only one lunch shift with this group of cantankerous, feebly lustful old men to know that I'd have to quit if Carol continued her quest. I was saved only by the fact that there were a few waitresses who preferred working this particular room and who were annoyed when I took their shifts. I never quite figured out why Carol had such a needle to me. Perhaps it was because I didn't seem servile enough. Perhaps it was because, even at that early stage of my waitressing career, I saw restaurant managers as mostly out of touch with what was really going on at the table and I didn't disguise those feelings well enough. Perhaps she just didn't like me. Whatever the reason, I felt I was always swimming against the tide with Carol and that whatever success I had on the job would be in spite of her and not because she helped me in any way.

I was not very popular with the contingent of veteran waitresses, either. I suspect that they felt somewhat threatened by my (and Belinda's) presence in the Dining Room. They'd received very little in the way of rewards for their service over the years, and some of them were understandably bitter. Most of them had children my age. Nevertheless, I made a few attempts to develop some sort of camaraderie between us. I'd spend time in the break room, for example, joining Agnes, Thelma, and Ethel as they drained countless cups of coffee and smoked several packs of cigarettes, and try to insinuate myself into the conversation. If they were talking about their children, I'd try to come in with some sort of story about my own family. If they were discussing the rules of the Dining Room, I'd add my own two cents about how I felt things were running. It was fairly hopeless. I had absolutely no experiences in common with these women and they knew it. Most times they simply ignored me until I went away. Strangely, they all seemed to love Deane although he never seemed to make any attempts to ingratiate himself with them. I began avoiding the break room unless I had Deane in tow. In a way, he became something of a protector. Belinda never spent time in the break room. She always showed up for her shifts already dressed in her work clothes (against the rules) and cut through the front entrance (really against the rules) to the Dining Room.

Despite the frosty reception I received from the ladies of the Dining Room and Carol's permanent dislike of me, I did manage to make some allies. Tracy (who I suspected was looking for an extramarital adventure) was very kind to me and consistently put in a good word or two about my abilities on the floor. Then there was Hans, who had been so impressed with my earlier improvisation at his table that he returned for lunch shortly thereafter and specifically asked for "the new little left-handed girl." Carol couldn't possibly ignore this.

The next week I was scheduled for my first Fish Fantasy.

The following Friday, Deane and I arrived at work with plenty of time to spare before the dinner shift began. He had assured me it would be a particularly long night and said he wanted to take a shower before it all began. It took us ten minutes to take the two elevators and navigate the series of hallways leading to our locker rooms. When we finally arrived, Deane tapped me lightly on the shoulder and raced by me on his way to the men's locker room. "See you inside," he said, his words blurry from too many cups of espresso. I'd had three cups of the stuff myself and I sensed a coffee headache starting at the back of my skull.

Rosemary, a waitress I'd worked a few lunches with, was alone in the women's locker room. Her preparations always took longer than anyone else's, and when I walked in she was just beginning her transformation. After greeting me, she changed carefully out of her T-shirt, jeans, and sneakers and stood in a bra and panties for what seemed like an inordinate amount of time. Finally she seemed ready for action and applied a feminine hygiene spray to herself and the locker room in general. Next came panty hose. Then deodorant (also in the form of a spray). She hummed to herself, occasionally interjecting lyrics. "Money for nothin'," she sang as she donned her white work shirt. And as she put on her tie, she added, "Chicks for free." My head buzzed with caffeine as I watched, transfixed, the meticulous care Rosemary took with every detail of her uniform.

"Have you seen that video?" she asked me. "It just came out. It's great. I can't stop singing the song. Aren't you going to get dressed?"

"Too much coffee," I told her. "I can't move. I've got some time anyway."

She slipped the regulation black 100 percent polyester pinafore-style dress over her head and stood on a bench so that she could see the full body effect in the small locker mirror. I loathed that dress and felt it was designed to make every woman who wore it look as unappealing as possible, but on Rosemary it looked like evening wear.

The last items to come on were her work shoes. The shoes were identical to mine and those of every other waitress in the building. Black, crepe soled, ugly beyond belief, they were sometimes a reason in and of themselves to look for another job. She whipped her long brown hair into a ponytail and doused it with hairspray. Whatever small sections of her body were without scent were then covered with several generous squirts from a perfume bottle. Rosemary's makeup came last of all because it required the most attention. With the easy skill of a professional, Rosemary proceeded to cover a black eye under careful layers of foundation. She kept a store of such makeup in her locker for good reason. This wasn't the first time I'd seen her cover a shiner and I'd known her for only a couple of months. By the looks of it, this one had already faded considerably since she received it. Her wounds were an open secret. Everybody knew that they came from her alcoholic husband, but nobody ever discussed them with her.

Rosemary's makeup was brilliant. She blended her eyeshadow with the colors of her bruises so well that by the time she was finished, they were mere suggestions of abuse. Rosemary had a final ritual she performed before leaving the locker room. She kissed her fingertips lightly and pressed them to a photograph of her two small children, which she kept, along with her array of makeup and sprays, in her locker.

"See you at dinner?" she asked, locking up her cubicle.

"I'll be in," I told her.

"You working the Fantasy tonight?"

"Yup, first one. What about you?"

"Card Room. Hey, good luck," she said and breezed out of the locker room, leaving a myriad of scents in her wake: baby powder, hairspray, gardenia. Rosemary had just turned twenty-one. Two years older than she, I felt immeasurably younger as I watched her leave the room.

I waited a few beats before changing into my own version of Rosemary's outfit. As she had done, I put my shoes on last, delaying the inevitable. I did not have Rosemary's long legs and felt I looked like an overgrown schoolgirl in badly fitting clothes.

By the time I made it into the staff room, Deane was already there, showered, shaved, and shined up like a new penny.

"More java?" he asked me as I sat down with my dinner, which consisted of a roll, some butter, and a cup of coffee.

"Can't find anything that appeals to me over there," I said, gesturing to the staff buffet.

"Well, I can't blame you," Thelma piped up, planting herself at our table. "This"—she held up a forkful of meat dripping with a suspicious sauce—"is supposed to be prime rib. It's so tough. Prime rib should melt in your mouth."

"Thelma, do you really think they're going to give you the good stuff?" Deane sighed, tucking into his own plate, which looked both symmetrical and color coordinated.

"I've been here twenty years," Thelma grumbled. "Why not?"

Deane shrugged and turned his attention back to me. "Nervous?" he asked.

"A little," I said.

"What're you nervous about?" Thelma asked, chewing her tough prime rib.

"She's working the Fantasy tonight," Deane answered for me.

"What?" Thelma looked both annoyed and incredulous. "They're letting you work a Fantasy after two months? I had to be here years before they let me work it." She swallowed and sized me up. Thelma was possibly the most hostile of all the older waitresses. Her husband was a retired beat cop, and a generous portion of his toughness had transferred to her.

"It's probably because you're so young," she added. "They're trying to get some young girls in there to mix it up. Foolish, is what it is."

I studied Thelma's face. Her skin was a mosaic of lines, every one of which, I assumed, had its own story. She shaved her eyebrows and penciled them in later, complementing the effect with electric-blue eye shadow. Her orange hair was piled precariously high in curls on top of her head, setting off the brick-colored frown of her lips.

"You're probably right," I told her. "But here I am."

"Hmm," Thelma mused.

Deane rolled his eyes. "C'mon," he said, "let's go work the Fantasy."

*♪ ♪ ♪*

The Dining Room was abuzz with fishy excitement. Looking around, I actually thought I was underwater for a minute or two. The best part of the Fish Fantasy, I found out, was that it was a prix fixe buffet. The waiters only had to provide hot towels, open wine and champagne (which came with the meal), and clear plates. Although much busier than an average night, it was actually easier and more profitable. The guests were also a sight to behold: all of Portland's oldest money dressed in tuxedos and finery, struggling to free lobsters from their shells. The whole thing had an aura of fuzzy unreality. I felt I was crashing a party that clearly I would never be invited to. A few of my customers asked who I was or how I liked working at the club, but most were simply interested in learning where Agnes and Ethel were. Since I was new, I had fewer tables than the other waiters and plenty of opportunity to watch the proceedings from behind the bus station. Belinda (who I noticed was violating both the nail polish and earring codes) was running her narrow behind off. Deane, usually smooth and evenly paced no matter how busy he got, was developing a line of perspiration on his brow. I knew they would both make much more money than I would by the end of the night.

I turned my attention to the buffet, manned by several chefs in starched whites. I recognized all but one, a tall, stocky newcomer who waved his hands in flourishes over the food and greeted all the guests. He stood directly in front of a giant salmon carved from ice and it framed him in rather a unique way. I saw him look up and over in my direction, so I averted my eyes. When I looked up again, he was still staring at me. I disappeared behind the bus station and busied myself organizing silverware and turning ice buckets. When it was time for me to reenter the fray to serve coffee to one of my tables, the tall new chef was standing right in front of me, blocking my path. I actually had to crane my neck to look at his face.

"Hi, little girl," he said.

I suppose I should have been offended at the term he used and the slightly lewd way he offered it up, but I wasn't. Perhaps it was the giddy atmosphere of the Dining Room or my own feelings of isolation from the festivities. For whatever reason, I was instantly charmed. He introduced himself as Leo and immediately adopted a conspiratorial air, telling me how silly he found the whole concept of a Fish Fantasy. I learned that he was a visiting chef, called in by his good friend Hans, and would be overseeing the menus in the kitchen for a few weeks. Leo didn't make any attempt to downplay his credits and listed the names of several restaurants and professional societies I had never heard of. It was almost as if he was presenting me with his résumé to see if it met with my approval. In the short time we talked (and it couldn't have been longer than five minutes), I learned that Leo was originally from New York (something in common, we marveled) and now lived in Colorado. We shared our thoughts on the Dining Room and its patrons and traded facetious quips (still more in common). When we'd gotten through all of this, Leo said, "I've been watching you all night." I was spared having to come up with a rejoinder to this impossible statement because Leo was interrupted by Hans and a very flustered-looking Carol, who was clearly annoyed at who I was talking to. Leo left me to greet more people and unveil another batch of lobsters and sauces.

"Please come and find me before you leave," he said. "You know where I'll be."

I am still not sure what attracted me to Leo. It might have been that he seemed so sure of himself or that he seemed to have a very sharp sense of humor. Perhaps it was that he was much older than I was or that he was obviously successful in his career. Physically, at least, he wasn't what I would have thought of as my "type." He was balding, for one thing, heavier than I would have liked, and had a pleasing, rather than handsome, face. Nevertheless, although I was wary, I was intrigued by his obvious attention to me. I really hadn't had much experience fielding pickup lines or parrying advances from men who weren't my own age. And then again, some of us are just born with a naïveté that no amount of experience seems to eliminate. I am, without doubt, one of those people. This romantic blindness has allowed me to maintain a certain optimism over the years, but it has also led me to make some very poor decisions.

For whatever reason, though, I did go looking for Leo at the end of my shift and we spoke a little longer. He said he wanted to take me out for dinner and claimed to know the chef at Portland's best restaurant. I told him I'd think about it and he seemed pleased that I hadn't agreed right away.

"Good idea," he said. "I could be an ax murderer, for all you know."

He had a certain talent with lines like that.

We had our first date soon after. Leo liked to do everything in a big way. He showed up at my apartment with roses and made a show of escorting me, holding doors open and pulling out chairs whenever possible. The restaurant he took me to had a 360-degree view of the city, allowing the lights of Portland and the Willamette River to twinkle erratically through every window. We had a special table reserved for us and the chef came over to talk to Leo, shaking his hand and chatting a bit about the state of the business before going off to prepare our dinners. I admit I was impressed with the display. Leo's plan for seduction, however, had only just begun. I'm sure that had I been older, he would not have told me the story he shared once our dinners arrived. But he had guessed (with amazing accuracy) at my need to collect the tales of others and fold them into my own experience. What he threw at me next was a guaranteed direct hit.

"I learned to cook in Vietnam," he told me, and my eyes grew wider. "I was drafted at eighteen, right out of high school. Marines. Spent two and a half years in Da Nang."

"Did you kill anyone?" I asked, half jokingly.

"Well, if somebody's shooting at you," he said, "you don't wait to feel bullets ripping through your stomach. You tend to shoot back."

I noticed for the first time that his brown tie did not match his blue jacket. In fact, there was something a little off about his whole outfit.

"You don't feel bad?" I asked. "Knowing you've taken lives? It doesn't bother you?"

Leo was eating a plate of veal. I noticed that he sliced it into very small portions before placing it carefully into his mouth. "You don't see them," he said. "You don't know who they are. It's not real. Anyway, if it comes down to a question of my life or someone else's . . . well, I'm not going to let myself be killed by somebody I don't even know."

"Why would you want to put yourself in that position in the first place?"

"I didn't." He shrugged. "The government made that decision for me."

"You could have tried to get out of it," I said.

"I would have if I'd known what it was going to be like."

There was a silence between us, punctuated by the sounds of silverware clattering against plates and the ambient hum of conversation.

"Well, how'd you get out, then?" I asked, determined to see the story through to the end. He had me and he knew it.

"It was an injury. They sent me home."

"So you did get shot?"

"No, I always managed to avoid that."

"Then what was it?"

"I stepped in the wrong place at the wrong time. It was a brilliant device someone dreamed up called a Bouncing Betty. It clicks when you step on it but it doesn't explode until you take your foot off. They told me I was lucky to have survived. I lay on the side of this road bleeding and unconscious for fifteen hours before anyone got to me."

"But," I said tentatively, "you don't have a limp or anything. Do you?"

"It didn't exactly hit me in the leg," he said. I was sure I detected a glint of excitement in his eyes. "More like upper thigh. Very upper. Not the sort of damage that shows." He watched my expression for a moment as if measuring his next words carefully. "Everything's in perfect working order," he said, "but I can't ever have children." I gasped a little and he said, "You don't like this conversation, do you? It bothers you, doesn't it?"

"I think it's interesting," I managed to say.

"We don't have to talk about it anymore."

"I don't mind."

"You keep staring at my tie. Did I get something on it?" He checked the tie, laughing a little.

"No, it's nothing. I was just kind of thinking . . . it's brown and your jacket is blue."

"I'm color-blind," Leo said.

He had an answer for everything.

The fact that Leo and I were dating soon became common knowledge in the Dining Room. In the kitchen, at least, it afforded me a unique, if wary, respect. I had broken through the ranks and obtained the unique status of being the top guy's girl-friend. The other chefs seemed quite in awe of Leo and his culi-nary abilities and they demonstrated their deference toward him by making my life considerably easier. My dishes always came out first, and I was instantly forgiven if I made a mistake on an order. And after word of our involvement spread, I received none of the ribbing that other servers got routinely, especially that of a sexual nature. Leo himself made no secret of the fact that we were an item. He cooked special meals for me and fed them to me on the side. Since he didn't work the line, acting more as a supervisor, he couldn't be accused of giving me preferential treatment, although he clearly was. He rarely called me by name, preferring to greet me always as "little girl."

As for the waitstaff, they were either oblivious to what must have seemed like an odd pairing or incredulous and vaguely disapproving. My enhanced status in the kitchen, especially, did not sit easily with servers who had been working in the Dining Room for years. Deane thought the whole thing was hysterical and teased me about it relentlessly, often making off-color remarks as he breezed by me in the kitchen. Belinda thought Leo was a dead end. There was something about him, she maintained, that was just not right.

Belinda, however, was more concerned with her own problems than my romantic wanderings. She'd had quite enough of the Dining Room and its politics. Carol had given her a number of pink slips already for various infractions and she was on the verge of being fired. Belinda was very resourceful. Within weeks of my first date with Leo, she was hired at an upscale Italian restaurant in a small, fashionable shopping center. She left the Dining Room without so much as a day's notice. I missed her sorely.

My relationship with Leo heated up, fueled by the fact that he was only visiting and would shortly have to return to Colorado and take care of business there. He owned a house, he told me, and managed a restaurant besides. He also told me that he had a couple of ex-wives, both of whom he was still on good terms with. He took me out to dinner frequently and we spent several afternoons sitting by the river, drinking up the last warm days of an Indian summer. He offered to buy me a new closetful of clothes and I turned him down. He was definitely coming back for me, he said. I was too good to let go. I was precious. A rare jewel, or something similar.

When Leo went back to Colorado, I was devastated. Despite my better intentions, I had managed to get myself entirely wrapped up in him and our little romance. I was also quite convinced that despite his protestations to the contrary, I would never see him again.

With Belinda and Leo gone, the Dining Room quickly became unbearable. No longer a complete novice, I had become comfortable with the more exacting aspects of fine dining. Belinda had taught me well. I was able to open a bottle of wine with as much panache as she and I was even overcoming my fear of being blinded by flying champagne corks. I could balance the large trays on my shoulder with ease and I could fold napkins with the crispness of origami. However, I could never get used to the Dining Room patrons. Deane had been completely correct in his description of them. They seemed like an extremely embittered lot, despite all their money. They were very demanding, besides, and truly regarded us as if we were a somewhat lower form of life. I had many customers who never so much as looked at me when I stood at their table. Others repeated their orders to me several times, slowly and loudly, as if my brain were limited and needed the extra time to process this complicated information.

Besides all of this (which would have been bearable if the payoff had been big enough), they were bad tippers. There was no cash in the Dining Room, since all the patrons were members of the club. At the end of the meal, the diner had only to write in the tip and sign the check. I saw some of the worst tips in my life scrawled on those checks. In fact, a standard rule of thumb was that the wealthier the guest, the lower the tip. As a final insult, all the tips were added directly to our regular wages, so the whole lot was taxed at a much higher rate. I hadn't paid much attention to this in my early days in the Dining Room because I was busy learning what I'd said I already knew, and then I was busy creating my own kitchen drama with Leo. With that behind me, though, I began noticing that I wasn't making very much money, after all, and I really didn't care for the people I waited on.

With Leo gone, too, Carol stepped up her efforts to make life miserable for me. She scheduled me for weeks of double shifts and broke up my days off so that I never had two in a row. I sensed that she was waiting for a reason to write me up, and I knew a confrontation between the two of us was inevitable. I got tired just thinking about it.

I shared my complaints with Belinda, whom I still saw frequently. Belinda was really enjoying her new job and told me that she was making much better money than she had in the Dining Room. All I had to do was say the word, she told me, and she'd arrange an interview with her manager for me. I told her I'd think about it.

Leo called me infrequently from Colorado. When I told him about the oppressive conditions in the Dining Room, he offered to speak to Hans on my behalf and arrange for me to interview "upstairs." The thought of working in the club's food and beverage office with Carol was totally repugnant. I told Leo to forget it.

"Well, it won't be long before you're out of there," he told me. "I'm coming to take you away from all of that." He went on to tell me how we would travel around the world together, spinning a tale that I couldn't believe but wanted to hear anyway.

Leo showed up in the Dining Room a couple of weeks later. I was working a Fantasy, and Deane came up behind me, covered my eyes with sweaty hands, and led me into the kitchen. "Guess who's here?" he said.

"Hi, little girl," Leo said, laughing. When he leaned over to embrace me, there was a smattering of applause from the chefs

behind him. As for me, I had become a believer. Leo had come
back for me. He might as well have ridden a white horse right
into the Dining Room.

Leo was a little more subdued than he had been a few weeks
before. He had a lot of business to attend to back home, he said,
and he was feeling the pressure. He was prone to migraines and
had to leave the kitchen a couple of times to lie in a dark room
until they subsided. He assured me that after he was finished
with his job for Hans, we'd make plans to take off and start our
lives together. So, although I was unhappy to see him go when
he left again for Colorado, I was convinced that he would be
back very soon.

Never one to wait patiently, I wanted to call Leo and discuss
our plans, but I found that the number he'd given me was dis-
connected. I held on for a couple of days, expecting him to call
me, but my phone remained silent. I called directory assistance
to find a new number for him, but they had no listing for anyone
by his name. A slow, insidious panic began forming in my brain.
Belinda shook her head and Deane clicked his tongue. Their
advice was to forget about Leo before I discovered things I really
didn't want to know.

After three weeks with no word from Leo, I did something I
can only marvel at now. I called Hans, as if he were a buddy of
mine and not my boss, and asked him if he had a working phone
number for his friend Leo. It took Hans a few minutes to figure
out who I was. Hadn't Leo talked about me? I asked him. Did he
know that Leo and I were seeing each other? Hans remained
silent for several seconds after I delivered this information. I felt
myself break out in a sweat. When Hans spoke again, it was in a
tone that indicated pity, annoyance, and a mild disgust all at the
same time.

"Didn't Leo tell you that he was married?" Hans asked me.

"Married?" I echoed.

"He has a baby son," Hans went on. "Leo Jr."

"But he can't have children," I said. "He was injured in Vietnam."

"Leo," Hans said patiently, "was never in Vietnam."

I'm still not quite sure how I managed to get through the rest of the conversation. I didn't hear anything else Hans said until he finished by saying, "I'm sorry," and hung up.

The only thing that remained clear to me after my phone call to Hans was that I would no longer be able to work in the Dining Room. The humiliation alone, with everybody knowing what a fool I'd been, was reason in itself to quit immediately. I called Belinda and asked her to arrange the interview she'd offered to get me. When I told her about Leo, she was compassionate, never once telling me that she'd told me so. She did offer to try to track Leo down so that I could exact an appropriate revenge. It was tempting, I told her, but what I really wanted was to bury the whole episode and never see the inside of the Dining Room again.

It took Belinda two weeks to set up an interview for me with her manager. During that time, I tried to keep as low a profile as possible in the Dining Room. I was sure that every time I turned my back I could hear snickering from Thelma, Agnes, and Ethel. What was almost worse were the looks of quiet pity I received from Rosemary. The cooks began treating me as if I were a recent amputee, staring at me out of the corners of their eyes but careful not to say anything that might upset me. Possibly the worst reaction, however, came from Tracy, who said he'd heard "something" about what I'd "been going through" and really wanted to help. Would I like to get together, say for drinks at my place? I told him I'd have to take a rain check.

Carol (had she been tipped off by Hans?) started scheduling me in the Men's Bar and the Card Room, where I made only a fraction of the already paltry tips. I had been removed from my Fantasy shifts. When I asked her about the scheduling changes,

Carol told me that my work performance had declined and that I'd have to work my way back to the Dining Room.

I gave notice.

My interview with Belinda's manager was very brief. I fell in love with the small, busy Italian restaurant right away. The waiters and waitresses looked to be closer to my own age, and what's more, they actually seemed to be having fun. He looked at my résumé and said, "I'll be honest with you, I don't really need any servers right now, but Belinda's given you a glowing recommendation. I'd have to squeeze you in on lunches to start. Would that be all right?" I hastened to tell him that it would be. "And the thing is," he went on, "you'll probably be able to move to dinners pretty quickly if you're as good as Belinda says." He looked at my résumé again and smiled.

"You've got great experience," he said.

I never heard from Leo again. Over time, my memory of him took on the quality of an unsolved mystery. I can't say I learned nothing from the experience. On a small scale, I realized how important it was to have a good relationship with the chef in any restaurant. This was knowledge I carried (sometimes to extremes) with me to every subsequent waitressing job. More subtly, I would never again fall for the kind of approach Leo used. Trust was not such a simple thing, after all, I thought, and the world was obviously filled with Trojan horses.

At the very least, Leo had allowed me to throw myself headlong into the type of real-life experience I'd been waiting for since my Yellowstone days. In fact, I'd gotten so caught up in this new real world, I'd forgotten that I had come to it, in the beginning, to generate enough "authentic" suffering and wisdom to make me a better writer. Aside from several spirited journal entries, I produced hardly any writing during my months in the

Dining Room. I wouldn't realize until later that the time between experiencing an event and effectively processing it can sometimes be quite lengthy.

I continued to see Deane after I left the Dining Room, but our visits became less and less frequent until we were meeting for coffee only once every two weeks or so. Some of the wind seemed to have been let out of his sails and he said that he missed me in the Dining Room, that things were just incredibly boring there without me. Laughing, he told me that Lisa and Tracy were expecting a baby, Rosemary had been named manager of the Card Room, and that a member had actually keeled over at the table. "See what I mean?" he said. "Nothing like what *you* managed to get into." He winked at me. To his credit, he never mentioned Leo by name, even jokingly. For someone who considered almost every personal tale fair game, this probably required great restraint on his part. He, too, was becoming tired of the Dining Room politics and planned to quit.

The last time I spoke to Deane was two years after I left the club. He had quit working altogether to stay home and nurse Bill, who had developed brain cancer. There was a deep sadness in his voice, which he tried, unsuccessfully, to cover by making his usual sarcastic quips about human nature. For several reasons, I wasn't in a position to offer much comfort at that point. Instead, I found myself talking about how difficult my own life had recently become.

"You'll manage," Deane told me then. "If there's one thing that's certain it's that you're a survivor. I can tell you that."

"That's probably true of both of us, isn't it?" I said.

"Maybe," he said softly. I arranged a time to meet Deane for coffee and told him I was really looking forward to seeing him, but because of pressing obligations for both of us, the meeting never took place. This is something I've always regretted because, soon after, we lost touch completely.

Brief, intense relationships such as the ones I had with both Deane and Leo are very common in the restaurant business. The transient nature of the job itself is often to blame. Waiters and waitresses are always moving on, leaving their coworkers behind. Everything about the movement of a dining room is temporary. The landscape of a particular restaurant during a particular season is one that constantly shifts. And each night becomes a part of several different personal histories the moment it is over.

I've never meant to leave behind any of the close friends I've made over the years, but the ones who remain today are the ones I am still working with. As for the rest, I have formed them into permanent parts of myself. Their stories, at least the ones they made with me, are now my stories.

This, in the end, is what I do.

# the art of waiting

**Tonight, everybody wants to sit** outside on the patio.
My station is inside, on the banquette, all the tables squashed
close together. I'm in the middle of calculating how much money
I'm not going to make when a party of five is seated at one of my
tables. They're well dressed, well seasoned, and look as if they're
in the mood to spend some money. I breathe a sigh of relief until
another waitress comes up to me and says, "Don't knock yourself out over those people."

"Why not?" I want to know.

"Because they stiffed me last week," she says. "They're Swiss
or French or something. They don't tip."

"This isn't something I needed to hear right now," I tell her.

"Just trying to help you," she sniffs.

The party is neither French nor Swiss, but they are most definitely high maintenance. In no time they have me running to all
corners of the restaurant with a thousand little demands. They've
brought promotional coupons with them and want all their appetizers for free. The manager knows them and tells me to make
sure they get free desserts. He is obviously unaware of the promotional coupons. They want a bottle of white and a bottle of red.

No, two bottles of red and a glass of white. No, just one red and two glasses of white. No, actually they'll just have the bottle of red and a glass of Fernet Branca.

"For me," says the one woman who is not part of a couple. "I need it for my digestion."

When the entrees arrive, the single woman makes a sour face over her lasagna and says, "It really should be hotter."

"Have them nuke it in the microwave," says another.

"We don't have a microwave," I say. "But I'll be happy to have them heat it up for you in the kitchen."

"That's exactly the problem," she says.

"You don't want it heated?"

"No, I want it hotter, but I don't want to wait a half hour until they make me a new one."

"We don't have to make a new one, we can actually heat this one. It won't take half an hour."

"I don't want to sit here without a dinner while the rest of my friends are eating."

"If you're going to complain about something," says another, "at least let the girl fix it."

"It's not a matter of having it fixed. It should have been hotter in the first place. Now by the time I get to to the end of it, it won't be hot enough."

"Why don't you let me take it? It'll only take a minute."

"That's not the point. It shouldn't have come out this way."

I gaze at the woman helplessly. This is the type of situation I've encountered many times before at the table, but I am still unable to come up with a suitable remedy. The woman doesn't want me to take her dish away and heat it up and she doesn't want to let me leave it at the table. Perhaps if I offered to turn back time for her so that the lasagna could be prepared to her exact specifications (or maybe a self-heating dish would work for her), I might be able to please her. But this is obviously not going to happen. Therefore, I am left with an impossible conundrum. Everybody else at the table is now watching me, waiting to see how I am going to handle it. I make a last attempt.

"Let me run it back to the kitchen," I say. "I'll have them heat it quickly for you and you'll have it back right away."

"No," she says, "I'll keep it. I'm hungry. You see, it's the right temperature for me to eat right now, but I like to talk while I eat. It's going to cool down too fast and then the last bit will be too cold."

"What would you like *me* to do for you, then?" I ask her.

"Stay close by," she says. "Maybe when I get to the end of it, I'll have you heat up what's left."

I have to smile and nod assent. This, I think, is what it's all about: complicated psychological interchanges with complete strangers taking place over contracted periods of time. I sign up for this kind of dialogue every time I approach a table. I am the waitress. My job is to serve. Of course, just what makes up the definition of the word *serve* is not nearly as clear.

My attitude toward service and servers changed completely with my job at Molto's, the little Italian restaurant where Belinda worked. During my brief tenure in the Dining Room, I'd met many servers who had made their life's work out of waiting tables. Had I been paying more attention, I probably would have noticed that most of them were quite skilled. At the time, however, I was more concerned with finding my own way through the requirements and duties of my job. I paid little heed to the art of the work itself. I found my coworkers an interesting group, and with Deane and Belinda, I'd formed strong friendships. But by the time I became involved with Leo, I'd stopped analyzing the job at all. If anything, my experience in the Dining Room had come perilously close to souring me on the concept of table service in general.

On my very first day at Molto's, however, I became aware of the sharp contrast in the landscapes of these two restaurants. For one thing, the staff at Molto's was much younger, hipper, and better looking. The bartender, Anne, was a tiny blond woman with beautiful green eyes, about my own age, who had a penchant for dating wannabe rock stars. She was so small, she had to use a stool to reach some of the liquor bottles. Naturally, bar patrons usually got a prime view of her sculpted backside every time she did so. Anne made very good money. Then there was Belinda, who'd really come into her own as far as tailoring her work outfits to be as appealing as possible. No more earring or hair codes for Belinda. Charlotte, in her early thirties, was the grande dame of Molto's. Charlotte, who taught an aerobics class during the day, had the lithe body of a dancer and a caring, almost motherly manner. When I arrived at Molto's, she'd already been working there for five years. Then there was Grace, a flame-haired single mother in her twenties, who was very vocal about the physical attributes of the many Molto's waiters she'd dated.

The waiters at Molto's exuded the same sort of sensuality as the waitresses. I was assigned to follow Chris, who looked like a Chippendale dancer and had the voice of Barry White, on my first day of training. Chris ordered a spinach salad and sent it back to the kitchen when it came out looking a little limp. The redone salad was a shiny green marvel. "Now look at this," Chris said. "*This* is a sexy salad. Mmm-mm." It was enough to make one swoon.

The cooks at Molto's, Sonny and Wes, were a whole story in themselves. In any restaurant, heat is a factor determining the mood of the staff. It's always hot in the kitchen, and in the dining room, a server is in a constant state of motion. During a busy shift, everyone gets a little sweaty. But at Molto's, the heat was more than just a factor, it was a salient entity. Molto's kitchen was tiny, encompassing barely enough room to swing the proverbial cat. On busy nights, five or six servers had to move in and out of this minute space, as well as the two cooks and single dishwasher. We were literally on top of each other, bumping hips and shoulders. It was impossible to avoid physical contact. The restaurant seated less than seventy-five people at capacity, and on some nights the kitchen would put out two hundred dinners in sweltering heat.

In the summertime, Sonny and Wes stripped down to jeans, aprons, and muscle shirts. We'd slam into the kitchen and see their arms outstretched, holding pans, flipping pastas, turning steaks, and stirring sauces. They were both gifted quipsters and they rarely turned around, knowing which waiter or waitress entered by scent. They were a vision at the busiest times, beautifully built, funny, creating fantastic food. We'd come in, order, and sigh. To maintain their sanity, the cooks kept a radio set to whatever the hippest FM station was at the time. So there would be music, too, and sometimes we'd dance around each other in the kitchen, making Sonny and Wes, who were separated from us only by a few inches of countertop, laugh out loud.

Charlotte and I often stood at the line together, watching Sonny and Wes as their muscles flexed and rippled in tandem.

"It's not really fair, is it?" she'd ask.

"Definitely not," I'd answer.

"Guys, you've got to put your shirts on," she'd tell them. "You're killing us out here." Sonny and Wes lived for comments like that. Really, there wasn't a waitress working who didn't lust after those two during the course of a shift. Sonny and Wes responded in kind.

Whether it was the heat, the proximity, or the relative youth of the employees, everyone at Molto's shared a peculiar kind of intimacy, which extended into the off hours. We shared rides to and from work, helped each other move, and often went out for

drinks after work. Of course, this wasn't paradise. Too much familiarity breeds contempt in any situation and this one was no different. There were flare-ups, romances that crashed and burned, and
occasional job dissatisfaction. As a general rule, though, there was
little competition among the staff at Molto's and we were very
close.

What made Molto's even more appealing was that it simply
ran well. For most of the time I worked there, all the waiters and
waitresses worked as a team despite the fact that they all had
very diverse interests and backgrounds. While not all of them
intended to remain in the business, for the time they were there,
the servers at Molto's actually enjoyed what they did and the
money they made doing it. There were several reasons for this
phenomenon. For one, we all loved the food we served. Molto's
was a bit ahead of its time, offering a menu of authentic Italian
dishes that were very unusual then, although they can now be
found in many trendy Italian restaurants all over the country.
The wine list, too, was eclectic but expertly designed. The owner
of Molto's held regular wine tastings for the staff so that we'd be
knowledgeable about what we were selling. Another factor was
our manager, Barry, who, although a perfectionist, was completely fair-minded and had a rare ability to cultivate loyalty.
Finally, the waiters and waitresses I worked with at Molto's truly
cared about how they performed on the job. It was a matter of
personal pride.

As a result, Molto's (which had already been in business for
ten years) did well enough for its owner to open a second restaurant. For me, Molto's formed a standard against which to measure not only my skills as a waitress but my ability to function as
a successful adult in the outside world. My time at Molto's
would bring a turning point in my life. Although I had no way of
knowing it, my reasons for waiting tables and my understanding
of my future direction would undergo some radical changes only

one year after my first shift. In a fundamental way, the restaurant itself was responsible for these changes.

But I'm jumping ahead of myself now. What I mean to say here is very simple: there is an art to waiting and to serving.

Allow me to illustrate.

According to the Bureau of Labor Statistics, there are almost two million people currently employed as waiters and waitresses in the United States. This figure accounts for a little less than half of all the jobs in the food and beverage service industry. A projection for the year 2006 estimates a net increase of about two hundred thousand. Of course, this statistic refers only to current figures and says nothing about those who, at some point or other, supported themselves waiting tables before moving on to other careers. One can only imagine how large that number would be.

It seems undeniable that the numbers of individuals and families who dine out several times a week have increased dramatically in the last two decades. This demand has led to a proliferation of restaurants catering to every dining need from formal to fast food. Time has become an elusive commodity, everyone is in a tremendous rush, and nobody wants to cook. The Bureau of Labor Statistics puts it this way: "Employment growth [of food and beverage service occupations] will stem from increases in population, personal incomes, and leisure time. Since it is common for both husband and wife to be in the work force, families may increasingly find dining out a convenience."

My own personal observations have led me to believe that dining out is not merely a convenience but a necessity for harried working parents, who feel so beaten up by the demands of their days that the last thing they want to do in the evenings is prepare a nurturing meal. They want, rather, to be waited on themselves. They want someone else to do the cooking and someone to serve them with a smile. They want someone else to pay attention to their needs and give them exactly what they want. More often than not, that special someone is the waiter or waitress.

Given the sheer numbers of waiters and waitresses who handle, touch, and serve the food we consume, it seems odd that the job is not given more respect. As a general rule, consumers expect their servers to be emotionally available enough to pamper them into a feeling of well-being that will last for at least the duration of their meal. I doubt that some of these patrons would expect the same from their closest relatives. Yet many guests (I can't say all) also assume that their waiter or waitress is a complete idiot. Who else but an uneducated fool would take a job waiting on them?

(In my experience, I've noticed that waiting on tables is one of two things that almost everyone thinks they can do. The other is writing. Perhaps it's no accident that there is only one letter of difference between waiter and writer. But this is a topic for an entirely different conversation.)

A general societal attitude toward waiting on tables was outlined for me a few years ago on the game show *Family Feud*. The question was "What occupation would you least like your wife to have?" The number one answer, gleaned from a variety of husbands, one assumes, was "waitress." Not stripper, mind you, or prostitute. Waitress.

Despite this, the Bureau of Labor Statistics estimates that job openings for waiters and waitresses "are expected to be abundant through the year 2006, reflecting substantial turnover—characteristic of occupations attractive to people seeking a short-term source of income rather than a career."

Well, sure, this is a job anyone can do, isn't it?

I beg to differ. Not everyone is up to this particular challenge. Some of the most talented, imaginative, and intelligent people I've met have been my fellow waiters and waitresses. All of those people were also very good at their job. I've also seen examples of the reverse, waiters and waitresses from hell, who, unsurprisingly, didn't last long in the game and who went on to jobs that supposedly require many more skills.

The Bureau of Labor Statistics offers an interesting definition of the nature of restaurant work and the skills needed by those who wait tables. What really stands out, though, in this rather perky description of the job held by millions, is the subtext, or the practical application of statements like "Waiters and waitresses take customers' orders, serve food and beverages, prepare itemized checks, and sometimes accept payments."

Sounds simple enough.

This is how it really works.

## Nature of the Work

"Whether they work in small, informal diners or large elegant restaurants," the Bureau of Labor Statistics says in its annual *Occupational Outlook Handbook,* "all food and beverage service workers deal with customers. The quality of service they deliver determines in part whether or not the patron will return."

*Quality of service* is a relative term. Some patrons seem to enjoy having a bad time when they go out to eat. I wish I had a dollar for every time I've heard a customer say, "I've had terrible service every time I've come to this restaurant." Why do they come back? My theory is that, in part, this customer is still looking for validation from his server. In some pathetic way, he wants the server to like him. Because it would be totally unacceptable for the customer to admit this (even to himself), he turns it around and projects hostility at his waitress. When the waitress picks up on this, she becomes automatically defensive and somewhat prickly herself (after all, why should she be held accountable for the customer's previous experiences?), and the customer's anticipation of another horrible dining experience becomes a self-fulfilling prophecy. He will rant and rave, ask to see the manager, have several items deducted from his bill, or perhaps be offered a free meal for the future. The waitress will get in trouble with her manager, have her night ruined, and go home talking about how she's learned to hate humans. The customer, however, will return. He has to. His waitress still doesn't like him.

This theory applies only to a certain type of customer, however. I strongly believe that there are others who simply feel compelled to complain when they dine out. For these people, venting frustration at a waiter, waitress, or manager is (possibly) their only form of therapy. I know who these guests are as soon as I approach the table. They scowl, bark, and let it be known that no matter what I do for them, they are *not* going to enjoy themselves. Before I'd even had a chance to take her order, a woman at one of my tables once told me, "I'm not going to be easy, you should know that. In fact, I think many of the people who have waited on me in the past are now in psychotherapy." She was as good as her word. Guests have also been known (and this is a fact) to place hairs, bits of glass, even bugs in their food in order to get a free meal.

Some restaurant owners and managers actually exacerbate problems like this with the draconian policy of hiring "spotters," or spies disguised as ordinary guests, to dine at the restaurant and report back to them on the quality of the service received. I was working at Molto's the first time I discovered this practice. My manager told me that a customer hired in this capacity had reported to the owner that my service was a bit below average, that I didn't seem very friendly, and that I didn't smile enough. When I discovered, through asking enough of the right questions, who this customer was, I was mortified. I remembered him well because he and I had gone to the same college at the same time. On the night in question, we'd talked about what it was like to be out of school and discovered a few mutual acquaintances. Why this person had chosen the path of a professional snitch was incomprehensible enough, but the fact that he'd turned what I thought was a rather pleasant conversation into a negative report for my boss was beyond belief. I've developed a finely honed hatred for spotters since then, but they can't take all the blame. I truly believe that these people really feel that they have to find fault in order to earn the free dinner they're getting. It's a no-win situation.

Take, for example, the restaurant I worked in recently. The corporate offices of this particular restaurant sent spotters out to each of its units twice a month with an itemized questionnaire and ample space for comments. Each question was worth a certain number of points, and restaurants (as well as servers) were penalized if the overall score was below a certain percentage. This would result in great quality control if the system actually worked. But how is it possible to assign point values to qualities as elusive as the server's personality (with which, more than anything else, the spotters found fault)? Naturally, I was the victim of one such report. The couple in question had been seated in the middle of an extremely busy Friday night. They were actually an extra table outside of my section, which I'd been assigned because their waiter was hopelessly buried. In her (extensive) comments, the woman wrote that I was knowledgeable about the menu, served them in a timely fashion, made several recommendations, and checked back with them to see how their meal was. Nevertheless, her dining experience was ruined, she said, because I didn't seem particularly "interested" in either her or her husband and didn't seek to engage them in "other" conversation.

Some spotters even resort to complaining about waiters other than their own. One woman griped that all the servers in the restaurant looked stressed out and cheerless. Apparently she had concerns about our mental health.

Spotter reports became something of a standing joke in this restaurant because the end result was that they did absolutely nothing to improve the overall quality of service. In fact, the reverse was probably true: all the servers developed a certain paranoia about the whole thing and behaved accordingly. Good waiters were still good, and bad waiters were still bad, but everyone slowly became guarded and unnatural in their approach to the table. Our monthly employee meetings began to resemble scenes from Shirley Jackson's story "The Lottery." We'd all sit around waiting to see whose number was up this time and who would end up being stoned by the court of public opinion.

So much for quality of service.

The *Occupational Outlook Handbook* goes on to further describe the "nature of the work" this way: "In fine restaurants, where gourmet meals are accompanied by attentive formal service, waiters and waitresses serve meals at a more leisurely pace and offer more personal service to patrons."

What exactly is meant by *personal service*? In addition to suggesting wines, explaining menu items, and offering variations on specific dishes, personal service extends into some very gray areas. Recently, for example, I found myself working a particularly busy Saturday night, managing five tables, four of which contained large parties. Each one of these tables expected very personal service and wanted me at the table almost constantly. One table of three couples insisted on ordering their drinks one at a time. Despite the fact that I repeatedly asked, "Would anyone else care for anything from the bar?" the host insisted that nobody did until I came back with the one drink he'd ordered. At that point, he asked me, "Are you going to bring the gin and tonic also?" Of course, by the time I'd made six trips for six drinks, the first person to order one was ready for the next, starting the whole cycle over again.

The adjacent table was celebrating a birthday and I was taken aside by each member of the party to make sure that I wouldn't forget to bring "our free birthday dessert—and we want candles and singing, also." After I'd assured everyone, individually, that I would not forget, the ninety-year-old matriarch whose birthday they were all celebrating yanked at my sleeve until I bent over close to her lips. "It's my birthday," she snapped, "and I don't want any damn singing. You got it?"

The third table consisted of a couple with three small children who began to slide out of their chairs almost immediately after being seated. "We're in a bit of a hurry," the mother told me. "The kids can't really wait. Do you think it will take a long time? Can you rush our food? But don't bring the main course until we've finished our appetizers."

Despite the strain, however, I was managing to juggle all these demands without falling into the abyss that waiters refer to as "hopelessly buried," until a man at the fourth table (two elderly couples and their married children) had a little too much to drink. As I was clearing their plates and getting ready to deliver dessert menus, the wife of the drunken man offered me a wad of vomit-soaked napkins. "This is for you," she said, placing them on my tray when I refused to touch them. "He's not feeling well," she said, pointing to her husband. "Can you bring us some napkins?"

My night more or less fell apart after that, but I still had certain decisions to make. I really couldn't contain my disgust at the gall of the vomit woman, and she took offense. I had to write the table off. As for the multiple drink table, they complained that my service was slow ("Are you having a bad night?" the host asked me) and tipped accordingly. After I called in all my favors with the kitchen, I managed to get the food for the couple with the children in record time. I didn't receive any thanks for this, verbally or monetarily, but I was relieved that I hadn't given them any cause to complain. The birthday table was a bit dicier. After weighing my options, I brought out a small cake studded with candles, along with several waiters who sang "Happy Birthday" in loud, off-key Italian. The matriarch shot daggers at me with her eyes and I shrugged. After all, she wasn't paying the bill.

In a more pleasant but no less extreme example of personal service, I once waited on a couple visiting the West Coast from Boston. They were expecting their first child and told me that it was their last time to take a vacation together alone. They were debating names, they told me, could I offer up some possibilities? I provided them with a few names and their meanings (because the names in my own family are so unusual, I've made an informal study of the etymology of names) and then told them what their own names meant. The couple became very excited and went on about how lucky they were to have been seated in my station. I wished them the best at the end of their meal and I meant it. The next night they came back and asked for a table in my section.

"We've come up with a list of names," they said, "and we really wanted to share it with you and see what you thought."

They came in for the next three nights (the last three of their vacation) and ate dinner at my table. I liked these two and felt a bit beholden to them because they'd been so nice to me and had tipped me so well, but after the first night, they came in expecting me to stand around and chat with them for the duration of their meal. I truly did not want to be rude to them, but I'd run out of things to say to them after the second night. It was almost like having relatives come to stay at my house.

Of course, there are still other types of personal service. I've been propositioned quite a few times at the table, sometimes directly, sometimes in the guise of genuine interest in my sparkling personality. Luckily, I don't remember most of these. One, however, still stands out clearly. It was another large party. Again, alcohol was involved. The host was a large, burly fellow and singularly unappealing. He told a few bad jokes and touched me every time I passed by the table. He ordered several bottles of very expensive wine and offered me a glass of each one, which I declined. By the time I ordered the entrees, the check was already close to three hundred dollars. Midway through dinner, the host motioned me over and gestured for me to come close. Thinking he was going to order another bottle of wine, I bent down to hear him whisper in my ear, "You're not very tall, are you?" I shook my head no. "Well, let me tell you something," he continued, his breath against my neck, "you're just the right size for me to fuck you in this chair." There was absolutely nothing I could do about this remark and he knew it. For all anybody knew, he'd said nothing at all, and so I pretended that he hadn't. However, I didn't let myself near his end of the table again, forcing him to raise his voice if he wanted to ask for something. I consciously chose not to think about why this man felt he had the right to talk to me in such a fashion and consoled myself with the thought that he was an ugly pig who would doubtless never get lucky in the way he wanted.

(As a related aside, most of the waitresses I've worked with agree that it is never a good idea to date their customers, but I've seen a few notable exceptions. One waitress in particular continually scanned the dining room for eligible men who might pluck her from her miserable fate. After a few duds, she met Prince Charming, a true sleazeball who brought his buddies in regularly to stare at her. Prince Charming sent roses to the restaurant, as well as a giant stuffed teddy bear. The waitress claimed to have been totally swept off her feet. It would only be a matter of time, she said, before she was released from the hellhole of restaurant work and was living in the style to which she planned to become accustomed. Time was certainly what Prince Charming got—ten to twenty for racketeering. The poor waitress watched his arrest on the news and went home to find the FBI camped out in front of her door.)

Well, personal service is as personal service does.

## Working Conditions

"Food and beverage service workers are on their feet most of the time and often carry heavy trays of food, dishes, and glassware. During busy dining periods, they are under pressure to serve customers quickly and efficiently. The work is relatively safe, but care must be taken to avoid slips, falls, and burns."

Actually, one carries heavy trays of glasses only when one can find the glasses in question. Or the spoons. Or the forks. My sincere hope for the health of the public is that very few restaurants operate like one that I recently worked in. In this restaurant (part of a chain), all the managers were given year-end bonuses based on the profit margin of their particular unit. There are several factors affecting profit in any restaurant: labor is one, food cost is another, and then there are supplies. Labor and food cost can be cut only so much if the restaurant is to remain operational. Supplies are a different story.

Claiming that silverware was being pilfered by the staff (or gremlins), the management of this particular restaurant refused to bring out spoons, forks, or steak knives when these items began running perilously low. And by perilously, I mean that after the first year of operation, this restaurant (which is still very busy and noted in several national dining guides) no longer served spoons with coffee. The coffee would arrive at the table with a plastic stirrer embossed with the restaurant's logo. The logic here was that spoons were too precious to waste on coffee. What if the guest ordered a dish of ice cream? Despite begging, pleading, and ranting by the waiters and waitresses, management stoically refused, for years, to bring out the supplies, which were stored, in abundance, in a locked room off the kitchen. This led to some truly nefarious activities in and around the table. Busboys regularly got into fistfights over forks and started hiding them under piles of tablecloths, stacks of menus, or next to garbage cans, where they assumed nobody would look. Ultimately, these busboys forgot where they'd hidden their stashes and raided the tables of other waiters for silverware, which led to heated arguments between waiters ("Let me see your pockets—I know you have at least four spoons in there!").

In the end, however, it was the guests who suffered the most, without even knowing it. Desperate waiters, faced with customers yelling for forks (it *is* difficult to eat without one), ran to the kitchen, frantically rinsed used forks (which were soaking in dirty water), and dried them with soiled linens. Those forks were then sent to the table.

Although I can't say I've seen this practice in any other restaurant, I'm alarmed by the thought that it might happen elsewhere. The fact that this particular restaurant is so well known and so popular leads me to believe that large restaurants with similar structures might employ the same tactics. Buyer beware. Or, as my father has often said, "Every time you eat in a restaurant, you take your life in your hands."

Well, what's life without an element of risk?

Risk is also an important factor in the working conditions of any waiter or waitress. And by this I mean the risk to one's mental health. Although I haven't seen waiting tables come up on many top ten lists of the most stressful occupations, it could certainly be included. There is enormous pressure on every food server (especially those in busy semiformal restaurants) to juggle an astonishing variety of mental and physical tasks over short, intense periods of time. Timing, as they say, is everything. What's more, a server is constantly being watched and, yes, judged. There is no room or time to lose one's cool at the table. True, I am not speaking of saving lives or putting out fires. However, how well one can perform under pressure in a restaurant directly influences one's earnings and therefore one's living.

For example: A typical weekend night might find me serving five tables at a time. Table One orders drinks and says they want to look at the menu for a while before they order. Fine with me. Table Two is seated and says that they're in a bit of a hurry because they need to catch a movie. They want suggestions on the menu because they're on a diet and have special needs. They also want to order a particular bottle of wine that they've heard about. Meanwhile, Table Three is being seated. They're regulars who've requested my table specifically and they're in the mood to chat. I have to signal them that I'll be right with them, knowing that I can't approach their table until I have at least five minutes to shoot the breeze with them. I go searching for the wine for Table Two and find that we're out of it. I have to go back to the table and suggest another wine, during which time they've all come up with impossible variations on the menu that the chef will make but that will take an extra forty-five minutes to prepare. After I've taken their order (my order pad looks like the rough draft of a short novel at this point), I make another trip back to the bar for the substitute wine that Table Two has decided to order. While this is going on, Tables Four and Five are being seated simultaneously. I look around for my busboy, hoping he's had the foresight to bring bread and water to the tables, but he's nowhere to be found. Later, I learn that he's having a snack in the kitchen. I pacify my friends at Table Three by telling them I'll put their order in and then come back to talk to them as soon as I've greeted my two new tables. Before I can even go to the new tables, however, I have to open the wine at Table Two. Unfortunately, the wine they've ordered is a bottle of Machiavelli Chianti, which often comes with a dry, hard cork. Sure enough, opening the bottle proves to be a herculean task, and as I'm huffing and puffing, I see Tables Four and Five craning their necks, looking for me. Tables Four and Five, it turns out, both want cocktails, and Table Five tells me that they're ready to order "right away." "Wonderful," I say, thinking that I won't have to spend too much time there, but no, the woman at Table Five is not at all ready to order. Her eyes scan the menu lazily. "What do you think is better," she wants to know, "the seafood linguini or the chicken breast?" I make a couple of recommendations and ask her if she'd like me to come back. "Oh no," she says, "I'm ready." As I'm taking the dinner order for Table Five, I glance over and see Table One ready to erupt. They want to order *now*. As I now have no time to stand back and observe the pace with which my tables are eating so that I can order their salads and entrees accordingly, I switch into overdrive and order everything—drinks, appetizers, and dinners—all at once. As I do, I offer up a little prayer that the kitchen is on its usual slow timer and that not everything will appear at the same time. It's too late for Table One, though. They're already angry that I've taken so long to get to them. My friends on Table Three are none too happy, either, and feel I'm ignoring them. My busboy has reappeared, looking as if he's just back from vacation, and wants to know what I need. "I don't know," I spit at him, "look around!" After I finally deliver the drinks to Tables Four and Five, I'm able to run to the kitchen to see what stage of preparation the entrees are at. "You're coming up," the chef says to me. He's sweating, red in the face, and looks totally pissed off at the world. I watch helplessly as the dinners for Tables One, Two, Three, and Five come up at exactly the same moment. There are ten plates altogether for four different tables. By all rights they shouldn't have come up together, because some of them are slower-cooking items like lasagna and steak. But the kitchen may have made a mistake on somebody else's order and be passing these off on me in the guise of trying to be speedy. They've played this game before and will never cop to it. "I can't take these all out at the same time," I hiss at the chef. "Then you shouldn't order them at the same time," he hisses back. "Don't bring anything back and tell me it's cold." It's pointless trying to argue with him. Obviously, my prayers have not been answered. When I deliver their entrees, Table Five tells me that I forgot to bring their salads. Table One says that their food is merely "OK." Luckily, the couple at Table Four is making out. At least I won't have to go there for a while. Table Three, however, is offended by the public display of affection and demands that I send the manager over to break them up. I find myself apologizing to everybody. My manager wants to know why I can't handle the pace. "It's not like you have any large parties," he says. There are now only two possibilities for me. The first is to fold completely, throw my tickets up in the air, and walk out of the restaurant. The other is to organize a triage system. With forced calm, I tell my busboy that he needs to go to every table in my section and give them whatever they want. I tell my friends on Table Three how sorry I am that I can't talk to them and that hopefully next time I won't be as busy. After checking with the manager, I offer Table One a free dessert for their troubles, which brightens their day considerably. I solicit the help of another waitress to check on Tables Four and Five before they, too, become hopelessly unsettled. Finally, I drop the check on Table Two, where the two men at the table fight over who will pay it. They both start yelling at me not to take the other's money and I have to tell them, "I'm sorry, but you two are just going to have to work this one out on your own. I'll be right back." As I walk away from the table, the hostess stops me and whispers frantically, "Are they just about finished? I'm running an hour wait." I laugh at her, at myself, and at the situation. I've become so stressed that I've actually entered into the eye of the hurricane and I enjoy a moment of complete calm.

This state of transcendence is not an easy one to reach, and most of the waiters and waitresses I have worked with have found ways to get to it by other means. When I began working at Molto's, I was amazed at how much my coworkers drank. This was a pattern I saw repeated in every subsequent restaurant. I've never met a waiter or waitress who could work a shift such as the one above and not need some sort of release at the end of it, whether it be through alcohol, drugs, sex, or, for the luckier ones, bursts of creative energy.

## Training, Other Qualifications, and Advancement

"Because maintaining a restaurant's 'image' is important to its success, employers emphasize personal qualities. Food and beverage service workers are in close contact with the public, so these workers should be well-spoken and have a neat, clean appearance. They should enjoy dealing with all kinds of people, and possess a pleasant disposition. State laws often require that service workers obtain health certificates showing that they are free of communicable diseases."

In my opinion, this description is understated to the point of hilarity. *Personal qualities,* in particular, is a term that, could it truly be defined, would illustrate perfectly what makes both the best and worst servers. (For the record, I have never placed myself in the former category. Being the best at serving people requires a level of selflessness I haven't come close to achieving.) I saw examples of both at Molto's and have forever used them as yardsticks to measure not only the service of my coworkers but my own.

Belinda was certainly the best waitress I have ever worked with. The moment I saw her open that bottle of wine in the Dining Room without ever letting it touch the table, I knew she had a certain facility for her job that I would probably never achieve. Belinda's personal qualities extended beyond her ease with a wine opener, however. At Molto's, we were not allowed to have order pads and were required to remember orders for parties of up to six people. Belinda was able to carry the most complicated orders for six or seven tables in her head without ever forgetting an item. She also knew instinctively what her customers would order before they did. Her predictions became something of a parlor trick for a while, in fact. Beyond such obvious attributes, however, Belinda was able to morph both her personality and her looks to suit whoever she was waiting on. For example, I'd watch her waiting on a group of young women and she'd appear reserved and fresh faced. Her conversation with them would be friendly but impersonal, never threatening. For couples, she'd become sophisticated, knowledgeable, and attractive. When waiting on men, she became girlishly flirtatious and subtly sexy. Were it not for her obvious sincerity at the table, Belinda would have merely been a good actress. But I don't believe that Belinda herself was aware of her transformations, and that detachment was part of the reason she made more money and received more compliments on her service than any of her coworkers.

None of the qualities that made Belinda a great waitress and a good judge of character made her an easy person to deal with when she was not on the floor, however. Although she remained a good friend of mine for years, she usually ran through managers, owners, and coworkers in short order. A born organizer, Belinda knew what would make a restaurant run smoothly and was very vocal about what she felt needed changing. Despite the fact that she was a natural at what she did, most of her employers weren't willing to put up with what they felt was insubordination for very long. As a result of this and her own restlessness, Belinda switched jobs quite often. I'd only been working at Molto's for a couple of months, in fact, before Belinda moved on to greener pastures.

Unfortunately, I was responsible for the hiring of the worst waitress I have ever worked with. Tiffany, a relative of mine, was new to the city (and perhaps the planet, I later thought) and needed to find work. Tiffany assured me that she'd had plenty of experience waiting tables and pleaded with me to help her get a job at Molto's. My manager liked me and found Tiffany amusing at her interview, so he hired her.

The disaster that followed was almost sublime in its totality.

For starters, Tiffany was completely unable to hold a thought in her head, let alone an order. She became the only waitress at Molto's to use an order pad, and even then she wrote down the wrong items. She took orders for entrees not listed on the menu and drove the cooks nearly insane when she demanded they prepare these dishes. Because she added every bill incorrectly, the bartender on duty was forced to total Tiffany's checks to avoid costly mistakes. But even with all this help, Tiffany had absolutely no sense of timing—a fatal flaw. Every day she came to work (and she often didn't make it in for her shifts), she acted as if she was serving a leisurely meal in her own home, to one table at a time. The word *multitasking* was not in Tiffany's vocabulary.

Perhaps all of this could have been forgiven, or at least managed, if Tiffany had been possessed of some of the personal qualities that make a good, or even competent, waitress. But although she was an attractive young woman, Tiffany selected variations on the standard black-and-white uniform that could only be described as garish and strange. Seeking to disguise an imaginary heaviness, Tiffany shopped at a clothing store named Renoir's Lady and came to work in a floor-length tent of a skirt that would have been better suited for a Wiccan festival. Her jumbo skirt caught on the edges of tables, collected spills of every kind, and tripped her quite often. In contrast, she bought white shirts that were way too small for her ample bosom and popped several buttons under the strain. As for hair and makeup, Tiffany was clueless. Suffice it to say that several strands of her dark tresses frequently wound up in the dishes she served. When I attempted to offer some advice on her attire, however, Tiffany accused me of being jealous of her sense of style. I countered by telling her that our manager, Barry, had noted that her clothing was inappropriate (what he'd actually said was "Where the hell does she think she is, a cabaret?"). Tiffany really took umbrage at this, telling me that she was quite sure Barry was "very attracted to me, if you know what I mean."

Barry did have a certain attraction for Tiffany, but it was the sort of fascination that makes people slow down when they pass a fatal accident on the freeway. For in addition to being a train wreck in terms of ability and attire, Tiffany was also unable to get through a single shift without dropping, breaking, or spilling something. Her penultimate feat at Molto's came during a busy lunch shift. The dining room was divided into a main floor and a balcony linked by a carpeted stairway. I was taking an order in the upstairs smoking section when I heard a tremendous crash. The wind whispered "Tiffany" in the silence that followed.

Sure enough, Tiffany had managed to wipe out on the stairs with two dishes of linguini and shrimp in cream sauce, which made the seating of any more upstairs tables a viscous impossibility. Tiffany was laughing. Horrified, I rushed over to the host's podium where Barry was watching silently, his jaw muscles working overtime in an extended clench.

"Barry, I'm so sorry," I said.

Barry, a chiseled New Yorker with a wit drier than the Sahara, looked at me and said, "I can't stand the way she moves. I can't stand the way she moves through my restaurant."

Wringing my hands, I told him, "Please fire her. I don't mind. Really."

Barry was no fool. He was also the first and last restaurant manager I have ever respected. "Oh no," he said, "I'm not going to fire her. You can do that. Go ahead, I dare you."

Neither one of us fired Tiffany. Miraculously, she found another job (serving cocktails, no less) after complaining that nobody was nice to her at Molto's. Before she left, however, she managed to create a final nightmare of epic proportions. In preparation for her new job, Tiffany got two-inch acrylic nails applied to her fingers. She then came to work at Molto's with said nails and proceeded to puncture several holes in the boxes that held the restaurant's house wines. Naturally, Tiffany never noticed the leaks. Since the wines were stored in the upstairs cooler, chablis soon began flooding out of the containers, down the stairs, and along the walls, dripping in a fruity waterfall onto the tables below.

Tiffany and Belinda represent opposite ends of the waiting spectrum as it pertains to those elusive *personal qualities,* but I've also seen everything in between. Unfortunately, many restaurant managers hire their waitstaff according to their own specifications regarding certain qualities. Breast size, for example. One owner I worked for hired a stunning Brazilian girl to wait tables even though she spoke absolutely no English and had never lifted a plate in her life. When it proved impossible to keep her on the floor, he paid her just to stand in front of the restaurant in a short skirt, holding menus.

As for state laws requiring that servers prove they are free of communicable diseases, I've never encountered such a request. Perhaps this is because most restaurant managers figure that communicable diseases on both sides of the table cancel each other out. A waiter may come to work with a cold, for example, but he would never approach a table with a visible open sore (what customer would tip *him*?). However, a customer thinks nothing of sharing his maladies with his server. The woman I waited on who handed me the napkins full of vomit is but one example. I've also had to clean up used dental floss, emptied syringes, and bloodied linens. Other servers I have known have not been as lucky, having been licked, kissed, and thrown up on.

## Job Outlook

Finally, the Bureau of Labor Statistics provides a telling paragraph in its description of the job outlook for waiters and waitresses:

"While employment growth will produce many new jobs, the overwhelming majority of openings will arise from the need to replace the high proportion of workers who leave this very large occupation each year. There is substantial movement into and out of the occupation because education and training requirements are minimal."

A recent survey projects that Americans spend almost a billion dollars a day on dining outside the home. Surely, this is a clear indication of the nation's increasing appetite for personal, gratifying service. Yet, as the Bureau of Labor Statistics rightly claims, the training and education requirements for the providers of this service are minimal. It's somewhat of a paradox that as a society we demand so much from those for whom we have such little regard.

Perhaps this is all a bit too profound. I don't claim that waiters and waitresses need advanced degrees in psychology or human relations to be successful at their work. Nor do I believe that waiting should be elevated to the status of health care, teaching, or any other occupation vital to the forward movement of the human race. However, I do believe that there is more to waiting than immediately meets the eye. Even servers themselves are often unaware of the subtle complexities of their job. My feeling is that for all the reasons above, waiting tests a server's ability to cope with much more than remembering an order and delivering it in a timely fashion. In addition to providing excellent training in personal organizational abilities, patience, and stamina, waiting also provides a test of a server's human relations skills. There are few jobs that offer such direct contact with such a wide variety of people. Those who are able to hone these skills, I feel, will be successful in whatever field they choose, whether they stay in the restaurant business or not.

Restaurants provide one of the last customer service industries to flourish. These days everything can be done via fax, modem, or phone. I can order my clothes from a catalog, furnish my house through home shopping channels, listen to music samples on my computer, and submit my written work via e-mail. The only thing I really can't do without a human being present is be served dinner in a restaurant. Somehow, there really is no substitute for the person-to-person contact involved in the simple act of sitting down in a restaurant and being waited on. Perhaps this is part of the reason why the interchanges between customer and server are often so highly charged and have emotional content far beyond what seems reasonable given the situation. The expectations for an "experience," be it pleasant or not, are great. On both sides of the table.

# molotov cocktail waitress

**After working for a while at Molto's,** surrounded by so many people on a daily basis, I found myself in one of the loneliest periods of my life. On the day I turned twenty-four, I railed against fate in my journal. What kind of ridiculous age was this to be, I wondered. I'd accomplished nothing and was on a fast track to nowhere. Although I'd continued to write between shifts, on my days off, and late at night when I couldn't sleep, I was a far cry from the successful writer I'd planned to become when I first started working in the Dining Room. In no particular order, I listed all that I had not accomplished: no great works, no mate, no children, no meaningful contributions to mankind. I couldn't even get a decent relationship together (and by this, I meant any kind of relationship, even the ashtray-hurling passion that flares and then dies). The few friends I had left from my college days were embarking on serious love affairs, which would later turn into marriages for all of them. They wanted very little to do with me and my connection to their recent pasts.

I worked at Molto's as often as I could without burning myself out on it altogether. After all, there was only so often I could rub up against the same five people in that tiny kitchen. Besides this, the configuration of Molto's was changing, slowly but perceptibly.

Following her usual MO, Belinda had quit and moved on to another restaurant. She'd been replaced by Sue, whose super-model looks and sunny disposition seemed too good to be true. We all wondered when she would crack and reveal a fatal flaw. Then the usually unflappable Barry set the events of his own undoing in motion by hiring Pamela, whom he was personally very attracted to, a married mother with a notoriously jealous husband. The developing tension between Pamela and Barry soon began affecting the moods of everybody on the staff. Charlotte reacted by taking a second job in another restaurant and worked fewer shifts at Molto's. Wes managed to win the heart of the beautiful Sue, and the two of them embarked on the most publicly physical relationship I'd ever seen. They kissed in the kitchen. They felt each other up at the dishwasher. They made eyes at each other over the line. They came into the restaurant after hours (they told us) and had sex on the floor of the smoking section. The fact that they were both incredibly good-looking only made things worse. Watching them was a little like watching a trailer for a home porno movie.

For a while, I managed to make my own life a little more difficult by dating Sonny. It was spring, after all, and I wasn't immune to the undercurrents flowing through the kitchen. Unfortunately, Sonny neglected to tell me that he was also dating Barbara, who bussed tables at Molto's. Barbara, who had an abusive speed-freak ex-husband stalking her, was a real hard-luck story. She was also very tough and very strong and she frightened me. I was extremely unhappy about being dragged into the middle of this drama when all I'd really been looking for was a little diversion. Of course, I still had to work with both Sonny and Barbara after it all hit the fan, which was interesting since on any given night one of them was preparing my food and the other was bussing my tables. Food was thrown, epithets were hurled, and feelings were hurt.

Finally, Barbara cornered me between Table Twenty and Table Twenty-One one night and said, "You can have him. I'm not good enough for him anyway and I'd only bring him trouble." She was weeping.

"Please," I told her, "I have no claims on Sonny at all. He's all yours and I'm sure he loves you very much."

I stormed into the kitchen and threw a handful of tickets over the line at Sonny.

"What's the order?" he asked, baffled.

"You are *such* an asshole," I spat at him.

"So, would that be rare or medium rare?" he asked.

It was getting—in more ways than one—too hot in the kitchen.

I decided that adding more work to my schedule was the only viable escape. Again, Belinda was the catalyst. She was working as a cocktail waitress at Le Jardin, an upscale bistro a few blocks from my apartment in downtown Portland, and offered, again, to get me an interview. In short order I was hired to work a cocktail shift on the two nights I was free from Molto's.

It soon became evident, however, that Le Jardin was not going to provide me with the type of distraction I was looking for. Nor was it particularly profitable. I barely made enough money on the two nights I worked to justify being there at all. With this in mind, I answered an ad in the local paper for a job as a writer. The ad didn't specify what kind of writing, for whom, or what salary, but none of that bothered me. My thought was that I had to try to get it.

I showed up to interview for the job in a small office piled high with papers, ashtrays, and half-filled coffee cups. It turned out that the job specifications didn't exactly match those in the newspaper. The two men who interviewed me were going into a joint venture developing a discount card for use in restaurants, movies, and amusement parks. Hank, the older of the two men, had been selling insurance for most of his life. Tim, the younger man, published a small newspaper that consisted mostly of advertising copy for the businesses that paid for space in the paper. What they really wanted was somebody to sell their discount cards over the phone. I was disappointed. I told both of them that I was hopeless at selling and what I really wanted to do was write. Tim hastened to tell me that I'd be doing a lot of writing for his paper (if that's what I wanted) and that my hours selling would be minimal. They offered me the job on the spot. I felt compelled to take it, even though the pay was pretty low and I'd be adding a long daily commute to my already crowded schedule.

The job was not without its generous dose of irony. Every morning I'd arrive in the office, take a seat in the glassed-off triangle of space that had been provided for me, and look at my assignment for the day. The writing assignments bordered on the bizarre. For example, Tim would leave a note on my desk saying something like "Write a story on San Francisco. About two pages should do it." Sometimes he'd want restaurant reviews. Of course, they couldn't be real reviews since the restaurants were paying to be mentioned. Instead, I'd get a faxed menu and have to create a fantasy tale about what went into the making of dishes I had never seen, much less tasted. I felt I'd really reached the apex of this type of writing when I was instructed to write about a motel in Capistrano, California. "Like the swallows," I wrote, "visitors will always want to return to Motel X in Capistrano. . . ." Hank and Tim loved my writing so much that my services soon became completely funneled into the paper. I was even listed on the masthead. The discount card never got off the ground. Despite the fact that I felt what I was writing was the height of silliness, I was actually getting paid to write for the first time. That in itself was no small thing for me. This, I reckoned, was a job worth keeping.

But by the fall of 1986, I'd had just about enough of everything. My plan to disappear into as many jobs as possible had resulted only in greater personal dissatisfaction. I had been writing short stories frantically in my spare time and had sent a few of them out to small literary magazines. I'd received a few nibbles, and this was enough to make me think that I should be devoting all, not part, of my time to writing. I was never going to get anywhere slinging plates, I reckoned (of course, all the stories I was writing were about people and events I'd come to know of through the restaurants I worked in, but I wasn't farsighted enough to realize this), and I was just wasting my time. Some of Portland's notorious dampness had settled into my soul. I was tired of watching it rain week after week. I felt as if my entire personality was becoming pale and washed out.

My writing job at the paper had convinced me that I would probably be able to scratch out a living writing something somewhere, and I decided I'd have to make a definitive move. San Francisco sounded like as good a place as any to try. A few college friends were living there and actually having some success in their chosen fields. However, I knew I'd never leave as long as I had my job at Molto's. Despite the fact that it had become a bit oppressive, the money I made there was still good, and I'd worked there longer than I'd worked anywhere up to that point. It was familiar. So I gave notice, telling Barry and my coworkers that I intended to move south and try to make it as a writer.

Because I'd given a month's notice instead of the usual two weeks, my leaving turned into an extended going-away party.

Every weekend night, I'd join Wes, Charlotte, Anne, and whoever else wanted to come along for drinks and pool. Wes was in
a state of desolation due to the fact that Sue had herself recently
moved to California in search of a better life. I started spending
more time with him on our weekly forays and listening to his
tales. Although he preferred to limit his banter to incisive barbs
in the kitchen, I learned that he had a razor-sharp mind as well
as an ability to quietly assess the personalities of his coworkers
with amazing accuracy. Wes told me that he was getting terribly
tired of Barry's disastrous flirtation with Pamela and was sure
that no good would come of it. Barry, he claimed, was getting
into some "bad shit" over the whole thing and it was affecting
his managerial skills. Wes also told me that he was sick of working himself to the bone for what he was paid. He was looking
into opening his own restaurant, he said. All very hush-hush, of
course. "Too bad you're moving," he added, "you could come
work for me."

But I didn't actually feel like I was going anywhere. I'd made
no plans and was, effectively, just waiting for the end of my time
at Molto's to force me into movement of any kind.

My last night at Molto's came on a Sunday. Pamela, who had
recently been promoted to nights, dominated the floor, scooping
up as many tables as Barry would give her. Barry himself looked
as if he hadn't slept for weeks and was irritable beyond what I'd
seen before. The whole shift was very anticlimactic. Charlotte
was off and everybody else went home early. I went about cleaning as Wes packed up the kitchen.

"I can't believe it's come to this," I said. "Seems like there
should be something more momentous to mark my last night
here."

"So wait for me," Wes said. "I'll take you out."

The two of us ended up at a bar near Molto's. Wes bought
me drink after drink and listened to my grand plans for the

future. I told him a bit about my past, too, such as it was. He talked about Sue and how disappointed he was that she had decided to leave. Our conversation began to take on the strange elastic shape of drunken exchanges that happen in the wee hours. After we closed the bar, Wes drove me home and walked me upstairs to my apartment.

"Can I come in for a minute?" he asked.

"Sure," I said. "What's a minute? It's almost three in the morning."

My apartment was very small, but Wes managed to walk around it as if there was much to be seen.

"I don't have much to offer you," I said from the kitchen. "Definitely nothing to drink here. I've got some oranges, though."

"Oranges would be good," Wes said. "I'll have an orange."

We sat opposite each other and I struggled to peel an orange with motor skills that were severely compromised by the number of vodka tonics I'd ingested.

"Why don't you let me help you with that?" Wes asked and took the orange from me. He peeled it gracefully without ever breaking the rind. I could see both the cat and the canary in the smile on his face. He sectioned the orange, handed me two pieces, and placed two in his mouth.

"Very good orange," he said. "Thank you."

The silence that followed soon became crushing in its weight.

"What are we going to do now?" I asked Wes.

"Well," he said slowly, "we got the orange together pretty well. Seems like it'll be easy from here on."

Today, I remember strange details of that night. For example, I remember distinctly the sweet citrusy taste of the fruit and that it was the last decent orange of the season. I remember that the weather turned cold that very night, going from Indian summer to frigid winter. And I remember that all night I had the sad sense of something ending but no vision of a new beginning with which to replace it.

*ø ø ø*

I began feeling nostalgia for Molto's as soon as I quit. The few days I was going to give myself to relax and make plans turned into weeks. I kept going to work at the office during the day, but my nights seemed absolutely vast and empty. Suddenly there seemed to be a huge hole in what had been passing as my social life. Despite the fact I had sworn to move on, Molto's still felt a bit like home.

It was with this feeling that I stopped in soon after I quit to say hello. Nobody seemed to understand quite what I was doing there since I'd so recently been adamant about not wanting to come in for as long as possible. As if to make me feel a little more comfortable, Barry invited me to a party he was throwing the following weekend.

"It's for all the Molto's survivors of the summer of eighty-six," he said. "You definitely fall into that category, so you should come by." I told him I would and wrote down directions to his house. "Tell Tiffany," he added, laughing. "She can come, too." Tiffany was still in town, although I saw considerably less of her at that point. After rehashing some of her most spectacular feats at Molto's, I told Barry that I'd let her know about the party.

"I'll just make sure she gets her drinks in a paper cup," he said.

I've often wondered about the strange chain of events that followed that visit to Molto's because, on the one hand, it seemed that what followed was merely a series of choices that could have been presented to anyone. On the other hand, what was to come seemed peculiarly predestined. I've never been able to figure out which was which.

I didn't want to go to Barry's party. In fact, as soon as I
returned home, I decided it would be a bad idea. I hadn't left on
particularly good terms with Sonny and I was sure that he and
Barbara would be there together. Hostility would be high and I
wasn't in the mood to be dragged into a catfight. Nor, after my
last night at Molto's, was I much in the mood to see Wes. I knew
from Barry that Sue was visiting Wes from California and figured
I was the last person he'd want to see at a party. There was
Barry, too, and his relationship with Pamela. I figured that the
party was probably Barry's way of safely inviting her to his
house. The guy was so desperate to see her, he'd risk seeing the
husband in a social situation. It could be quite ugly. Besides, I
told myself, I'd resolved to leave this all behind. Why would I
intentionally place myself in the lion's jaws?

Then Tiffany dropped by. I have no idea how she'd learned
about Barry's party, but by some wrinkle of fate, she knew all
about it and was determined to go. She was also determined to
take me with her. I argued with her about it, but without sharing
too many personal details I couldn't come up with any valid reasons why I shouldn't go. When she pointed out that I'd probably
spend the night alone watching *Miami Vice* instead of going out
"and having some fun for a change," I found it difficult to turn
her down.

So we went.

Barry's party was exactly as I had suspected it would be.
Barry was, if possible, more uptight than he was when managing
the restaurant. I soon understood the reason: Pamela was there,
without her child or her husband, nervously fussing around
Barry's kitchen. The torturous byplay between these two served
to add an element of freneticism to the whole affair. Barry was
besotted with Pamela by that point and she was playing quite a
number on him. All the while he was trying to act as cool as possible, which wasn't working very well. Out of the corner of my

eye, I noticed him drinking heavily and making various trips to his bedroom with various friends and various envelopes of white powder.

I paid little attention to this, however, since I was caught in the generous swell of my own soap opera. As I had predicted, both Sonny and Wes were in attendance and so were Barbara and Sue. Sonny had no idea what approach to take with me and ended up using several in the course of a few minutes, which made him appear like an utter fool. Barbara had decided to be extremely nice to me, which was much more frightening than if she'd leaned over and pulled out my hair—which was clearly what she would have preferred.

Sue's looks had only been improved by her time in California. She looked ready for the cover of an alternative lifestyle version of *Vogue*. Wes made sure he had at least one of his hands on some part of her body at all times. For me, he had only a glower and this question: "Weren't you leaving town?"

"Nice to see you, too, Wes," I answered and escaped to the kitchen, where I was rescued by Charlotte, who knew all about uncomfortable restaurant encounters, having been part of a few in her day.

"There's someone I want you to meet," she said, leading me to a tall, dark stranger who was leaning awkwardly against a cabinet, looking as if he'd wandered into the wrong party. "This is John," Charlotte said, smiling. "We worked together at Molto's years ago. John's a writer, too."

With my eyes, I telegraphed a message of dismay to Charlotte, but she shrugged and smiled again as if to tell me that I might actually like this John person and promptly melted into the scenery.

While John and I spent the next half hour standing in exactly the same spot, we covered a tremendous amount of conversational ground. He, too, had wandered into Molto's out of a sense of nostalgia a few days earlier and received an invitation to the party from Barry. He, too, was working on a first novel. He, too, was planning a move to San Francisco in the near future, having been convinced that finding work in Portland was impossible. We talked about Molto's, past and present. I learned that not much had changed over the course of the last five years. We talked about writing and discussed the plots of our novels. I wasn't at all surprised when he told me he'd love to read what I'd written. John was, quite obviously, very eager. In fact, it occurred to me that he'd come to this party specifically to meet somebody he could leave with. I wasn't about to go anywhere with him, but I was intrigued by him and told him that I was planning to attend a lecture a local literary agent was giving the following week.

"Why don't you give me your phone number?" he said. "Maybe we could go together."

"Sure," I said. "Maybe."

"I'm really glad I came to this party," he said impulsively. "Until the last minute I wasn't going to come at all. I didn't actually think there'd be anyone here for me to talk to."

I'd almost forgotten about John by the time he called me a few days later, but I was happy to hear from him. The lecture by the literary agent became our first date and was rapidly followed by a second. Within a couple of weeks we were inseparable. There was a level of intensity to my relationship with John that I'd never experienced before. The whole thing seemed to be operating at an accelerated speed. It almost seemed that if we slowed down, spent less time together, what was building between the two of us would vanish. It was actually a bit frightening to get so close to someone so quickly, especially since what was developing between us had the feeling of something serious.

At the height of our romantic bliss, we took a trip to Molto's for dinner. It was only fair, we reckoned, that we go in and thank both Barry and Charlotte for helping us meet.

Barry seemed nonplussed but relatively amused at our gushing declarations of love for each other, but Charlotte just laughed.

"I knew you two would hit it off," she said.

John and I continued to spend as much time together as possible, but it soon became apparent that both of us were going to
have to start thinking of a future beyond the dawning of the next
day. Neither one of us wanted to leave the other, but we hadn't
known each other long enough to suggest leaving together, so
both of us put our plans to move on temporary hold. John had
recently left a job working in a halfway house for troubled teens,
because of the high stress and terrible pay. While he scouted
around for a teaching position, he took a night job as a prep
cook in a small Mexican restaurant to make ends meet.

My part-time writing work wasn't nearly enough to float me,
and without the income from Molto's, I was days away from dip-
ping into the meager savings I'd so carefully accumulated over
the previous few months. Despite my new romance and subsequent lease on life, I began to have nagging feelings of insecurity.
If nothing else, waiting tables had provided me with a sense of
self-reliance. There was a certain security within the walls of a
restaurant, which I was missing. Not wanting to admit that my
plans to try to make it as a writer had been relegated to the back
burner, I told myself that I wouldn't be going anywhere if I let
myself run out of money entirely. Waiting seemed, again, the
only option. And again, it would be a temporary measure, something to gain a financial foothold while my future unfolded. The
only question remaining was which restaurant I would work in.

I wanted to synchronize my hours with John's, so I went
looking for a restaurant with late hours. This meant that I'd be
looking at restaurants that doubled as bars. I had only looked at
a couple of these places before learning that The Columbia, an
extremely busy, high-volume bar close to my apartment, was hiring cocktail waitresses.

I liked the idea of cocktailing and, even after my unprofitable stint at Le Jardin, still thought there was something that sounded very glamorous about it. Of course, my ideas about these things were predicated on some decidedly nonfeminist notions. I had grown up idolizing Barbara Eden's character on *I Dream of Jeannie*. And though I'd never admitted it to anyone, I thought that the bunny outfits the waitresses wore in the Playboy Clubs were really cute.

The cocktail waitress, I learned, is a unique breed. Her financial success often depends on her physical attributes as well as her ability to take any number of rude, sexist, even abusive comments with a smile and a quick comeback. Her job is to serve alcohol, but she is held accountable for those who become overly intoxicated. She has to carry several drink orders in her head and make change instantly with one hand while the other balances a tray of glasses, coins, and bills. Most of the cocktail waitresses I've known go home late at night and dream about the job.

Belinda, veteran of so many waitressing jobs, once told me, "Cocktailing dreams are the worst. It's not like you're dreaming about not being able to catch up with your tables. When you dream about cocktailing, it's like you're going crazy. People are shouting drink orders at you, you drop all your change, and you spill everything on your tray over and over again." She was absolutely right.

When I set out to apply for a job at The Columbia, I was hoping not to repeat my experience at Le Jardin, which was both interesting and challenging but stressful beyond belief. The reasons for the stress had little to do with the physical demands of the job. Rather, the depression I felt after almost every cocktail shift had to do with watching the interaction between people and alcohol. The transformation I saw in average humans after the consumption of a few drinks seemed to me both raw and desperate—something I'd just as soon forget. It is often said that what one dislikes most in others is what one dislikes most in oneself. Perhaps my negative impressions of the cocktail hours I worked had something to do with my state of mind when I worked them: a bit raw and a little desperate.

Le Jardin, filled with blond wood, houseplants, and, every evening at happy hour, suited men drinking scotch and bourbon, was the most depressing place I've ever held a tray in.

Up to that point, my cocktail experience had been limited to a few shifts serving highballs to octogenarians in the Card Room. Le Jardin was different only in the fact that the mean age of its patrons was about thirty years younger. During the shifts I worked, at least, the clientele was almost exclusively male. They came down from their offices at five or five-thirty, picked list-lessly at the cocktail wieners dying slowly on the happy hour buffet, and then buried themselves in booths, waiting for me, Belinda, or whatever other cocktail waitress was working to walk over in her high heels and little black skirt and offer to get them whatever they wanted. And what they wanted was usually a martini or a scotch and conversation. There were a few ques-tions I heard repeatedly:

"How long have you been working here?"

"Are you going to school?"

"You got a boyfriend?"

There was a little game that went along with the cocktail ser-vice on these tables. I'd take the order, arrive back at the table with the drink, and set it down on the table. Most of the time, the customer would position himself so that I'd have to lean over him to get the drink within reaching distance. I'd ask if he wanted to run a tab or pay as he went, and he'd ask, "How much do I owe you?" I'd tell him and he'd pull out a large bill from which I'd make change. The customer would then fan the change out on the table, indicating that one of the bills was meant for me, but before he'd give me the tip, he'd ask one of the above questions. I'd have to answer, and the conversation started rolling. How long the dialogue went on depended on how eloquent I was feeling on a particular night, how drunk the customer was, and how personal the questions got. Usually we'd go back and forth a bit before he was satisfied, at which point he'd select a bill from the pile on the table and place it on my tray. The most talented customers would drink as they talked so that by the time there was a lull in the conversation, they could ask me for another drink and start the process over again.

I got be very creative at Le Jardin in the scant few months I worked there. Sometimes I was still going to school, studying psychology, biology, even archaeology. I was going to be a dentist, interior designer, chef. I was never single. Sometimes I had a boyfriend who was a childhood sweetheart. Sometimes I had a husband who was a policeman. Occasionally, I had children. Twins. The specifics of these tales were irrelevant. All the customer ever heard was "unavailable," and he stopped listening after that.

Often, the customer shared his own story with me. These tales were striking in their similarities. Wives who had lost interest. Ungrateful children. Divorce. Le Jardin wasn't the type of place where people came to celebrate. It was more a place of quiet desperation. Alcohol was the common theme and the great equalizer. When I worked with Belinda, I was sometimes able to have a laugh or two at how pathetic our customers seemed. Most of the time I was just struck with a sense of the overwhelming loneliness around me.

Although my experience at Le Jardin was still fresh enough to provide vivid memories, I was sure that The Columbia was a different type of establishment altogether. There was a younger crowd here, I thought, one that was surely less lonely and less desperate.

The application process at The Columbia closely resembled an open audition. I arrived at the appointed hour to find all of the front tables filled with cocktail hopefuls, busily filling out their applications. I counted at least twenty young women sitting poised, pens in hands, waiting for an interview. It was easy to understand why this position was such a coveted one. The Columbia was one of the most popular, busiest places in town. An old establishment, it had survived several changes in identity, going from bohemian to preppy, sophisticated to sloppy, and back around again. Part of The Columbia's draw were its twice-weekly dollar-drink nights. Tuesdays and Saturdays, patrons could be found lined up around the block waiting to get extremely drunk for as little money as possible.

The Columbia's bartenders also put on quite a show for guests every night of the week. The bartenders were all large, brawny men who tossed bottles of liquor back and forth, spun glasses, and poured drinks in seconds without ever spilling a drop. They were able to prepare several orders at a time, including those shouted at them by cocktail waitresses and those they read from the lips of patrons across the smoky room.

I'd logged many hours at The Columbia, and all of them flashed across my mind in Technicolor when I walked in there to fill out an application. The bar had been one of the meeting places of choice when I was in college, and later I'd spent time there with both Belinda and Deane after our shifts in the Dining Room.

I was waiting in line for my chance to speak to one of the managers conducting interviews when I felt a tap on my shoulder and turned to see a very familiar face.

"Hey, what are you doing here?" Belinda said.

"Same as you," I answered, looking at her application. I hadn't seen Belinda since I'd left Le Jardin a few months before. Both of us, it seemed, had gotten very busy doing nothing. We caught up with each other as we sat and waited. I told her about John and she told me that she'd recently met someone with whom she was getting very serious. I filled her in on what had been happening at Molto's and she reminded me of the various times we'd crawled out of the very place in which we were currently trying to get hired.

"Wouldn't it be great if we ended up working together again?" she asked. I agreed that it would, but I was doubtful that I'd get the job. I had little direct experience cocktailing. Somebody like Belinda had a much better chance.

I was interviewed by a harried woman of indeterminate age wearing expensive clothing and too much eye makeup.

"Are you willing to work very late hours?" she asked. "Sometimes we don't get out of here until two or three in the morning."

"That's fine," I told her. "I want to work late."

"Do you think you can carry up to six full beer glasses at a time?"

"That's definitely not a problem."

"You don't have any back problems, do you? There's a lot of lifting." She eyed me carefully. "You're kinda little," she added.

"It's not a problem unless I have to reach anything on the top shelf," I said, pointing to the towering bar.

"Why'd you leave Molto's?"

"I needed a change of pace."

"What about Le Jardin?"

"It was very slow there. I really couldn't make enough money to justify staying on."

"What's the difference between a martini and a Gibson?"

"Martini has an olive, Gibson has an onion."

"Which has more alcohol, a glass of red wine, a bottle of beer, or a shot of scotch?"

"They all have the same alcohol content."

"OK," she said. "Thanks for coming in. As you can see we've got quite a few applicants here, so it'll take a while to get through the interviews. But we'll definitely let you know."

Belinda and I left together and went out for coffee. Belinda was sure she had nailed her interview. I was sure I had failed mine. A few days later, the woman who interviewed me called and offered me a job. Strangely, Belinda never got a call.

I suspected that I was in over my head at The Columbia immediately, but I couldn't bring myself to admit that I'd made a mistake. I understood right away why the manager, Donna, had wanted to know if I had any back problems. Unlike Le Jardin, where I'd barely had to balance more than two drinks at a time on a tray, the high volume at The Columbia necessitated that I carry several orders at once. The weight wasn't so bad in itself, but trying to navigate the crowded bar without spilling anything required a combination of both grace and skill.

Donna's comment about my size took on new meaning as well. As the course of an average night at The Columbia wore on, patrons became drunker and less inclined to move out of the way of fast-moving cocktail waitresses. Customers would sometimes be stacked up three deep at the bar and I'd have to fight my way through them to pick up my drinks. Once I'd filled up my tray with orders, I'd have to turn around and bully my way out again. Every cocktail waitress at The Columbia carried her tray aloft over her head. When I first saw this, I was sure I'd never be able to do it, but the first time I was jostled badly enough so that my drinks went sloshing all over my tray, I automatically raised the tray out of harm's way. When other waitresses raised their arms, however, their trays were over the heads of the patrons. Because I was considerably shorter than most of the waitresses, my tray met most people at eye level when I raised it over my head. Although I thought this was going to be a disadvantage at first, it turned out to work in my favor. I found that most people will tend to either duck or move over when they see a tray of drinks headed for their foreheads. Nevertheless, the amount of pushing I had to do just to get to my tables was unbelievable. On the advice of some of the veteran waitresses, I started to kick at the shins of some of the most rooted customers to get them to move. This was sometimes the only way to avoid losing valuable time trapped in a human gridlock. The Columbia was certainly no place for anyone suffering from claustrophobia. In addition, I was often assigned to work the balcony, since I was a new hire and the upstairs tables made up the least desirable stations. Fighting my way up the stairs with drinks and food made every night quite a workout.

Coming home every night feeling as if I'd run a marathon wasn't a bad thing in itself. It was the utter lack of personal space that gave me pause. On any given night (although the busier ones were worse), I was knocked into, poked in the ribs, and brushed up against. I lost count of the times I felt anonymous hands sliding across my behind as I squashed my way through the crowd. Most of the cocktail waitresses at The Columbia (myself included) avoided wearing skirts to work. It was just too easy, especially when we were climbing the stairs, for men (and occasionally women) to "accidentally" slide their hands along our legs. Of course, this was part and parcel of the job and I knew it. Complaining about being touched while working at The Columbia was about as futile as a fireman complaining about smoke.

And as for smoke, there was plenty of it at The Columbia. The patrons smoked as much as they drank and the employees kept up the pace. Waitresses smoked in the service stations or kept cigarettes burning at the bar. Bartenders had cigarettes tucked behind their ears. There was no area, even the kitchen, that was smoke free.

The kitchen, in fact, was staffed with a collection of the scariest characters I have ever worked with. One cook in particular delighted in terrorizing waitresses with the stump of one tattooed arm while he chain-smoked with the other. I'd heard that The

Columbia had been shut down a few times in the past for health code violations and it was easy to see why when I entered the kitchen for the first time. Everything, including the cooks, was layered with a coating of grease that smelled as if it had been around for years. There were large cockroaches visible in every corner. Fortunately, most of them were big enough to be detected in the food before dishes went out to the table. Really, food was a secondary commodity at The Columbia. Almost all the dishes on the bar menu were either grilled or fried and dripping with fat. The occasional salad offerings were simply frightening to look at and didn't get ordered very often. I felt that it was entirely unsafe to eat at The Columbia, yet many did, and none, to my knowledge, ever died from it. Perhaps the alcohol killed any existing bacteria.

Food, however, was not an issue on dollar-drink nights, which I started working immediately after being hired. No training in the world could have adequately prepared me for the mania of Buck Night. Every drink in the house was a dollar, including draft beer and glasses of house wine. Drinks with higher alcohol content, such as Long Island Iced Tea, were two dollars, as were "call" liquors (pricier name brands, such as Absolut vodka or Tanqueray gin).

(Some stalwart—or deranged—patrons even managed to avoid paying a dollar for their drinks. In this case, they'd opt for a drink known as a Bar Mat. A Bar Mat is made when the bartender picks up the rubber mat on which he's been mixing—and spilling—all his drinks and dumps the contents into a glass. The alcohol content is high. The taste—well, you be the judge. Bartenders gave these drinks out for free.)

Every bartender in the place took some kind of stimulant before and during a Buck Night shift. Before I worked at The Columbia, I'd wondered how the place could make any kind of profit on these nights. It took putting on an apron to figure it out. To begin with, the bartenders poured every mixed drink short. And unless the customer was standing right in front of the bartender and watching him pour, call liquors were magically transformed into well liquors. If patrons knew that this was going on, they didn't seem to care. A dollar drink is tough to beat, even if it is watered down. Usually, I averaged a 100 percent tip on each one of these drinks. Although we had specific stations, the crush of people was so great inside the bar on these nights that we could count on doubling our tips just from people who were wandering the floor waiting for a place to sit. But money aside, dollar night was absolute madness. A typical interchange went something like this:

Customer pulls on my sleeve, taps me on the shoulder, or waves frantically.

I say, "What can I get for you?"

Customer, who can't hear me because the music and the din of voices drowns everything else out, says, "Hey, can I get a drink?"

I shout, "What can I get for you?"

Customer can finally hear me but still feels he has to move his mouth precariously close to my ear and says, "Hey, how much is a screwdriver?"

I roll my eyes and shout, "Everything's a dollar!"

"How much for a beer?"

"One dollar!"

"I'll have a beer and a screwdriver. That's two dollars, right?"

"I can only bring you one drink at a time."

"What?"

"I can only bring you one."

"One what?"

"OK!" I scream. "I'll be right back!"

But the customer is not finished. He grabs me again as I'm turning toward the bar and shouts with such force that he sprays me with spit, "Hey, *smile!*"

Unlike Le Jardin, which was a haven for lonely men looking to fall into the bottoms of their glasses, The Columbia was an active meeting place for singles. Somehow, this was no less depressing than what went on at Le Jardin. Again it seemed to me that I was surrounded by an awesome loneliness. Fortunately, I was usually too busy to focus on the mating dances around me. Nevertheless, the feeling of desperate, forced gaiety in that bar was one that stayed with me forever and I am reminded of it each time I so much as smell an alcoholic drink.

Working at The Columbia had certain advantages. Unlike the other jobs I've had serving cocktails, The Columbia was usually too loud and crowded for patrons to really get personal with the cocktail waitresses. Touching aside, customers couldn't make themselves heard with rude comments, so most times they opted just to communicate their orders.

Surprisingly, the rudest customers I've ever encountered were in the cocktail area of an upscale restaurant where I worked many years later. Here patrons had much more money, much more free time, and much less human decency. When I worked cocktails in this restaurant, I found that after the first tip, and it was usually quite meager, the customer felt he had purchased me for the evening and expected service bordering on slavery. I also received some comments bordering on harassment, such as the ones I got from three golfers one evening. After a few beers, these three men started asking all kinds of personal questions about what kind of men I liked to date, how old I was, and whether I liked to go skinny-dipping. I finally cut them off and passed them over to the bartender after one of them stared hard at my breasts as I placed his beer in front of him and said, "Are those real?"

The Columbia also had the advantage of being quite profitable. Most nights I collected so many bills it took an extra half hour to count them all when I cashed out. I was averaging over a hundred dollars in tips on dollar-drink nights, which was very good money at that time. Often I would limp home at two in the

morning and be too wired to sleep but too exhausted to undress
or even move. I'd throw all my singles, fives, and tens on my bed
on those nights and just lie there in a pile of money. The green
bills, smelling vaguely of gin and beer, were visceral reminders of
why I had just spent the night beating myself up. Unfortunately,
at the age of twenty-four, I felt like I was already too old to keep
up the pace it took to maintain that kind of cash flow. When I
calculated that I was making about a dollar a drink and then
thought of how many drinks it took to reach the hundred-dollar
mark, the work-to-profit ratio didn't seem very good at all.

I hadn't been working at The Columbia very long, however,
before I started having problems that overshadowed those of the
job. As quickly as it had blossomed, my relationship with John
was beginning to unravel. I have never been able to put my finger on the exact reason why it came apart so rapidly. Perhaps
part of it was the fact that we hadn't allowed ourselves sufficient
space to step back and evaluate whether or not we were truly
compatible. We had both leaped headlong into the relationship
with our feelings unguarded and exposed. We had been so
caught up in the thrill of each other that when some basic differences began to surface, we were both surprised and disappointed. I believe that for a time we were really in love with each
other. But it soon became apparent that love (by whatever definition of the word) was not going to be enough to keep us from
trying to change each other to more closely resemble what we
expected or wanted to find in a mate.

It was John who pointed this out while we were having
lunch one day. Over dessert, he told me that he thought we
should stop seeing each other for a while and then see how we
felt. I saw this as his way of trying to dump me "nicely" and
walked out of the restaurant in tears.

The next few weeks at The Columbia were almost impossible. I was nursing my own broken heart while watching others

start drunken liaisons. It had been less than a year since my last birthday, a day that had found me taking stock of all that was missing in my life and vowing to move on. Such a short period of time later, I found myself missing even more. I had embarked on a "real" relationship, only to see it burn into cinders. This loss, which ran deeper than the physical absence of John, had left me even lonelier than before. At Molto's, at least I had counted some of my coworkers as friends. In exchanging this job for the one at The Columbia, I'd lost that camaraderie as well. My coworkers at The Columbia were truly a hard-living crowd. There was not one among them I could really connect with. And, I had to face it, I really hated my job. I saw a reflection of deep misery in the face of everybody I served. Cocktailing and that old feeling of raw desperation were now interchangeable.

It became supremely difficult for me to serve alcohol while in this state. I started getting upset over things that had never bothered me before. For example, it was par for the course for an inebriated customer to claim that I'd brought the wrong drink by the time I got it to the table. Most of the time, the customer himself had forgotten what he'd ordered. Usually I'd just ignore the complaint and keep going, but I began taking it very personally and finding myself on the verge of tears every time it happened.

Up to this point, too, I had experienced a certain elation after every shift. It was the kind of endorphin-based euphoria that I'd felt since my days in the luncheonette. After a hard night's work, I'd feel that I'd successfully completed a singularly demanding task. In a way, it felt as if I'd conquered the odds. But a few weeks after my breakup with John, I ended my shifts with only a feeling of depression. The odds, it seemed, were conquering me.

Besides the psychic disturbances, I was experiencing some brand-new physical discomforts. The late nights, cigarette smoke, and close quarters seemed to be getting to me. I felt exhausted all the time and vaguely nauseated. The sight of the one-armed cook smoking Marlboros over the onion rings, alone, threatened to make me vomit.

It was Belinda (on whose shoulder I'd regularly been crying) who gave voice to what should have been obvious.

"You're not pregnant, are you?" she asked.

"Well," I answered, "*that* would certainly make things interesting, wouldn't it?"

Belinda and I went shopping for a home pregnancy test at an all-night supermarket at midnight. She'd come into The Columbia and drunk scotch and milk until I finished work. There was something surreal about the whole adventure. We stood in line with several transients buying fortified wine and she babbled on about how exciting it was, what was I going to tell John, would I want a boy or a girl. . . .

"It's probably all moot, because I don't think I'm pregnant," I told her, realizing as the words left my lips that I most definitely was.

"Want me to come over tomorrow morning?" she asked. "I could be there with you when you take the test."

"That's OK," I told her. "I'll call you and let you know."

The following morning I sat by myself for a long time watching the sky change from white to dusty to the gunmetal color of rain. It was only December and already one of the wettest winters I could remember. I stared at the results of the pregnancy test for thirty minutes while I held a blanket around my cold feet. Too many thoughts had crowded themselves into my head, and all I could hear was the brain equivalent of white noise. I picked up the phone and dialed Belinda's number. It was very early for cocktail types like us and she answered the phone sleepily.

"Well," I told her, "it looks like I'm going to be somebody's mother."

# in the family way

**If work at The Columbia** was difficult before, it became just about impossible soon after I learned I was going to have a baby. I finally confided in Sherry, another cocktail waitress, and told her that I didn't know quite what to do. Sherry was rail thin with a witchy shock of curly red hair. Of all my coworkers, she seemed the most competent, energetic, and articulate. It had been Sherry, in fact, who had helped me through my first Buck Night, taking me over to the bartenders before the shift began and telling them to be extra patient with me since I'd never "worked the meat market before."

"How exciting!" she gushed. She was my age and already had two small children she was raising without the benefit of a husband.

"Exciting, yes," I told her, "but I'm thinking that maybe this isn't the best environment in which to grow a new life."

"Oh, don't worry about it," she said, taking a deep drag from her cigarette, "you'll be fine." She smiled as if to reassure me. "I've just got one piece of advice," she added. "When you have the baby, make sure they give you an episiotomy. That way they can sew you up *tighter* than before. Know what I mean?" She winked, nudged me, and put out her cigarette. "Back to work, then."

I didn't find Sherry's advice the least bit comforting, and every day the smell inside The Columbia (a combination of alcohol, grease, cigarette smoke, and bar fruit) grew stronger and more oppressive. On a few nights, the only thing that kept me from running to the bathroom was the fact that it smelled even worse in there.

I'd gone into something of a "one day at a time" mode since discovering I was pregnant. I had a suspicion, before ever speaking to John, that I'd probably be marching into parenthood alone. We had ended our relationship on bad terms and he was in no way interested in a reconciliation. We hadn't so much as spoken to each other for weeks. I was almost positive that he had very little room in his future plans for me, much less a child. Given these misgivings, I decided that I could probably manage without John's active participation. My family's reaction to the news, on the other hand, would be critical. I knew I would be lost without their support. I broached the subject as diplomatically as I could at a family dinner.

"You know, I think that possibly I might be . . . that is, I think there's a chance I could maybe be pregnant," I said. In the silence that followed, I added, "And I need to know how you all feel about that because I'm going to need your help."

Their response, immediate and uncensored, was overwhelmingly positive. Not only were they willing to help, they were actually excited at the prospect of a new baby. Not one member of my family expressed a single doubt or misgiving. How could I even ask, they wanted to know, of course they would be with me 100 percent. When would I know for sure?

"I know," I said. "It's a fact."

"I thought so," my mother said.

After this discussion, I decided that the best plan for the moment was to continue working at The Columbia until I started to show. Very few shifts later, this plan was rapidly derailed. I scheduled a meeting with Donna and told her that, through no advance planning, I was going to have a baby and I didn't think I could continue working. To my surprise, Donna literally begged me to stay. It wasn't at all a problem with her, she claimed, and I could take a leave when the baby came and be assured of having my job when I came back. It would be fun, she said, for all my coworkers to follow my pregnancy. She was sure everyone would be very supportive. She even offered to take me off Buck Night and schedule me for less physically demanding shifts. I must admit that I was actually thinking about this option and had almost decided it would be worth a try when she said something that changed my mind completely.

"It'll be great," Donna claimed. "You'll probably make twice as much money as before. People will tip you *and* the baby."

I suddenly had a vision of what I'd look like in my last trimester, carrying drinks around the bar. I thought about how much secondhand cigarette smoke I'd inhale and how unhealthy the atmosphere was on every level. It was a fairly disgusting picture.

"I'm sorry," I told her, "I can't do it."

Waitressing is a singularly difficult job to hold while pregnant, and not just because the physical demands are so great. Rather, I've noticed a certain attitude toward pregnant waitresses, made up of both pity and consternation, that makes the work quite trying. Pregnancy just doesn't fit the commonly accepted profile of a waitress—especially a cocktail waitress.

I've worked with two women who went through their pregnancies in restaurants. Neither had an easy time of it. The first was a young unmarried woman whose pregnancy was totally unplanned. The managers of the restaurant hated the very idea of it and asked her if she didn't think it would be best to work in a less stressful environment. She didn't. Powerless to fire her for being pregnant, the managers cut this woman's hours and scheduled her to work the least profitable shifts. Their efforts to squeeze her out didn't work and she stayed on until the week before she delivered.

The second woman was married and had planned her pregnancy. She had also been waiting on tables for most of her adult life and knew her rights as a pregnant employee, having gone through her first pregnancy at another restaurant. Still, the managers weren't particularly pleased at her expanding presence and griped that she wouldn't be able to keep up with the demands of her job. She often got some unpleasant reactions from her customers. Viewing her as a piece of public property, men and women alike would rub her belly and ask her very personal questions, like whether or not she was married and why she was working in a restaurant.

"They always look here," she said, holding up her left fourth finger, which was bare due to swelling. "They don't see a wedding band, so they think I'm some kind of loser. Like it's shameful or something. As if it's any of their business anyway."

Even I had felt sorry for pregnant servers who waited on me. I felt as if I should be doing the work, not her. It was this feeling, more than any other, that convinced me I couldn't stay on at The Columbia.

Donna had asked me to work through New Year's Eve and I agreed to do so. The week before Christmas, however, I developed a bad cold and found myself unable to move from my bed. I called Donna and asked if I could be relieved of a shift or two.

"Why don't we just call it a day?" she snapped at me. "It's obvious you don't really want to be here." I suppose I should have felt some remorse, but I was merely relieved. She wasn't wrong, after all.

On the face of it, things were starting to look a little bleak. I now had no job at all and no steady income for the foreseeable future. My office job had recently come to an end as well, since

Hank and Tim could no longer afford to pay me a salary of any kind. Tim had promised to keep me on as a freelancer for the paper, but those assignments would provide very little income.

I was also about to experience motherhood without the help or even the presence of the baby's father. John had not reacted well to the news that he was to become a father. He had, in fact, given me a series of conditions under which he would provide me with support. Since most of these conditions involved terminating the pregnancy, we soon came to an unbreachable impasse. There followed arguments, tears, and plenty of accusations on both sides. The end result was that John left the city, the state, and any hope I might have had of his involvement in my life before I felt the baby's first kick.

In addition, I had no idea what I was going to do once the baby came or where I was going to live. There was only so long I could manage in a studio apartment with a child, and besides, I didn't know how the apartment managers would react to my adding a new tenant.

This was one side of the situation. There was a much rosier outlook on the flip side. I had no income, to be sure, but I did have all the money I'd saved from working so many jobs over the previous months. It wasn't going to last forever, but it was something. I obviously wasn't going to be using it to move anywhere. I didn't have John, but I had the unconditional support of my entire family along with their promises to be with me every step of the way. This was no small thing; it was an absolute lifesaver. As for my impending motherhood, there are some things in life it's just better to know less about before they happen. My lack of vision into my own future was a blessing that allowed for unlimited optimism.

It also looked as if there might be something of a solution to my joblessness. My father had been wanting, once again, to venture into the restaurant business, and by the time I quit The

Columbia, he had rented a storefront in northeast Portland. This time the theme was New York–style pizza, and again he wanted it to be a family-owned-and-operated business. After much voting, debate, and names drawn out of hats, Peppy's was settled upon as the name of the new place. My sister Maya was taking some time off from college to lend her culinary talents, and the rest of the family planned to muck in as needed. My father's hope for Peppy's was that it would soon support our entire family. While the idea for Peppy's had been germinating, I had gone from working at Molto's to The Columbia and had thought I'd be able to help out only when I had days off. A few weeks into the construction of our new business, however, it became clear where I'd be spending most of my days.

My father had a vision of the way he wanted Peppy's to look, which was a return to the old-fashioned diner style of his childhood. With this in mind, we laid down black-and-white checkerboard flooring, installed Naugahyde booths, and painted the walls in pinkish lavender. There were little touches, too. We bought old-style fountains for lemonade and grape juice, had a neon sign made for the front window, and I painted a giant pizza on the back wall so that it was directly in the line of vision of anyone ordering at the counter. We even rented a jukebox and two pinball machines. The jukebox, played only by members of our family, was a complete failure, but the pinball machines were extremely popular.

The menu was simple but specific and the taste had to be just right. My father had grown up in New York and both Maya and I had spent a good portion of our childhoods there. All of us had distinct memories of what New York pizza looked, smelled, and tasted like. Anyone who is a fan of real New York pizza knows that there are very few substitutes. There is a certain je ne sais quoi to a large, cheesy, aromatic slice of Brooklyn pizza that my father was determined to replicate. To this end, Maya and my father experimented with a variety of doughs, sauces, and cheeses until they produced something that satisfied their palates. I can't say that New York–style pizza was unheard of in Portland at that time, but it was certainly a novelty. Franchise pizza shops and thick-crusted Canadian-bacon-and-pineapple–laden pies were more the accepted norm. Nevertheless, a couple of places featuring Big Apple pizza had recently sprung up and were developing devoted followings. My father was hoping for the same kind of response.

Our summer in the luncheonette had been the last time we'd all worked together like this and the memories were inevitable as we set up the restaurant. But while the dynamic in my family remained relatively unchanged, almost everything else about this venture was different. The luncheonette had been temporary. Peppy's, we hoped, was permanent. The stakes, both financial and emotional, seemed quite a bit higher. As for me, I didn't view Peppy's as the gateway to romantic adventure as I had the luncheonette. The butterflies in my stomach had been replaced by morning sickness. I was still waiting to meet someone who would change my life, but this time around that someone was growing inside my own body. During the early days of Peppy's, I couldn't see much farther than that. Nor did I want to.

Pizza was one of Peppy's selling points. The other was the fact that it was owned and run by a family (*our* family). My father felt that capitalizing on the whole family-values theme would appeal to our customers and make them want to buy pizza from us instead of a nameless, faceless franchise. With this in mind, we went around to introduce ourselves to our neighbors, all of whom we hoped would be eating their weights in pizza in the near future.

The district we'd set up in had no clear identity and was an eclectic mix of small businesses. One thing it had plenty of was character, and our neighbors, as it turned out, were quite an interesting group.

Our neighbors on one side were the husband and wife owners of a Vietnamese bakery. The wife was always there, day and
night, sweating over various doughy creations. The husband
came in and out, making deliveries and buying supplies. He
spoke no English at all and the wife spoke very little. Nevertheless, she was usually quite chatty in a broken-syllable kind of way.
There were always a few of her family members around the bakery: young girls, babies, sometimes a boy or two. We had no idea
what relation any of them had to each other. The wife (who never
actually told us her name) appreciated the fact that we were a
family working together. Every morning, we'd come in and buy a
baguette for breakfast and she'd give us coffee on the house.

"No, no pay," she'd say. "F'ee for you."

Later, when my "delicate condition" started becoming obvious, she'd attempt to press pastries and strange turnovers with
fillings of undetermined origin into my hands.

"When baby come?" she asked.

"July," I told her.

"Good. You take. You eat. Good for baby." I took, but couldn't
eat. I believe she and her family felt more or less the same way
about pizza. Although they were very friendly and very generous, they never came over to eat at Peppy's.

Our neighbor on the other side was a cobbler. A tiny Asian
man who spoke even less English than the bakery owners, he
kept very much to himself. In the entire time that we owned
Peppy's, we heard only two words from him. We could set our
watches by him as every day at 5 P.M. he'd walk into Peppy's,
slap a couple of quarters on the counter, and say, "Small Coke."
He never ordered pizza.

There was a faded single-screen movie theater across the
street, which hadn't yet figured out that it would have to become
either an art house or a historical monument to compete with
the multiplexes everywhere else. The theater manager, Leonard,

was unkempt and extremely grumpy. When we devised a pizza special for matinee goers, Leonard flatly refused to place any flyers or menus in the lobby but came in himself to take advantage of the price breaks.

There was a florist on one side of the theater, owned and operated by a couple of middle-aged men, both named Ben. The Bens eschewed traditional arrangements for their flowers in favor of more artistic designs, most of which tended to be rather depressing if exotic. Because we liked to support all the local businesses, Maya and I purchased an arrangement from the Bens for our mother's birthday that year. "You decide," we told them. "It's her birthday, so something cheerful and springlike would be good." The resulting bouquet looked like it had been taken from the back of a hearse. It was so grim, in fact, that my mother actually laughed at the sight of it. The Bens, at least, stopped in for pizza once in a while, although neither one of them could tolerate tomato sauce, so we ended up designing a special "white pizza" just for them.

On the other side of the theater was a store that defied definition. Everything in this warehouselike space looked as if it had either fallen off the back of a truck, been manufactured in a Third World country, or both—a dizzying collection of televisions, bicycles, baby strollers, lunchboxes, kites, and brightly colored plastic toys (the kind that had several removable parts suitable for choking small children). The store kept odd, erratic hours and was never staffed by the same people two days in a row. None of the staffers ever came in for pizza, incidentally, even before a fire swept through that store (and only that store) several months after we opened.

We set up an account for Peppy's at a local bank at the end of the street. The tellers, all women, were usually dieting at any given moment, so we added salads to our menu to accommodate them. They were generally a very pleasant group and took a genuine interest in how well we were doing. Unfortunately, they were often too traumatized to lunch at Peppy's. Whether it was the location, lax security features, or simple bad luck, this particular bank seemed to be one of the most often robbed institutions in the area. One particular teller, Rose, a divorced mother of two teenagers, had the misfortune of staring down the barrel of a gun twice in a two-month period.

Our happiest neighbors and our favorite customers by far were Kev, Mike, and Jeff, a trio of flamboyantly gay hairstylists located next door to the bakery. Kev was tall, barrel-chested, and had a long mane of ringlets. He dressed in billowy shirts, boots, and tight pants. The overall effect was Robin Hood meets the Cowardly Lion. Both my mother and I went to Kev to get our hair done and he regaled us with one outrageous story after another. Kev had little regard for public health warnings and swore to live his life exactly the way he wanted to. He told us tales of various hustlers he'd picked up, which we didn't believe until one of them showed up at the salon one day and ended up eating pizza at Peppy's. While he waited for an additional slice to go, Kev's boy toy offered to marry me and "give your baby a name." When I politely declined, he said, "No, really, I think pregnant women are very sexy."

Mike was a little more restrained in both looks and attitude. He actually admitted to having a crush on my father, with whom he flirted shamelessly. Subject to huge mood swings, Mike either complained bitterly about the state of the world and all the people in it or was in a state of giddy ebullience. We never knew which it would be on any given day. Mike's bipolar behavior bothered Kev, and Kev's unapologetic posturing bothered Mike. The two would often come in separately, eat lunch, and complain about each other. On the fringes of these dramas was Jeff, who came in only a few days a week to service an established clientele. His uniform was simple: tank top, leather jacket, jeans, and a belt buckle with the word QUEEN stamped on it in four-inch metal letters. Jeff spoke very little, laughed a great deal, and smoked constantly. All three were big fans of our pizza and patronized Peppy's almost daily. Of all the businesses in the neighborhood, they were the only ones to do so.

The grand opening of Peppy's was hardly the rush we'd hoped for. In fact, business was decidedly slow for the first few months. My father had hoped to gain many regular customers from the foot traffic around the area. There was foot traffic, all right, but generally not the kind that generated income. For example, one regular visitor was a blind traveling salesman who poked his head into Peppy's every other day or so and demanded to know "What is this place?" When told, he responded, "Wanna buy a handmade belt?" Since nobody ever did, he usually backed out with the parting shot of "Ah, the hell with ya." Then there were a regular contingent of night crawlers wanting to know "Where's that titty bar at?" And we had a host of people who came in, walked up to the counter, stared at the menu, and then asked to use the bathroom.

We began advertising free delivery in the hope of generating sales from families in the surrounding neighborhoods. Maya and I called every friend and contact we had in the greater Portland area and invited them in for pizza. A few became regulars. Belinda came in to eat soon after we opened and told me that she had gotten a job as a bartender/cocktail waitress at a bar near her apartment. She was really enjoying it, she said, but for some reason she had recently gained quite a bit of weight. In fact, she showed me, she could barely close her jeans.

A month later, Belinda called to tell me that she, too, was pregnant. Her boyfriend wasn't happy about the news, either, she said, and was refusing to speak to her. Her due date was less than two months after mine. Perhaps, she suggested, we could have a double baby shower?

Gradually, each member of my family began to assume a role at Peppy's and our days started to follow a predictable routine. My father did all the ordering, buying, and deliveries. He prepared fresh sauce every morning, spending hours peeling garlic, sautéing mushrooms, creating salads and, later, lasagna. My mother spent her days working in an office and her evenings sitting at a booth in Peppy's. My youngest sister, Déja, who'd been an infant when we had the luncheonette, was now nine years old. She perched behind the counter most afternoons, alternating between pinball and homework. Maya made pizza and more pizza. In fact, she had touted her cooking skills so highly in the early days of Peppy's that soon she was the sole pizza maker. Her position, seated or standing in front of the ovens, was one she would hold for the duration of the restaurant. The task of customer service was more or less relegated to me. With my doctor's appointments, growing belly, and baby preparations, I wasn't able to log as many hours at Peppy's as Maya or my father. As it turned out, I was also unable to eat tomato sauce without getting sick, effectively eliminating pizza from my diet. All of this served to remove me from consideration as a cook of any kind. Besides, with all my experience at the table, I was a natural choice for front-of-the-house operations.

Every morning, my father and Maya picked me up at my apartment. The three of us ate breakfast together and planned out the day in terms of what had to be prepared and stocked or what flyers had to be designed and printed. Maya made dough and grated mozzarella cheese. I went to the bank for change. My father peeled garlic and, every half hour, moved his car into another temporary parking space. If it was slow and it looked as if I was becoming too sedentary, my father would leave notes for me at the cash register.

"The doctor says that walking is good for you," one of these notes said. "P.S. We need tomatoes."

As the days grew warmer and longer, we all spent more time waiting, although very little of it involved waiting on tables. We waited every day for customers to arrive and all found our own ways to fill the downtime.

Perched by the ovens with her apron on, Maya read dozens of romance novels over the course of the days. She also indulged her penchant for soap operas. I watched with her as the soaps ran between what passed for a lunch rush and what might turn into a dinner rush. (We watched so often, in fact, that when my son was born he became his own study on the effects of prenatal stimulation. If he was fussy after lunch, I noticed that he became soothed as soon as one of the familiar soap theme songs played within his earshot. To this day, as well, pizza remains one of his foods of choice.)

Pinball was also a particularly popular time waster, and various family members competed for the highest scores. One machine, titled Centaur, featured a beast that was half man and half motorcycle. Periodically, as the balls zipped around, the machine would chant "Destroy centaur" in a particularly demonic tone. I heard it so often that my dreams often featured this phrase.

On a larger scale I waited to give birth. Pregnancy is a singular challenge for those short on patience. The baby was due in early July. By mid-May I had read half a dozen books on pregnancy and early motherhood. I'd given myself a baby shower at Peppy's and had collected a substantial layette. I'd bought a crib and set it up in my apartment. I'd selected a name, Blaze, for the baby I was convinced was a boy. Maya was to be my labor coach, and by early June we'd completed childbirth classes together. I started beginning conversations about the baby with "When he gets out. . . ."

"When he *gets out?*" Maya scoffed. "You make it sound like he's in jail in there. Why are you in such a hurry? Leave him alone and let him develop at his own pace, why don't you?"

It was very difficult for me to wait it out after coming to this stage of readiness. Before this, my working days had been fast-paced and high pressure. Quiet gestation, therefore, was not a condition that came very easily.

I did have occasional writing jobs, which would periodically keep me busy. Tim would come into Peppy's, eat a slice of pizza, and pick up the copy that I'd written. I never told him about my pregnancy, and although he sometimes stared directly at my belly, he never made a single comment until he called with an assignment a month after the baby was born and heard the unmistakable noises of an infant in the background. "Say, did you have a baby recently?" he asked. "I was just wondering. . . ."

Going through my pregnancy under the watchful eyes of not only my family but a daily host of strangers taught me how very public restaurant work is. Prior to Peppy's, I had always felt there was a certain anonymity to waitressing. After all, with the exception of regulars, one's customers are different every day. Each table is a chance to display a fresh persona, even a new identity if one so desires. But in truth, one really has to have an act to wait tables. A certain shtick is necessary at the table. This is what the customer is paying for. The average patron couldn't care less if you've had a bad day, week, or month and he resents it if he's forced to even consider this. He wants a smile, a dance, a bit of mystery.

Every waiter and waitress I've worked with has developed a personality especially for use at the table. One waiter I worked with, for example, was a dead ringer for the actor Rowan Atkinson. He exploited this resemblance for all it was worth. Customers often came in saying, "We want Mr. Bean to wait on us tonight." The waiter added little quirks to his behavior to add to the general persona he was developing, telling his customers in the middle of a meal, "Enjoy your dinner. I'm going to go smoke a cigarette, I'll be right back." Later he managed to up the percentage of his tips by telling his tables that he was a struggling single father (never mind that his daughter was over twenty-one and that parenting was probably last on the list of his priorities). Another waiter I worked with performed magic tricks at the table. His pockets were constantly bulging with colored scarves and playing cards, and he was usually late picking up his food since some of his tricks required quite a bit of time.

Waiters and waitresses who hail from countries other than the United States generally have an easy time presenting a restaurant persona. I've been consistently amazed at how easily impressed most people are by an accent of any kind. In fact, I've seen countless transgressions forgiven by customers just because the waiter or waitress was French, Italian, or Spanish. I've experimented with this one myself. One of my "talents" is the ability to mold my speech patterns and accent to whomever I'm talking to. A British accent is especially easy, as is a New York twang. At the table, I've utilized both, usually to great effect.

Many years after she sat behind the counter at Peppy's rehearsing for her first performance in an elementary school production of *The Wiz*, my sister Déja, an aspiring actress, would rehearse for other roles and develop characters at the tables of restaurants where she worked. For her, the restaurant literally became her stage; every shift was an opportunity for an improvisational performance.

At Peppy's, our shtick, such as it was, involved our family and the dynamic inherent within it. My pregnancy was unquestionably a part of this. Certainly, all of our neighbors knew that I was going to have a baby and they all seemed to wait for the blessed event with me, at times less patiently than I did. Mike, especially, was fond of walking into Peppy's, looking at me, and saying, "Haven't you had that baby yet?"

There was a high school close by from which we began to draw a lunch crowd of teenagers. I became a walking cautionary tale for the high school girls who came in and watched my expanding midsection. Most of them thought I was in my teens and had been forced to drop out of school. I saw them sometimes, huddled in the booths, whispering about what might have happened to me. The high school girls weren't the only ones who held these opinions. Many of our adult customers, who knew that we were all family at Peppy's, sought to unravel the circumstances behind my condition with considerably less subtlety:

"When's your baby due?"

"Are you going back to school once it's born?"

"Where's the father? He run out on ya?"

"Looks like you're carrying low—must be a boy."

"You're having a girl, aren't you?"

"Are you gonna call your baby Peppy? Ha ha."

"Is this your first baby? You're in for a treat. You can't imagine how wonderful it's going to be."

I can't say I minded the attention or even the fact that my unborn baby was up for discussion as often as whether we made our pizza with a thin or thick crust. In a way, it helped me feel a sense of community and commonality with people outside of my family. Perhaps, too, there is a bit of the exhibitionist in everyone who chooses waiting as a profession. At the very least, it's not a job for shrinking violets. A certain gregariousness is required of a person who must strike up pleasant conversations with dozens of strangers on a daily basis. And although my pregnancy was a distinctly personal experience, I've witnessed and been part of several other public episodes of bonding between seemingly disparate people, together only because they all happen to be eating in a restaurant.

I saw a striking example of this kind of bonding, for example, in September of 1997 when Princess Diana died. I worked the dinner shift on the night after the funeral. Without exception, every customer and employee of the restaurant had stayed up all night watching the funeral on television. Many customers were actually still tearful, their eyes red-rimmed. There was a feeling of shared sadness at every table. Some of my customers even took my hand as I took their orders and said, "Isn't it just the saddest thing?" It was the topic of conversation for the entire night, with everyone united in a sense of overwhelming grief.

Although business improved over the first few months we were open, it never really took off. My father was disappointed by the lack of support among the local businesses and felt that for the amount of effort we were putting in, the returns were quite small. He couldn't understand what we were doing wrong and why the neighborhood hadn't responded more positively to our pizza. He and Maya, together for more hours at a stretch than anyone else in the family, often lapsed into a routine argument when it was particularly slow.

"Where are all the customers?" he'd ask her. "It's Saturday night."

"I don't know," she'd answer.

"Haven't you had any orders for delivery?"

"No."

"Maybe the phone's not working."

"There's nothing wrong with the phone."

"Go call the operator, make sure it's working."

"It's working."

"Why are you still sitting in the same position? Why don't you make a fresh pizza?"

"For who? There's nobody here."

"There's not going to be, either, with that attitude."

The "Saturday Night Fight," as it was soon dubbed, became as much a ritual as the daily peeling of garlic and grating of mozzarella.

My father redoubled his efforts to make Peppy's a place where everybody would want to eat. It was all about pleasing the customer, he maintained. This was another distinct truth about restaurant work I learned at Peppy's: The customer is always right.

When I was a sixteen-year-old working at Maxman's, I hadn't truly understood why my father consistently gave Mrs. Zucker more meat on her sandwich or filled up Mr. Grubman's platters. A few years later, I found myself outraged at the lack of support given to waiters and waitresses by restaurant management. It took Peppy's to make me understand how truly expendable waiters and waitresses are. It is extremely easy to replace a server. In fact, most restaurants don't even bother advertising when they need to hire staff. A "Help Wanted" sign in the window or, in the busier restaurants, a predictable stream of prospective employees is usually all that is needed for a plethora of server hopefuls. The customer, however, is not so easy to replace. For some people, even one slightly negative experience in a restaurant is enough to warrant a flood of complaining letters, phone calls, even a potential lawsuit. The unhappy customer's ultimate threat is that he will never return and, what's more, he's going to tell all his friends about how poorly he was treated.

Because their cash flow is greater, larger restaurants are better able to handle disgruntled customers. Still, with the exception of one restaurant where the owner was certifiably insane, I have never worked in a place that didn't fall over itself trying to make sure that the customer's last words were "I'll be back." For a small, family-run operation like Peppy's, unhappy customers would signal a quick end to the business. Even with various enticements (free delivery, coupons, and specials), it was difficult enough to convince people to come in for the first time.

It was with this very intimate understanding of why the customer is always right that we restrained ourselves from cracking wise when a potential customer asked us "How big is your sixteen-inch pizza?" or "What comes on a cheese slice?" or even "Want me to tell you how you should really make pizza?" We said nothing when half of our high school crowd showed up with bags of food from McDonald's. The other half, after all, were eating pizza. We listened patiently while people gave us decorating tips, menu suggestions, or told us that we should lower our prices.

In a way, it was Mrs. Zucker all over again. This time around, we took it only slightly less personally.

By the beginning of July, I couldn't stand, sit, or lie down comfortably. I was so distracted, heavy, and full of baby that being at Peppy's became an impossibility. It was the hottest summer on record and I sweated it out alone in my apartment for what seemed an eternity. Finally, in the last week of July, I checked into the hospital to give birth.

My father placed a sign in the window at Peppy's that said simply CLOSED FOR DELIVERY, and my entire family joined me in the hospital, talking, eating, and milling about while I went through thirteen hours of labor. I wouldn't have had it any other way.

My son, Blaze, was born very early the following morning. Several hours later, Maya and my father went back to Peppy's and fired up the ovens. But it would never be business as usual for me again. The change in my life was staggering in its enormity.

Blaze's delivery had been complicated and he had to spend an additional week in the hospital. When I finally brought him home, I was amazed at the sheer emotional chaos my new baby created for me. He cried and I cried along with him. He seemed, quite simply, angry at having been removed from the womb. And after his time in the neonatal care unit, I was afraid that every sound he made was an indication of some strange mysterious illness. Neither one of us slept. For a week, I doubted all my instincts, terrified that I would be unable to understand or give him what he needed.

After about a week of this, I brought him to Peppy's. Exhausted and bleary-eyed, I sat in a booth near the counter with Blaze next to me, wrapped up like an enchilada in his car seat. The pinball machines rumbled. Maya made pizza. My father peeled and chopped garlic. Customers walked in and out. My mother sat with me and we gushed over what an unbelievably cute baby I had. Blaze slept peacefully. I felt safe for the first time since his birth. Nothing bad could happen here. From that moment on, my son and I developed a certain rhythm. He became a very contented baby, and I became not a woman who had just given birth, but his mother.

I spent only a couple of weeks at home with Blaze before coming back to Peppy's to resume my position behind the counter. We came back to a warm welcome from everyone in the neighborhood. The ladies from the bank presented me with a tiny blue suit and the request that I bring the baby in to see them as often as possible. Kev, Mike, and Jeff brought over a bag of toys and the Bens sent flowers. I was genuinely touched.

I brought Blaze with me every day and kept him beside me at all times. He always had a full bag of teething rings and toys, but he preferred playing with paper cups, rolls of tape, and take-out containers. He was never as happy as when the restaurant was full of people, noise, and the smells of pizza.

In the months following his birth, I couldn't have been more besotted with Blaze or happier in my new identity as his mom. That was the easy part. The difficult part was knowing that the quality of another person's entire existence depended on me alone. Peppy's, as it turned out, was the perfect buffer. As long as I was there, surrounded by family, food, and the endless sound of the pinball machines, I felt secure. For a short period, I not only ceased waiting for anything but sought to freeze time as it was, wrapping myself in the warm glow of new motherhood. And for a little while, Peppy's allowed me to do just that.

I believe now that the comfort I experienced at Peppy's is shared in some small way by everyone who spends time in restaurants, whether dining or working. A restaurant is a place where several basic human needs are met all at once. Within these walls there is food, shelter, and warmth. Often, there is a sense of family. At the very least, there are plenty of people around. One is never really alone at the table. There is certainly some security in this, even if it is only temporary.

Unfortunately, not everyone in my family was feeling the same euphoria as I following Blaze's birth. My father's initial disappointment in the lack of business had deepened into something resembling disgust. It had become evident, after a year of operation, that Peppy's was not going to take off anytime soon. Maya was wearying of making pizza day in and day out, and everyone had the feeling that Peppy's was highly underappreciated. The neighborhood was just too tough for the business to work, my father felt, and he didn't have the time, resources, or energy to keep flogging it. What's more, he and my mother had become heartily sick of Portland in general and were thinking of moving to California, where life, they were sure, was easier.

Morale finally hit a low point when Peppy's was robbed one brisk autumn evening. A scraggly thief held a penknife to my nine-year-old sister's throat and demanded she turn over the contents of the cash register. My father and Maya, discussing an order in the kitchen, never saw a thing. What kind of place was this, my father later questioned, where a man would hold up a little girl in a pizza place? Shortly thereafter, he put Peppy's up for sale and all of us started thinking about what we were going to do next.

It was around this time that my long friendship with Belinda began to falter and eventually fade away. I found it ironic that after spending so much time together, both working and playing, and sharing the most intimate details of our lives with each other, it took motherhood, an experience that could have bonded us even further, to expose the most fundamental differences in our personalities.

Belinda's daughter, Celeste, was born a few weeks after Blaze. I took my infant son to visit her in the hospital and the two of us laughed at the fact that our lives seemed to be running on such parallel tracks. We talked on the phone almost daily at first, comparing notes and exchanging information on any number of the topics that new mothers are singularly consumed with. We saw each other frequently as well, going out for walks in the park with our babies secured in front packs. After the first few months, however, Belinda seemed to tire of full-time motherhood. Perhaps she was more interested in the idea of having a child than in the actual child. Her attitude toward her daughter seemed alarmingly like her attitude toward her many jobs: when things ceased to be interesting enough for Belinda, she found a way to move on. It was this, more than anything, that upset me. I knew that my feelings toward Belinda were very critical, and the last thing I wanted or felt qualified to do was to stand in judgment on my friend. Belinda had come to my aid many times and had asked for little in return. She was very accepting and always gave generously of herself. I couldn't stand harboring negative feelings about her.

We began to see less of each other in part because of this and in part, I believe, because Belinda probably felt similarly about me. The last time we saw each other, Belinda told me that she and her ex-boyfriend, softened by the birth of his daughter, had started dating again and that she was hopeful that they'd end up getting married. He was worth a lot more money than she'd originally thought, she told me, and he was starting to part with some of it for the baby. And why shouldn't she be getting some of it, too; she'd had the baby, hadn't she? It would work out for the best, she believed, and when it did, she planned to have at least one more child, maybe two. We toasted our futures with cups of herbal tea and promptly drifted into noncontact.

I think of Celeste every time Blaze has a birthday and I remember the two of them dressed up in blue and pink bunny outfits, ready for a stroll in the park. I think of Belinda almost every time I open a bottle of wine at a table and offer her silent thanks for all the help she gave me. I wonder, too, if she's happy and if she's found a way to satisfy her restless spirit. And I wonder if she's still waiting.

After several months on the market, my father finally got a prospective buyer for Peppy's. He'd listed the restaurant's price in the paper as a "sacrifice" and was so eager to be rid of it and move to California that he was throwing into the cost every piece of equipment (including the kitchen sink, which he'd bought), training on how to make the pizza, and all of his recipes.

Our buyer was in his early twenties and went by several different names, Bud being the one he used most frequently. He drove a very expensive sports car and dressed in silk jackets and tight black jeans. He came with a buddy who had followed him up to Portland from Los Angeles. The two of them couldn't have looked more out of place behind the counter. When they donned aprons and apprenticed under Maya, we had to stifle our laughter at their total ineptitude. We had no idea why Bud and his partner wanted to buy a pizza place, and we were all afraid to ask. Our wonderment at the whole scenario only deepened when Bud paid for Peppy's, not with a check, but with a large brown paper bag filled with crumpled tens and twenties.

"Hmm," Maya mused, "small bills."

"Dug up from the backyard?" my mother speculated.

"Sshh," my father warned.

My parents packed up everything they owned along with my three younger siblings and drove to California within a fortnight of the sale. We heard nothing from Bud or his friend, and after spending almost every day of the previous eighteen months in Peppy's, we never set foot in there again. We heard that Peppy's lasted a scant few months after we left and was replaced by a video store, which in turn went out of business shortly thereafter. Years later, however, I found myself working in a restaurant with a waiter who had recently relocated from Portland. It turned out that we were truly ahead of our time at Peppy's. The district, so amorphous and scattered when we were there, turned into a happening hangout a few years after we left. Apparently it is now one of the busiest thoroughfares around.

A few months before the sale of Peppy's, Maya moved in with me and Blaze. My apartment managers, as it turned out, did not mind at all that I was adding a new tenant to the building. In fact, they had been trying to conceive a baby of their own for some time. When Blaze was about nine months old, they moved out of their roomy but gloomy three-bedroom basement apartment and offered it to me and Maya. My sister and I have been living together ever since.

As soon as Peppy's had been sold, Maya found a job in a bakery near the apartment and rose before dawn every morning to prepare dough of a different kind. My savings were long gone and I was well on my way to amassing considerable debt.

I went in search of another job.

The experience of Peppy's had represented something different for everybody in my family. For me, Peppy's had provided a bridge between two very different phases of life. I had a new identity, that of a single mother, and all of my decisions from that point on would be predicated on the needs of a person other than myself. I was no longer an observer of my own life, I was an active participant. I was amazed at how irrelevant the "problems" I thought I'd had before having Blaze seemed. Self-indulgent crises about my place in the world seemed meaningless when compared to the visceral reality of a baby's midnight fever. Blaze's health and well-being came first, and everything else would have to get in line behind it. I had become, in effect, one of the "real" people in the world around me.

Then, of course, there was the question of my writing.

When John and I had first started seeing each other, he had encouraged me to submit my novel to the literary agent whose lecture we attended. The agent had returned my manuscript with the comment that it was long on creativity but short on content. Part of the reason that it was, in her words, "seriously flawed," was that I was too young and had not experienced enough of life. "Love, separation, birthing, poverty, etc." were the words she used to describe the kinds of experiences I would need in order to effectively tell a good story on paper. Strangely, although I felt I'd pretty much experienced all of these in one fell swoop with Blaze's birth, writing about them was the furthest thing from my mind. In fact, I wouldn't write a thing for five years. This wasn't a conscious decision, more a shifting of priorities. Survival was now paramount on the list. As for my creative energy, all of it went into Blaze. Perhaps if I'd been married and financially secure, I would have found the time to devote to what had always been my passion. I suspect, however, that I would have done the same no matter what my circumstances. From the first seconds of his existence, I knew that Blaze was not a project to be worked on sporadically or when I felt inspired. He could not be gone back to later, and I couldn't edit my mistakes. I could never rewrite my part in his life. He was, therefore, my work. Everything else would have to wait.

Once again, restaurant work seemed like the only option, but this time for very different reasons. Waitressing would now provide me with the greatest financial return for the least amount of hours. My goal was to spend as much time as possible with Blaze during his waking hours. Working nights, I'd be able to accomplish this and also make more money than if I worked lunch shifts. Maya and I would also have opposite schedules, and I was most fortunate that she was not only willing but happy to take care of Blaze while I worked.

Whether out of a desire for the familiar or a need to avoid a protracted job search, I packed Blaze into his front pack and went directly to Molto's. To my extreme disappointment, Barry had recently quit Molto's and was planning to move back to New York. I couldn't imagine the restaurant running as well as it had without him. I also noticed that Pamela had hung on and had gone from being an occasional lunch waitress to a full-time dinner waitress with quasi-managerial status. Almost all of my former coworkers had moved on to other restaurants, and as I sat and waited to talk to the new manager, I noticed very few familiar faces. Even Sonny had gone off to parts unknown. Wes, I learned from the bartender, was still working and had been promoted to kitchen manager.

"He's here today," the bartender told me. "Why don't you go in and say hello?"

If it was strange just sitting in the restaurant where I'd spent so much time in what I considered my former life, it was downright bizarre walking through the swinging doors that led into the kitchen with a baby in tow. Wes was standing behind the line contemplating a recipe when I walked in and it took him a minute to look up. He went a little pale at the sight of me and Blaze together.

"How are you doing?" I asked him.

"Pretty well," he responded. "You?"

"Well," I said and gestured to Blaze, "I've been busy."

"Yes, well . . . and how's, er, John? That's his name, right?"

"I don't know," I said. "He's not around."

"Oh?"

"Long story," I said. "This is Blaze, by the way."

"Blaze. Cool name." Wes walked around from behind the line and stood next to us, awkwardly studying my son's face.

"So, I think I'm going to work here again," I said.

"Yeah? Why?"

"Why not?"

"Right, why not?"

"Maybe you could put in a word for me with the new guy?" I asked. "He doesn't know me."

"Yeah, OK."

"OK," I said, suddenly exhausted. "Nice seeing you. Maybe I'll be seeing you again soon."

"Hey, uh," Wes faltered, "so when was he born?"

"End of July," I said, shaking my head in disbelief.

"Oh." I watched as Wes did some calculations in his head. He laughed finally and said, "He's a beautiful kid. Congratulations."

I didn't need any help from Wes, as it turned out. The new manager was happy to hire me based on my prior work history at Molto's and confirmation of my abilities from Pamela. I experienced a feeling of déjà vu when he told me I'd have to start on lunches and work myself into dinners when shifts opened up. For the sake of my financial survival, I hoped this wouldn't take very long, but I was almost relieved to have a few "training" shifts before going back into the fray. I felt seriously out of shape and, after speaking nothing but baby talk for the previous year, didn't know if I could have a sustained conversation with an adult, even if it were just to take an order.

My return to Molto's was a perfect example of why you can't go home again. Although the physical structure and menu of the restaurant were the same, everything about the mood inside had changed. There was no longer the camaraderie among the waiters and waitresses that I had found so appealing. Nobody sang and danced in the kitchen. Servers argued over sections, tables, and who would go home first. I was moved to dinners fairly quickly and felt a subtle wave of hostility from those waiters who had logged many more lunches. Aside from Pamela, who had taken a very proprietary attitude toward the restaurant, I was the only server with a child. This placed me immediately in the "no fun" category, and absolutely nobody was interested in hearing my tales of the old days at Molto's. I went through the motions at my tables but felt curiously out of place and uncomfortable. It was as if I was attempting to wear clothes that no longer fit.

I began thinking that a major lifestyle change was in order. After years in Portland, I was tired of constantly having wet feet and waking up to gray skies. Our basement apartment was starting to become downright depressing with its insidious mold and lack of light. Maya began complaining of hearing snoring noises in the middle of the night. Although I laughed at her and dismissed her forbodings as hallucinations, I considered them to be another bad sign.

My parents called frequently from Southern California and raved about the quality of life there. They told both me and Maya how beautiful it was and how much easier things seemed to be. We had to move, they insisted.

"There are *plenty* of restaurants down here," my father insisted, "and they're all busy." Still, Maya and I were slow to start packing up our lives and kept putting off a move until "next month." It took an event that was both comic and frightening to finally spur us into action.

Maya burst into my bedroom at three o'clock one morning and screamed, "I'm *not* crazy! There *is* someone snoring outside my window! And he's about to roll into my bedroom!"

I followed Maya into her bedroom, unsure whether to laugh or cry, and saw something that, at first, my sleeping brain refused to accept. There was a vacant parking lot on one side of our building, which ended in a shallow ditch at the level of Maya's bedroom window. One of Portland's many homeless people had taken up his nightly residence in said ditch and, in an alcoholic stupor, had managed to roll right into her window. The windowpane, in fact, was all that was keeping him from crashing right into her bed. He lay peacefully against the glass, snoring loudly, an empty bottle beside him.

"What are we going to do?" Maya asked me.

"What can we do? He's not going to fall in. Probably." I had to laugh.

"Sure, very funny. It's not *your* bedroom. I don't think you'd be laughing if a drunk fell on *you* in the middle of the night."

"Look," I reasoned, "he didn't exactly fall on you."

"I'm sleeping in your room," she said, turning out the light and grabbing the blanket off her bed. "And you know what else?"

"What? Tell me."

"We're outta here," Maya said. "This is the last straw."

I had to agree with her. Within two weeks, we had shipped everything worth keeping to our parents and given away what wouldn't travel. I gave notice at Molto's for the last time, taking some photos of the place on my way out even though I knew I'd never forget it. Again, I finished my last shift with no fanfare. Only hours after it ended, Maya, Blaze, and I boarded a midnight flight to California and were gone for good.

# a diner in california

**Diners have a certain image** in the collective imagination. Soda fountains, for example. Endless coffee. Inexpensive but filling meals. Bright Formica and stainless steel. Waitresses in pink outfits, on roller skates. Red Naugahyde booths. An innocence of the all-American variety. There is something comforting in the warm glow of a diner, a feeling of safe haven. Diners evoke nostalgia, sweet as cherry pie, of a time when some things, at least, were simpler.

There is, of course, a darker version.

I worked in one.

When I moved to California with Maya and my year-old son, the logical first step was to find a job in the new land of low-fat milk and raw honey. My parents had raved about the quality of life in California:

"People walk around in shorts in the middle of the day!"

"Everybody's on a permanent vacation—nobody works here!"

"Beaches! Sunshine! Vegetarian restaurants!"

People, it seemed, survived in style down here. Maya and I both reckoned we could get decent waitressing jobs, which would at least pay the bills until we got on our feet and began doing whatever it was that we were really meant to do. For Maya, who had been playing violin since the age of nine, that whatever involved music. For me, a small voice in my head still whispered (although not very insistently) that I should be writing something. Anything.

Our initial approach to the job search was fairly simple. We'd found an apartment to rent that was close enough to the beach to sport an ocean view (if we craned our heads in a very specific way out of the living room window) and within walking distance of a town very popular with tourists. Because we'd moved without a car, or much of anything resembling furniture, for that matter, I strapped Blaze into his stroller and both Maya and I walked along the ocean from our apartment into town, stopping in at every restaurant along the way. Usually, we took turns going in. If the restaurant looked more upscale, Maya would wait outside with the baby while I filled out an application. Having only Maxman's and Peppy's to her credit, Maya felt unsure of her waitressing skills and, despite tales of my Dining Room experience, was unwilling to try to bluff her way into a fine dining situation. As a result, I filled out countless applications and Maya spent a lot of time with Blaze.

After a couple of days of this pavement pounding, we stopped in at Hoover's, an eclectic diner only steps away from the azure surf of the Pacific. The restaurant was decorated in shades of black, pink, and seafoam green down to the flecks in the Formica tabletops. There were whole wheat muffins under glass and Warholish prints on the walls. Next to an old-fashioned industrial coffee maker was a very high-tech cappuccino machine. The overall effect was Mel's Diner meets the Twin Peaks café.

Maya and I filled out applications together while I rocked Blaze in his stroller with my foot. The diner's owner, Adrian, seemed highly amused at our team approach. He was in dire need of help, he said, and had to hire someone immediately. I marveled at our good fortune and the fact that he wasn't even planning on checking our references.

"Can you girls start Sunday morning?" was all he asked.

It all seemed so easy.

Within a few weeks, however, Maya and I both discovered why, despite a steady flow of customers, Adrian had the highest staff turnover of any restaurant in town. We also learned a style of service that I have come to label "guerrilla waitressing." Within a scant couple of months, we were preparing for our shifts as if we were going to war. And Hoover's was nothing if not a battlefield.

Allow me to illustrate . . .

I wake up on Sunday morning at 5:30 A.M. and pack a bag for Blaze with toys, diapers, and bottles. He'll be spending the day with my parents until I finish work. I take a five-minute shower and hurry myself into a pink T-shirt and shorts. For the first time in my life, I've eschewed the traditional black waitress footwear for an expensive pair of cross-training athletic shoes. As I strap them on, I realize what a good choice they are. What I will be doing for the next several hours will be more of a work-*out* than work. I can't leave Blaze without saying good-bye to him, so I pick him up out of his crib and kiss his sleepy face before tucking him into bed with Maya.

"I'm leaving," I tell her.

"Hmmm . . . OK," she mutters. "See you there."

I walk to work while the rest of the world sleeps. My twenty-minute route takes me along the ocean, through quiet streets. It's still fairly dark outside and the salty air has a little bite. But this is California. I'll be sweating by noon, no matter that this is the middle of January.

I arrive for my shift at Hoover's at 6:30 A.M. My first task is to rouse Danny from his stupor so that he can unlock the restaurant and prepare the popovers.

I should explain. Adrian had a very successful business, which he was doing his best to run into the Indian burial ground that his restaurant was suspected of being built upon. By the time my sister and I were hired, he was about three quarters of the way to complete ruin. There were two things that kept Hoover's busy and saved Adrian from going under: a spectacular ocean view and popovers. Every single day, Adrian, or whatever hapless cook happened to be employed at the time, made dozens of popovers, which were served with every breakfast and lunch. Most mornings the popovers came out late, half burned or half raw. They were sent back regularly by customers screaming with indignation. Yet, amazingly, these same customers came back time and again, lining up for forty-five minutes on a Sunday morning in order to wait another forty-five minutes at the table with seven refills of coffee until they received an omelette that contained not what was ordered but whatever was left in the kitchen and that was garnished by a misshapen, ill-conceived attempt at a popover.

But I digress.

"Danny!" I shriek for the third time. "Get up! Danny, can you hear me?"

Danny Davidson is one of two cooks Adrian refers to as "my international staff of chefs." Danny found his way to Southern California from New Zealand and entered almost immediately into a Faustian bargain with Adrian. At twenty, Danny has been an alcoholic for more than five years. Adrian, seeing a prime opportunity, offered to pay him mostly in beer. While the arrangement suited Danny, it didn't allow him much spare cash to live on. Magnanimously, Adrian provided Danny with a room off the restaurant, which had been serving as a spare office. Thus, Danny, who had never so much as fried an egg before being hired at Hoover's, has become something of an indentured servant. He drinks steadily all day and finishes with several six-packs when his shift is over. By the time his next shift begins, he is usually deep in a bottomless blackout.

I pound on the locked door until my fists hurt and I experience a familiar flash of panic. Could Danny, whom I like but am unable to help, be comatose this time? Or worse? I bang and scream one more time. There is a muffled groaning behind the door.

"Danny! The popovers. It's getting late—please."

The door opens and I am assaulted by a wave of alcoholic fumes. Danny, half dressed, bloodshot and pasty, looks worse than a train wreck.

"Where's Adrian, the scabby prick?" Danny mutters. "It's not my shift this morning."

"He's not here," I say, desperately. "Please unlock the door for me, Danny."

Spewing barely intelligible curses, Danny stumbles down to the diner and lets me in. I have to beg him to stay vertical and start cooking. The restaurant is scheduled to open in an hour and we'll be full to capacity within a half hour afterward. Reluctantly, Danny staggers to the kitchen and begins whipping up a batch of popovers destined to reach a new low point in culinary standards.

It's seven-thirty and Sheryl, the next waitress on, is half an hour late. I'm running around frantically trying to get the coffee made, the tables wiped down, and the condiments filled and lined up. We're not going to be ready.

The phone rings and I lunge for it, hoping it's Adrian to say he's on his way. No such luck. It's Sheryl, sounding none too happy.

"I'm sorry, I don't think I'm going to make it into work today," she says.

"Sheryl, please, even if you're late, it's no big deal. But it's going to be really busy and we really need—"

"No, I'm really not going to make it."

"Are you sick?"

"Not exactly."

"Can someone come pick you up?"

"Well, I'm kind of in Mexico."

"Well, you could make it back in a couple of hours, couldn't you?"

"Not really. I'm kind of in jail. In Tijuana."

There is a long silence. My brain is refusing to process the information.

"Listen," Sheryl continues, "can you let Adrian know what happened? Tell him I'm really sorry. Also, I think you should know that Frank's with me. I mean, he's also in jail, so he probably won't be able to make it for his shift, either."

I don't want to know the details and Sheryl doesn't offer them. What I do know is that we're now two servers short. This day has all the earmarks of certain disaster.

Adrian shows up at eight. He's wearing a pink sweatshirt, black tights, and loafers with no socks. His hair is matted and his eyes are wild. He looks as if he hasn't eaten, slept, or bathed for at least a month. He barks, "Cappuccino, make it a double!" at me and heads to the kitchen. By this time my first customers have arrived, a couple of regulars who bring the Sunday papers and fold them into neat sections to read one at a time. One of them watches Adrian, smiles, and shakes his head.

"Crazy guy," he offers. I smile and fill his coffee. "It will probably be a few minutes before the popovers are ready," I tell him. "We're running a bit late today."

"So what else is new?" Mr. Regular tells me grumpily. "I'll take the omelette first, then. Bring me the popover when it's ready. And since I have to wait for it, you can bring me an extra one for free."

Thank you, thank you, Mr. Regular. I'm happy to serve you
and really earn my $1.57 tip. How empty would your life be
without the chance of that free popover for all your troubles? I
ring up his omelette, but I'm dubious that anyone is paying
attention to the order in the kitchen, where shouting is audible.

"You call this a popover?" Adrian is screaming as I approach
the kitchen. "This is an abortion!" Adrian takes the first batch and
throws them into the trash. "Now, make some real popovers!"

Danny is staring at his feet, taking the abuse. His misery
emanates in tidal waves.

"Um, I've got an omelette on order," I begin tentatively.
Adrian and Danny stare at me as if I'm speaking Greek.

"Can you believe this fucking kid?" Adrian says, pointing at
Danny. "Can't even get a fucking popover together. Where the
fuck is Oaxaca?"

"Oaxaca" is the other international star in Adrian's chef ros-
ter. A Mexican national with no green card, Oaxaca is illegally
employed by Adrian and treated even worse than Danny, if that's
possible. Sweet, timid, and unable to understand almost any
English, Oaxaca regularly works twelve- to fifteen-hour days. I
don't know how much Adrian pays him, but I'm sure it's crimi-
nally low. Oaxaca is not his real name, it's the region in Mexico
he comes from, but he is never referred to any other way—
another attempt on Adrian's part to keep him in his place.
None of us know what his name is, exactly, and he's too shy to
tell us.

(This type of hiring practice was a fact of SoCal kitchens I'd
discovered very soon after moving to the area. Inevitably, restaurants would hire illegal, or dubiously legal, aliens to work in the
kitchen for ridiculously low wages. Thus, restaurants of every
nationality—Greek, French, Italian, Indian, Thai—ended up
with Mexican cooks. One restaurant I worked in later carried
this policy to extremes, hiring illegals and raising their wages by

minuscule increments until Immigration did a sweep. At this point, the restaurant would "fire" the cooks, only to hire them back with new names at the old wages.)

"Um, Adrian? Sheryl called from Tijuana. She's in jail with Frank. They're not going to make it to work today, obviously, so I was wondering if maybe we could call somebody else?" I run from the kitchen after delivering this news, not wanting to hear its effect.

At nine the restaurant is almost full. Maya and one other waitress, Jessie, have arrived. Maya takes one look at me and reads the morning in my face.

"How bad is it?" she asks.

"Don't ask," I tell her. "I need you to take Twelve, Fourteen, and Fifteen. And Twenty's been waiting for ten minutes. How's Blaze?"

"Fine," she says, tying on her apron. "Mom and Dad have big plans for him today. They're going to the Wild Animal Park."

I raise my eyebrows. "They could just bring him here and avoid the cost of admission," I say.

Maya and I are soon waiting on at least ten tables each, while Jessie is struggling to handle two. Jessie explains that she's hung over this morning and will need a little time to ease into her shift. Adrian doesn't care about this because Jessie's father coaches a professional football team. Even though Jessie has been disowned by her father for drug and alcohol problems, Adrian figures some of the gravy will eventually drip over onto him if he employs the daughter. Oaxaca has shown up and started cooking, but Adrian is on a rampage, criticizing every plate that comes out of the kitchen, so that now we are at least ten plates behind and not a popover in sight.

"I don't know why I keep coming here," a woman says to me, waving her diamond-encrusted hand in disdain. "The service is slow and the food is terrible."

I don't know why, either. Go to another restaurant, I want to tell her. Please. Better yet, go home and cook something yourself for your bratty children. Instead, I make her a free latte and locate crayons for her two screaming kids, buying myself ten more minutes before she erupts again.

At ten, Chris and Terry arrive, replacements for the jailed Sheryl and Frank. Terry and Chris feel that since they have come in on their day off, they should be given the best tables, which are located on the patio, up a rickety flight of wooden stairs.

While the popovers were subject to the vagaries of human nature, the ocean was consistently beautiful. Since my episode at Hoover's, I have learned that people will do just about anything to secure themselves an ocean view, even if the table they are viewing it from is made of dirty white plastic, shaded with an ancient Cinzano-emblazoned umbrella, and laid with barely edible food. This was certainly the case at Hoover's, which in addition was laid out so eccentrically that it was almost impossible to give decent service to its prime tables.

Chris and Terry are arguing their point when the question of who will serve up on the patio becomes somewhat moot. We all hear a spectacular crash and a gasp of "Ooh" from the upstairs diners. On closer investigation, it seems that Jessie has fallen up the stairs with a tray full of cappuccinos.

"I think I blacked out," she says. "I think I twisted my ankle. I can't walk. I'm going to have to go home. Or maybe to the hospital."

At Adrian's command, we begin handing out free mimosas to the patio tables to assuage the trauma they've sustained watching the accident. Several tables feel they have to justify receiving freebies that they haven't yet had the chance to demand:

"You'd better make sure you get that cleaned up. If I slip on those stairs, there's going to be a lawsuit."

"Only one mimosa? Can I get another one if I don't get my breakfast in the next half hour?"

"Are you sure you use fresh-squeezed orange juice in this? Doesn't taste like it."

"I don't drink champagne. Can I get a free Bloody Mary instead?"

The downstairs tables get wind of the situation and begin complaining bitterly:

"Hey, I've been waiting thirty minutes for two eggs and toast. Where's my free drink?"

"What kind of place is this? Free drinks for half the restaurant?"

"Get that fascist Adrian out here now."

The downstairs tables get mimosas. This ploy actually works quite well. Enough diners get tipsy enough not to notice the wait or the escalating entropy. The only trouble now is that we've run out of orange juice. The juice man hasn't made a delivery for a while since Adrian is at least two months behind on payment. We are also running out of eggs, bacon, sausage, and hamburger because the meat distributor is in the same boat as the juice man. At this rate we will be out of every menu item but the tuna melt by noon.

"Tell them that this is Vegetarian Day at Hoover's," Adrian says. "This is California, isn't it?"

Despite the chaos, business continues to be brisk. I even have time to converse with some of my customers about topics other than the lateness of their orders. One man, for example, asks me: "What is this awful music?"

Adrian has two tape loops he insists on pumping through the restaurant. One is a medley of relatively current pop tunes and the other is a collection of standards that would work well in an underground French bistro. Today we are listening to the latter.

"I believe this is Eartha Kitt," I tell him.

"Eartha Kitt? You mean Catwoman? You gotta be kidding me. This place . . . "

I approach another table and offer them something to drink. "I just want you to know," one man says, "that the last time we were here, we had a terrible experience. The food was cold and we were not given any attention from our waitress."

"I'm so sorry," I say.

"Well," he continues, "we've decided to give you one more chance. Now, what do you recommend?"

"The tuna melt is excellent," I tell him and he orders it.

A couple I've waited on before comes in with their baby girl and sits down at one of my tables. There is dread in my heart. "How's it going?" they want to know. "You remember us, right? Greg and Kate? And this is our little Annalisa. Your name's Brenda, isn't it?"

"Uh-huh," I say. I don't have the energy to correct them. I've already told them what my name is at least six times before.

"Is it *crazy* today?" They are both grinning ear to ear, as if they'll be disappointed if I say no.

"A little," I say hopefully.

"We thought so. We're so glad you're waiting on us today, you're so nice. I hope the popovers aren't soggy today. Sometimes they're pretty soggy. But we don't mind because it's always so much *fun* to eat here."

"Like Dinner Theater?" I ask.

"Ha ha ha, you're so *funny*. She's so funny, isn't she, Greg?"

"Cute, too," Greg says. "Say, Brenda, we'd like to have a couple of omelettes, but Kate doesn't eat the yolks. Do you think you could get her an egg white omelette? If it's too much trouble, don't worry about it, we'll understand. We know things can get a little wild around here. Also, do you think you could find some kind of cereal for the baby? Maybe some polenta or something like that. Do you have polenta? If you don't, that's OK, but she does need to eat, so if you could get something soon for her, that would be great. But don't worry, we're not in a big hurry. If you could bring us a few popovers while we're waiting for our food that would be terrific. Also, can you check and see if you've got any asparagus? It would be fantastic if I could get a side order of asparagus steamed with a little olive oil. We'd like to start with some coffee drinks, if you've got time. I'll just have a double decaf latte. What would you like, Kate?"

"Yes, Brenda, can you make me a half-decaf low-fat cappuccino?" Kate asks. "Nonfat would be better, but I know you might not have it. If you do, I'd be so happy. I love your cappuccinos here, they're so *good*. Except the last time we were here, it was a little cold. If it's not too much trouble, could you make sure that my cappuccino is really hot? Can you do that for me, Brenda? By the way, how's your sister? What's her name? Myra, right?"

"You guys are both so cute," Greg adds.

I hate these people.

In the kitchen, a new storm is brewing. Terry rushes up to the grill and tells Adrian, "Can you fix this omelette? The woman says it's not done in the middle."

Adrian opens the omelette with his fingers and pokes at it. "It's fine," he says. "It's the best fucking omelette we've ever made. Tell her—"

"Well, she's right behind me," Terry says. Indeed, the woman in question, wearing workout clothes and a huge attitude, has waltzed right into the kitchen.

"Are you the owner?" she demands of Adrian. "I've got to tell you, this is the worst omelette I've ever had in my life. In addition"—she checks off the list on her fingers—"it came late, the coffee is cold, I couldn't get orange juice, and this bimbo"— she points at Terry—"is rude."

Time stops as we wait for Adrian's reaction. The hum of the restaurant fades against the crackling of static in the air. Calmly, Adrian walks out from behind the grill and puts an arm around the woman.

"Let's not talk about this here," he tells her softly. "Let's go outside." He opens the screen door for her, and as she exits the kitchen, he slams it at her back.

"First of all," he growls, "don't call my waitress a bimbo. Second of all, get the hell out of my restaurant. Learn some manners."

As she strides off speechless and fuming, Adrian mutters, "Ah, fuck her. In fact, fuck everything. Close the kitchen. Shut down the restaurant. I'm outta here." He throws his apron on the floor and walks out. Terry shrugs and Oaxaca grins broadly.

"You know he'll be back," Danny says hopelessly and picks up a frying pan. Oaxaca inspects the tickets, which have continued to roll in from the printer. "Garden salad," he says, "side of potatoes, two short stacks . . . "

At two there is a brief lull in the madness. I take the time to start my portion of the day's cleanup, which mostly involves trying to clean the cappuccino machine, which now looks as if several gallons of milk have exploded and then dried on its surfaces. Because I can feel someone staring at me from across the counter, I turn and see Dominic holding a couple of pink cake boxes.

Dominic is one half of Cake and More, a tiny company he runs with his partner, Ian. These two make some of the most beautiful confections I've ever seen, which is why Adrian, who can't even keep up with his juice payments, has lately decided to sell their cheesecakes. I have to smile when I see Dominic because, despite the fact that Adrian refers to him and Ian as "those pastry fags," I know that he's come all the way out to Hoover's on a Sunday afternoon mostly to see me. We've had a running flirtation going since he started bringing his cakes to Hoover's. Right now, I couldn't be happier to see him.

"Hi, how are you?" I ask him.

"Pretty good," he says. "Just thought I'd bring these by. We're working on something new and I thought maybe you'd like to try a sample." He opens one of the boxes and shows me a tiny round gâteau coated with dark chocolate and topped with a pink sugar rose.

"Wow," I tell him, "you guys are really talented."

"Maybe you can share it around," he says a bit nervously.

"Thank you," I tell him. "Cup of coffee for your troubles?" Dominic smiles and nods assent. I make him a double espresso and rummage in my apron pocket for money to pay him for the cakes. At Hoover's, we have to pay our distributors out of the day's sales. Lucky for Dominic, I've sold more than enough today to cover his bill. It won't last, I know. Sooner or later, we'll have to stop paying him. But for now, I want to keep him around, so I give him the cash and he hands me a receipt.

"Busy day?" he asks.

"This place is insane," I tell him. "Two of our servers are in jail in Tijuana."

Dominic laughs and I start telling him about my morning. For a moment, things feel almost normal. I'm just a waitress in a pretty diner, leaning over the counter I'm polishing, flirting with the good-looking cake man.

But it can't last.

A clot of hungry beachcombers, crusted with sand, stumble through the door demanding immediate service and wanting to know if they can get popovers to go.

"Sorry," I tell Dominic, "I've got to get back to work."

"Right," he says. "Thanks for the coffee." He pulls himself up from the counter and starts to head for the door. At the last minute, he stops himself and comes back, behind the counter this time, so he can speak close to my ear. "Maybe we can get together sometime?" he says.

"That would really be nice," I tell him and pause. "You know, I've got a kid," I add.

"No, I didn't know," he says, smiling. "How old?"

"One and a half."

"What's her name?"

"It's a boy. Blaze."

"Well, where's Blaze today?" he asks.

"He's with my parents." I've said everything I need to with those four words. There's no boyfriend, no husband. I'm a single mother, plain as day.

"So Blaze can come with us," Dominic says. And now he's said everything he needs to. Ah, the modern rites of courtship, I think to myself.

"Why don't you call me?" I say and scrawl my phone number on a paper napkin and hand it to him.

"OK, good," he says and, in another second, is gone. I head toward the kitchen and am immediately body-slammed by Terry, who is coming around one of Hoover's many blind corners. Terry happens to be carrying a pot of scalding hot coffee, half of which splashes across me and sinks, still steaming, into my chest.

"Oh, I'm sorry," she mumbles as I yelp in pain. "I didn't see you."

I spend the next thirty minutes trying to assuage the burning pain in my chest with icy towels. There's not much for me in the way of sympathy. Terry is claiming that *I* walked into *her* and has actually become indignant. I finish my cleanup and my last few tables. My enthusiasm for Dominic and his cakes translates into cash as I am able to happily sell several slices of the cherry cheesecake to the late lunch crowd.

By three-thirty, the flow of business is slow enough for me to leave. I can identify at least four different food stains on my apron and my legs threaten to fold at any moment. I have been in a state of constant movement for eight hours. I prepare my cash drop and take it upstairs to Adrian's office, where he's been hiding for the last two hours. He says nothing as I dump cash and tickets into a cardboard box near the door.

When I come back downstairs, my parents are waiting for me with Blaze.

"We thought we'd just drop him off here," my mother says, "so he can have a nice walk home." She hands me Blaze's stroller and diaper bag. "You look tired. Long day?"

"You don't even know," I tell her and tuck Blaze into his stroller. "Un un un," he says and, right now, I'm interpreting that to mean, "Hi, Mom, let's go home."

On my way out, I pass Danny sitting outside the kitchen, drinking a beer, taking his first break of the day. Oaxaca is attempting to scrape dried popovers from the kitchen floor.

"Look at the little mite," Danny says, smiling at Blaze. "He's so sweet. Hey, chum."

"Un un un," Blaze responds.

"You going home?" Danny asks me.

"Yes, if I can make it there."

"Y'know," he says, "I'd like to have a son someday."

"Why's that, Danny?"

"Well, so I could name him Harley."

"Harley? Is that a family name?"

"No, it's so his name would be Harley Davidson. Isn't that a great name for a kid?"

"Have a good night, Danny."

When I get home, I am too tired to ponder the riddles of the day. Why, for example, people keep coming back to Hoover's. Or why Danny and Oaxaca don't take a kitchen knife to Adrian. Or how much longer I can work in this restaurant without having a nervous breakdown. I am, however, sure of two things. For one,

I have the day off tomorrow. I will take Blaze down to a park by the beach and push him on the swings while he watches the ocean. On the way home, I'll stop in somewhere and have a cappuccino for myself and an apple juice for Blaze. It will be warm and sunny. The taste of life will be sweet.

The other certainty is that I have a hundred and fifty dollars in cold cash tucked into my apron pocket. Whether or not the trade-off to earn those dollars has been worth it is a question that will have to be addressed tomorrow or as soon as I can lift my aching body off the couch.

Maya arrives home at 5:30 P.M. and falls onto the other couch. "I can't believe I have to go back there in the morning," she says.

"How'd it end up?" I ask her.

"Not good. When I left, Adrian was giving Danny and Oaxaca a lesson on how to make popovers properly. I think they might be there all night. Oaxaca missed his bus and Danny looked like he was on his fiftieth beer."

"How much did you make?" I ask her.

"A hundred. You?"

"One-fifty."

"Not bad," she says. "What shall we have for dinner?"

I lasted six months at Hoover's. The final weeks were grim. Adrian stopped paying everybody, including staff. Because our paychecks bounced regularly on paydays, and this was a wonderful sales incentive, we'd have to sell at least the amount on the check in order to collect any wages at all. The muffin and doughnut man was not that lucky. He stopped coming around after issuing the following edict: "Tell Adrian to pay me or I'm comin' back here to break both his legs." Because Adrian engendered such unbridled hostility among his distributors, many of us actually started fearing for his life. Maya, for example, had a real fear that one morning she would arrive at work and find Adrian's dead body stuffed in the Dumpster. As a result, she avoided going into the back of the restaurant until she saw Adrian, still alive, walk in the front door.

Poor Danny managed to scrape enough money together to go back to New Zealand. Before he left, Maya and I invited him over for dinner. He arrived with a bottle of wine and twin turquoise necklaces, one for each of us. "You girls have been so nice to me," he told us, "and I know I haven't always been easy to work with. I don't know how to thank you." I couldn't decide which was more heartbreaking, the fact that Danny had such a low opinion of himself or that, aside from our apartment, all he ever saw of the United States was the view from inside Hoover's kitchen.

Oaxaca, whose name turned out to be Francisco, worked like a galley slave for many months before finally quitting. He resurfaced years later at another restaurant where I worked, hired as a busboy. We greeted each other like survivors of a particularly nasty accident. Unfortunately, Francisco seemed permanently scarred by his experience at Hoover's. He'd lost his edge and wandered around the restaurant as if lost, spilling coffee and showing up late. He just wasn't used to being treated fairly and quit after a couple of weeks.

As I had predicted, Adrian soon canceled orders for Dominic's cakes. Dominic, however, did call me for a date. Ultimately, we ended up seeing each other for almost a year. Dominic had a few talents. He was a very hard worker and a good businessman, and he made a Linzertorte to die for. Unfortunately, he was also peculiarly old-fashioned when it came to women and believed in traditional roles for males and females, which bordered on outright sexism. This attitude also led him to assume that I had an immediate need to provide Blaze with a father. Dominic was the first man I'd dated since John and I wasn't even sure if he was the right man for me, let alone my son. At any rate, I wasn't about to let him experiment and audition for fatherhood with Blaze.

"He's two years old," Dominic would say. "He shouldn't have a bottle anymore. He needs to be potty trained. Why don't you put him in day care?" It was a rude awakening to one aspect of single motherhood and a call for me to put as much distance as possible between myself and a similar situation in the future. This, I assumed, virtually assured that I'd spend a long period outside of any other serious relationship.

Perhaps, when he first met me, Dominic mistook me for an image of some diner waitress he had in his imagination: a poor working girl struggling to raise a kid on her own and desperately in need of a man to fix everything for her. I couldn't fault him too much for this. For a brief while, I thought I was that waitress, too. In any case, though, I'd been paving my own way for much too long to become the "girl" Dominic was looking for. The end of our relationship, when it came, was not pleasant. Anything started at Hoover's, it seemed, was destined for failure.

After the local sheriff showed up for a "till tap" to make good on bad debts, Adrian managed, through witchcraft, we all assumed, to sell Hoover's. The unsuspecting buyer was unaware of the curse on the place and he eliminated popovers from the menu to boot. After accusing Adrian of falsifying the books, the buyer and Adrian actually came to blows one day when Adrian refused to renegotiate the sale. Adrian sued the buyer for assaulting him and won a settlement. He, too, showed up later in a restaurant where I worked and insisted that I wait on him.

"Hey!" he shouted drunkenly, although he wasn't drunk at all, just mad as a hatter. "See this girl?" He pointed at me. "I taught her everything she knows!"

"Do you *know* that guy?" my manager asked me incredulously as I hung my head in abject embarrassment.

"I used to work for him," I answered.

"That's a relief," my manager said. "By the way he was talk-ing to you, I thought maybe you used to date him."

Hoover's itself maintained a certain aura of madness and drama that drew customers for quite some time. Without Adrian's unique brand of insanity, however, it just wasn't as much fun. Slowly, business died. Today, Hoover's is no more, having been replaced by an upscale restaurant specializing in designer salads and fresh fish.

As for me, I leaped from the sinking ship as soon as I saw the opportunity. I headed for a new Italian restaurant that arrived in town with a sterling reputation and the promise of big money. Ironically, it was Adrian himself who pointed out this restaurant while it was still under construction.

"See that?" he said one morning. "There's a big fancy Italian place coming in there. They think they're going to do so well. I've got news for them. They're never gonna make it in this fucked-up town. Not with their overhead."

Not surprisingly, he was completely wrong about this.

Desperate to escape the vortex that was Hoover's, Maya and I both climbed over construction rubble and bits of pink Italian marble to apply and interview at the new place. Once again we took the tag team approach, with one of us interviewing while the other sat with Blaze. These people, I realized, were serious. There were four separate managers conducting interviews and quizzing us on our knowledge of wines, fine dining, and Italian food. They spoke of "teams," "expansion," and "opportunity." It sounded a bit like they wanted to take over the planet rather than open a restaurant, but I didn't care, I just wanted to be hired. There was a second interview and then a third. All my ref-erences were rigorously checked. Finally, after I'd almost given up hope, I received a call inviting me to "join our team at Baciare." There would be three weeks of training and testing before the restaurant opened and could I be at the site at ten o'clock the next morning to complete the paperwork? I said I'd be there with bells on.

My sister, told that she didn't have enough experience, was not hired. She was destined to suffer through another nine months of hell at Hoover's before her release.

Despite its obvious mental tolls, I still look back on my Hoover's experience with great amusement, even fondness. There was something almost sublime in the insanity of each shift. I also learned a great deal about human psychology and crisis management working at Hoover's. These were lessons that would stand me in good stead later, in every area of my life. There were other advantages as well. Hoover's afforded me the ability to start over in a new place with a new child and a new life. Maya and I made enough money there to buy ourselves a car, some furniture, and a little peace of mind.

And there was also something quite beautiful about Hoover's. Every day I walked outside at least once and stared at the ocean, which was close enough to be practically in my lap. The crazy pink and green curves of Hoover's provided a perfect frame around the horizon whether it was sunny or stormy, blue or gray. When a smiling waitress and the smell of popovers and fresh coffee were added to this tableau, Hoover's seemed, however briefly, like a little piece of heaven. Surely, I think now, this is why Hoover's was always so busy despite the darkness behind its pastel exterior.

After all, everybody loves a diner.

# food and sex

**Several years ago,** a waiter friend and I rented a video after a shift and went to my house to watch it. After much debate, the film we'd decided on was *The Cook, the Thief, His Wife, and Her Lover.* My friend and I settled in on the couch for a comfortable evening. As the tape played, we found ourselves moving closer to the TV, our jaws dropping in amazement at the scenes unfolding before our eyes. Filmed in vividly colored detail, the story revolved around characters in a swank restaurant. There were scenes of greed and food, revenge and food, violence and food. Most pervasively, however, there were scenes of that most tantalizing of combinations, sex and food. There was sex in the kitchen, sex in the bathroom, sex at the table. My friend and I looked at each other. Although the reality portrayed in the film was clearly bent, we were both thinking the same thing: had the filmmakers visited the restaurant where we both worked? Surely, we thought, they must have.

"You know," my friend told me with the seriousness of a weighty confession, "I had sex on Table Fifty."

"Right on the table?" I asked.

"Right on the table."

"And?"

"Well, the sex wasn't that great, it was a little rushed, but it makes working there so much easier."

"And why is that?" I asked.

"Well, every time I see someone seated at that table, I know what happened on it. I know that they don't know, and somehow just knowing *that* and remembering *it* makes my night go a little smoother—if you know what I mean."

I thought about this for a minute and then I asked him, "So, who'd you have sex with on Table Fifty?"

"Ah," he said, "*that* I cannot tell you."

*♪ ♪ ♪*

With few exceptions, the restaurants I've worked in over the years have all been breeding grounds for amorous liaisons. There seems to be an almost chemical reaction that occurs when food, alcohol, and heat are combined in an enclosed space with the freewheeling movement of people in a restaurant. More is stimulated than just the palate. The call of the wild often seems loudest in a restaurant, where it is heard by those sitting at the table as well as those waiting on it. For me, one of the most entertaining aspects of table service has always been watching the parallel mating dances of staff and patrons. The convergence of these very primal urges creates drama of the highest order and, often, true comedy. It's an irresistible combination.

Of course, one expects to witness a certain amount of romance from patrons who are out on a date. It's almost too easy to identify the couples who will be headed to a bedroom as soon as dinner is over. They are holding hands at the table, kissing over the appetizers, whispering in each other's ears. Waiters and waitresses train themselves to understand body language as carefully as the spoken word. Therefore, we can tell by how close patrons sit to each other, how he touches her arm and pulls out her chair, how she feeds him little pieces of chocolate cake, and (the surefire one) how little she eats of her dinner, which way things are headed. For example, a couple on a date early in their relationship will either both have garlic in their meals or request that it be entirely removed from their dishes. There are also telling questions such as "Does it have a lot of bones?" Nobody wants to be seen picking apart a chicken if planning later to strip naked in front of a virtual stranger.

It's not always this subtle, however. There was the man who gestured to his date and told his waiter, "She says she'll have sex with me if I get her drunk, so line 'em up." And there was the woman who received a pearl earring and necklace set from her husband over dinner. Thrilled, she gave him a squeeze and said loudly, "Blow job for you tonight, honey!"

Inevitably, there are couples who seek to embroil their server in their personal sexual politics. Several times, I've had the displeasure of serving a table where the man is overtly flirtatious with me with the express purpose of irritating his partner. The desired effect is almost always obtained in these instances. For example, after her husband had commented separately on my eyes, hair, and figure one evening, a wife once told me, "Don't take him seriously, honey, it's got nothing to do with you. He's just trying to piss me off." To her husband, she added, "Why don't you leave this poor girl alone?" Her bitter tone and defensive body language told me that "poor girl" was quite the opposite of the way she viewed me, though. The best a waitress can hope for in this situation is that the couple won't make up during the course of the meal, because when that happens the waitress always becomes an instant enemy.

Of course, borderline flirtations are not limited to male patrons and waitresses. There are plenty of female customers who ditch their dates and leave waiters with their phone numbers. And generally, waiters who come on to their customers fare better than customers who come on to their waitresses. One waiter friend of mine (and all his male coworkers) had great success with the following trick when he worked in a small Italian restaurant in Alaska. When waiting on a table comprised entirely of women, my friend would offer a free dinner to anyone at the table who was wearing a teddy and was willing to prove it. Without fail, my friend claimed, women unbuttoned their blouses, showed off their lingerie, and ate for free. My friend got to see a number of teddies over six months before finally offending a table containing a mother and daughter.

But this is light fare on the menu of dining dalliance. Sometimes passion just can't be denied and couples in a restaurant will cross all conventional boundaries—overwhelmed by lust or merely the need to be naughty in public—and find a way to consummate their desires at, under, or near the table. Although I've personally witnessed many instances of this kind of trysting, two in particular stand out as shining examples.

The first happened on a sultry summer evening. I was waiting on a couple who were seated in a dim section of the open air patio. I had already delivered drinks to the table and I approached them to take their dinner order. The male half of the couple looked a little flushed as I stood before them. The woman, sitting beside him with one hand below the tablecloth and the other casually holding a glass of wine, had a sly smile on her face.

"Do you have any questions about the menu," I asked, "or are you ready to order?"

"I have a couple of questions," the woman said. She began moving her hand under the table in a rhythmic motion as she spoke and the man leaned in closer to the table, looking mildly uncomfortable. "Do any of your entrees come with salads, or is everything à la carte?"

"Everything is à la carte," I said. "But we do have several salads and appetizers to start."

"Great," she said and began moving her hand a little faster. Her date began breathing heavily, his face reddening into a shade of crimson. "And can I get this pasta without oil?" She pointed to an item with her free hand.

"Sure," I said, wanting desperately to leave the table and whatever unseen acts were progressing beneath it.

"Oh, good," she said. "Well, I'll have that, then, and why don't you bring me one of the house salads?"

"OK," I said. "And what can I bring for you?" I asked her date, although I knew full well he was getting everything he needed and more.

"Aah, uhnn . . ." he replied.

"You know what?" the woman interrupted, without ever breaking the rhythm of her hand motion. "Why don't you just bring him what I'm having? That'll be fine."

"Great," I said. "Can I bring you anything else?"

"Yes," she said, smiling broadly, "extra napkins, please."

The second encounter, at the same restaurant, involved a woman who was a regular patron and who had definitely had too much to drink. After groping her date at the bar, which is where she'd picked him up, she disappeared with him to the back of the restaurant, where they ended up in the ladies' room. They might have really made a night of it had a particular waitress not needed to relieve herself. The waitress came out reporting that the two were going at it full tilt in one of the stalls, complete with groaning, moaning, and the sound of zippers going up and down.

"So what did you do?" we asked her.

"Well, I really had to pee," the waitress said, "so I used the other stall."

"You mean they're still doing it?" we asked.

"I think so," she told us.

That information was pretty much all that was needed to turn the ladies' room into an instant attraction. Every waiter and waitress on the floor headed over to the bathroom and listened while a busboy held the door open. The waitress hadn't lied. The couple were still quite involved judging by the sounds they were making and the tangling of their feet visible beneath the stall door.

Eventually, our eloquence-challenged manager was forced to go to the bathroom and break it up.

"What I am supposed to say?" he sighed.

"Why don't you try using a stick?" one waiter offered helpfully. "Sometimes that works with dogs."

"Sing 'That's Amore,' " offered another.

"But what they are doing really? Do I have to go there? I am a man and it is the ladies' room."

"Yes," we chimed in a gleeful chorus, "you have to go."

Shaking his head and muttering at the vagaries of fate, the manager reluctantly entered the bathroom and, quite politely, knocked on the stall door.

"Hello?" he called. "Can you come out of there, please?"

"Can you give us a minute?" the woman said, sounding somewhat annoyed.

"No, you must come out now. This is a public place." After repeating this two or three times, the manager, who felt he had gone above and beyond the call of duty, left the bathroom and sat down heavily at a vacant table, still shaking his head and blushing furiously. The couple exited the restaurant through the back door a few minutes later.

What drives certain people to turn their table into a makeshift motel room? Aside from the fact that the above-mentioned couples were seriously lacking in any kind of paranoia, part of the appeal seems to be the built-in audience in a restaurant. The woman in the first scenario was clearly carrying on for my benefit as well as her date's. As for couple number two, it's not as if they couldn't hear a crowd of people snickering by the bathroom door. The fact that everybody knew what was going on added an irresistible naughtiness, making the encounters much more exciting.

In the face of these public displays of "affection," the attitude of the waiters and waitresses I've worked with is generally one of amusement. Occasionally, someone will take a moral high road ("Really, can't they wait until they get home?"), but the feeling is usually that if people want to make fools of themselves in public, so be it as long as they tip well. Besides, the staff usually have much more pressing issues with which to concern themselves—their own affairs, for example.

Before coming to work at Baciare, I'd seen plenty of affairs behind the scenes in various restaurants and been part of a few myself. As far as I was concerned, a restaurant without some kind of ongoing soap opera was an anomaly. But no restaurant ever came close to approximating the kind of steamy, volatile passion I saw at Baciare, which also won points for the sheer creativity of its staff in finding places and time to fulfill their desires. Within the first few months of its operation, this restaurant had as much of a reputation for its "scene" as for its food. Weekend nights, especially, became festivals of consumption on every level. The word *orgy* often sprang to mind. There were so many pairings that it soon became impossible to keep current with the various players. On any given night, there were trysts planned in the kitchen and consummated in the linen room, kisses stolen at the bar and on the cocktail patio, relationships starting and marriages ending. All of this heat made for an explosive atmosphere, and almost everybody got into the act, from the managers to the busboys. But perhaps the best way to describe what went on is to provide an illustration, the "dish," if you will, from the menu of an average night.

✐ ✐ ✐

Consider the scene: It's a Saturday evening in early summer. The sun hangs low over the ocean, coloring the water with a million blue diamonds. The restaurant, which has a prime view of the Pacific and the lightly swaying palm trees along the beach, prepares for a busy dinner. In the kitchen, a prep cook chops carrots, zucchini, and red new potatoes. Another ruthlessly hammers several pounds of steak into tenderness.

Behind a cage, the two dishwashers take their meal break. Because he can't find a clean fork, one dishwasher is eating a caesar salad with a steak knife. Very carefully, he spears the lettuce on the tip of the knife and slowly places it in his mouth. The other dishwasher has given up on silverware altogether and is eating chicken with his hands.

Tonight there is rabbit on the menu, so one of the line cooks is in the kitchen stuffing several rabbits with rosemary and garlic before he ties them to the rotisserie for their final ride. After the rabbits come the chickens, whole and stuffed to bursting with herbs and still more garlic.

In another corner of the kitchen, the sous chef, Mario, cuts an entire Pacific salmon into fillets. Using a swordlike knife from his own personal collection, Mario expertly slices the three-foot salmon in half and plucks the bones from its pink flesh. Diminutive and intense, Mario works fast and says little. He looks up from his task only when he hears the sound of the time clock punching the staffers in and out. His bright blue eyes scan the kitchen quickly to see who has come on shift and then, not finding the one they're searching for, drop back down to the fish.

Stefano, the executive chef, consults with the pantry cooks on the state of the desserts. He watches as they sprinkle cocoa powder liberally over the trays of fresh tiramisu and inspects a tray of the same that has seen better days. Although he leans in toward the dessert as if he's actually going to do something, Stefano rarely touches the food. Most nights his chef's whites remain spotless, which, considering that the kitchen averages five hundred dinners a night, is quite a feat.

In a tiny office off the kitchen, the managers have their daily conference, which basically entails sitting around, gossiping to each other in Italian, and drinking several demitasses of espresso. They insist on at least an hour alone to do this without interruption from any staff members. Rome might burn to the ground and still there they would be, blithely fiddling away.

The last two members of the lunch crew prepare to leave. They look bedraggled and tired and stand in the kitchen staring into space, gnawing on discarded crusts lying around the bread station.

"When's this torture gonna be over?" one says to the other.

"Five minutes," responds the other, checking his watch. "And I don't care if the openers show up late, I'm leaving. Fuck 'em."

As he speaks, the night crew begins arriving for work. These waiters and waitresses are showered, fresh, clean, and perfumed.

I must make a brief note about style here as it pertains to waiting. Waiters and waitresses don't get much leeway in this area when they are required to wear a uniform, so some become quite creative in finding ways to make the most of their physical attributes. In this restaurant, the uniforms were designed with old Italian waiters in mind and consisted of a jacket, pants, and tie. One waitress put darts in her work jackets so that they tailored her torso. Combined with her skintight black pants, this made her look like some sort of futuristic cyberbabe on assignment from the future. A less outrageous touch employed by various waitresses involved wearing a black bra under the white shirt so that the design of the undergarment was just visible enough for the imagination to run wild.

Waitresses also got creative with hair design and a variety of sparkly clips. Some of the waiters spent quite a bit of time on their hair, too, making liberal use of gels and sprays. Although facial hair was highly discouraged, some waiters experimented with sculpted goatees, moustaches, and sideburns.

Makeup, as Belinda had once shown me, took on a whole new meaning as well. Every waitress carried lipstick in her jacket pocket and reapplied it throughout the night, using butter knives as makeshift mirrors.

And of course, we all wore earrings of every imaginable design. I began experimenting with earrings early in my wait-ressing career. I found that if I wore fish earrings, I would invari-ably sell more fish, earrings in the shape of grapes or bottles equaled greater sales of wine, earrings in the shape of pasta— yes, I actually own a pair—were always noticed and invariably spurred orders for pasta.

In effect, the uniform was the costume for the night. What waiters and waitresses did with that costume and the body within it became a form of subliminal advertising. And as fright-ening as it seems, this kind of advertising really works. For example, if I was tired and wanted the table to leave, I'd try this one: "Would you like dessert or coffee?" and subtly shake my head no as I said it. At least seven times out of ten, the customer would say, "No, I don't think so. Just the check." Nodding helps in the reverse situation as well: "Would you like to see the wine list?" nod, nod. "Why, yes," the customer would say, "I think we will."

But now I've really gotten off the topic.

The night waiters and waitresses march through the kitchen on their way to the dining room and shout greetings at the kitchen staff before they go outside to polish silverware, straighten tablecloths, and argue with management over the sta-tion they've gotten for the evening. The busboys straggle in, pick at the leftover staff meal, and sigh heavily before checking to see which servers they've been assigned to for the night.

The two hostesses also arrive at this time. The first to enter is Maggie. Not constrained by any dress code, the waifish Maggie is wearing spike heels, fishnet stockings, and a clingy black mesh dress. Her hair, done up in a complicated chignon, begs to be released in a fit of passion, which, in fact, is likely to happen tonight because Maggie, not yet twenty and already married to someone she can't stand, is having a red-hot affair with Mario. Maggie heads over to Mario, who sends her a smouldering look over the salmon. The two whisper for a moment and then she strides out to her podium, where she will reign over the reservation book for the next six hours.

"*Porca miseria,*" Mario says to himself as he watches her retreating back. Mario is completely besotted with Maggie and can't stand not being able to show his feelings. The general consensus is that he's going to blow up at some point soon. The hope is that he won't be in possession of one of his many knives when this happens.

The second hostess to arrive is Kathy, bigger, louder, and much less graceful than Maggie. Kathy is dressed in a frumpy sweater, a too-tight skirt, and pantyhouse that have already started to run. She looks as if she's going to work in an office. Unlike the hush that greeted Maggie's arrival, Kathy is hailed with catcalls and whistles, all of which she seems to enjoy.

"Hi, guys," she says, smiling, and heads immediately to the office, shutting the door behind her. Stefano, noting Kathy's arrival, leaves the tiramisu sitting near the sink and follows her into the office.

By five o'clock, the entire crew is present and on the clock. In all, there are over thirty staff members working, ten of whom are servers.

In the dining room, the late sunlight streams through the windows, creating a mini heat wave inside the restaurant. In the display kitchen, sauces are steaming, mushrooms are simmering, and rabbits are turning over a large open fire. Fire, in fact, is everywhere: there are two wood-burning ovens, a mesquite grill, and fifteen gas burners all going full blast. The smells of garlic, onion, balsamic vinegar, and olive oil waft through the air. At the bar, a healthy happy-hour crowd has gathered and the alcohol is flowing, creating another kind of warmth. One of the bartenders flirts with the cocktail waitress while the other sets up martinis.

"Go stand in the sun and turn around," he tells her. "I want to see if you're wearing thong panties."

"You're a dog," the cocktail waitress says, but she complies with his request anyway.

In another corner of the restaurant, a clot of waiters and waitresses have formed around the computer, where they place their orders. Because the space in which they've gathered is so small, their bodies touch, bump, and rub against each other. David stands behind Sarah and puts his hands on her hips as she attempts to enter the order for Table Seven. He sniffs her neck. "Mmm," he says, "I like your perfume, honey."

"I don't have time for this, David," Sarah says. "Hands off."

"Come on, baby," David says and starts rocking her back and forth.

"David, I'm busy!" Sarah snaps. "And anyway, weren't you gay last time I checked?"

"No, honey," David says without releasing her hips, "I'm bisexual. I sleep with gay men *and* straight men."

"Can we save the sweet talk for another time?" interjects Frank, another waiter. "I've got a party of six I need to put in here."

"No sweet talk," David says and gestures toward Sarah. "She's saving herself for Gino."

"Shut *up*," Sarah says. "Go make trouble somewhere else, David." Frank and David exchange a meaningful look. Sarah completes her order and stomps off just as Gino arrives at the computer.

"Go talk to your girlfriend," David says to Gino. "She's in a bad mood tonight."

"What are you talking about?" Gino says and nervously spins his wedding ring around on his finger.

A thick line of diners gathers at the podium. Sheeplike, everyone in town wants to eat at exactly the same time. Within a matter of twenty minutes, the restaurant is full. Waiters and waitresses run an endless maze, which goes from the table to the bar to the pantry to the kitchen and back to the table again. The pace escalates along with the noise, which is now a low roar made up of conversation, clinking, sizzling, and Italian pop music. Both managers have emerged and stroll through the dining room, greeting customers and putting out various fires, which come in the guise of questions and demands. For example:

"Why is the kitchen so slow?"

"Can you delete this steak from my check because I meant to order a lasagna?"

"My busboy spilled water on Table Six and they want to see a manager."

"Can I leave first tonight?"

"I can't find any forks/spoons/knives/plates. . . . Yes, I've looked everywhere."

Vito, the elder of the two managers, is somewhere between Julius Caesar and Tony Bennett in looks and demeanor. Charming and sly as the proverbial fox, he has the ability to inspire trust from men and lust from women. He has already worked his way through affairs with one waitress, one cocktail waitress, and a hostess. The restaurant, in effect, is his henhouse to guard.

The younger manager is Giancarlo, recently reincarnated from a position as a waiter. Although Giancarlo aspires to receive the same respect as Vito, his lame efforts as a waiter are too fresh in the recent memories of the staff to inspire much of anything except a low-grade contempt.

It's getting hotter on the floor. Several waiters and wait-resses have begun to perspire and have the shiny look commonly found in print ads for cologne and underwear. Intermingled now with the smells of food are the various scents worn by the staff and the ambient fragrances worn by the customers.

At the grill, Frank and Sarah wrestle over an order of calamari.

"This is my order," Sarah says. "See, here's my ticket." She holds up a shredded piece of paper that has been soaking in a plate of red sauce next to the squid.

"No, my love, it's definitely mine," Frank says. "I've been waiting twenty minutes for this piece-of-shit order." As he speaks, Frank dips his hand into the calamari and shovels a few hot pieces into his mouth.

"You're a pig," Sarah says, "and it's still mine." She turns to the bemused grill cook, who has been watching the proceedings with great amusement, and says, "Whose order is this?" To inflame Sarah further, the grill cook shrugs and raises his eyebrows. "Look at the ticket," he says.

"It's mine, isn't it?" says Frank. "I'm taking it." Two more pieces of squid disappear into his mouth.

"No, *pinche puto*," says the grill cook. "You take it, Sarah."

"Couldn't you have said that before he ate half of it?" Sarah says, making an instant enemy out of the grill cook, and marches off with the rapidly cooling calamari.

Mario comes out from the back of the kitchen and stands at the line, expediting the orders as they come up. Maggie breezes by him with menus and customers once, twice, three times. Finally he grabs her arm as she walks back to the podium and whispers something in her ear. While he has his head turned, several cooks nod and wink at each other. Moments later, in the middle of the dinner rush, both Maggie and Mario disappear for several minutes. As if on cue, Vito immediately takes Maggie's place at the door and assists with the seating.

Gino and Sarah are standing at the pantry, waiting for salads. "What did you tell him?" Sarah asks Gino.

"Nothing," says Gino.

"Then why did he say I was saving myself for you?"

"I don't know," Gino says. "It doesn't matter, anyway."

"It matters to *me*," Sarah says angrily.

"Sshh," Gino says. "Are you going to make a scene now?"

"Would it *matter* if I did?"

"What's wrong with you tonight?" Gino says, wounded. "Do you have your period or something?"

"Lord, help me," Sarah sighs and then adds, "Is this my spinach salad? I needed one with no onions."

"You want no onion?" the pantry girl snaps and dives into the salad bare-handed. She grabs a fistful of onions off the plate and flings them in the trash. "There, no onion!"

"I hate this place," Sarah says, collecting the battered salad and marching off to her table.

In a dim section of the restaurant, another waitress, Tina, is setting a table with her busboy, Jesus. The two of them lift the tablecloth high so it waves like a white sheet in the breeze and set it tenderly down on the table. She strokes his hand as he lays the forks on the linen. If they weren't wearing uniforms, they would appear to be a couple making up a matrimonial bed. Jesus has recently become the love of Tina's life. There are, however, a few problems. For one, Tina receives no end of derision from her co-workers ("A busboy! Can you believe it!") and her situation is considered laughable. For another, Jesus is married with five children.

Sarah is standing close by at one of her own tables, watching the byplay between Tina and Jesus with dismay. Jesus is also her busboy for the night, but distracted by Tina, he hasn't managed to come anywhere near her section. While she calculates how long it will take for Tina and Jesus to finish their romantic moment, Sarah takes an order from her party.

"I want the steak," her customer says.

"How would you like it cooked?" Sarah responds.

"I'd like it between medium rare and medium."

"I don't think there is anything between medium rare and medium," Sarah says.

"Well, that's how I want it," the customer says.

"OK," Sarah says and writes "medium rare" on her order pad. "Would you care for a salad or appetizer to start?"

"No, but I want a side of spaghetti instead of the potatoes."

Sarah launches into a monologue she's delivered many times before about how the restaurant doesn't offer substitutions of pasta, but if the customer wishes to purchase a half order of pasta, she'll be happy to bring it along with the meal, or he can get a whole order of pasta and she'll be happy to split it with the others at the table. Sarah has given this speech so many times before that without any interruption in her narrative, she's able to look over at the line and see that two of her orders are up, across the aisle to see that another table has been sat, and over her shoulder to see that Gino is walking toward her with two plates of scampi.

"*Voglio fare l'amore con te,*" Gino says as he goes by and Sarah doesn't even flinch.

"What did he just say to you?" the customer wants to know.

"He was just telling me that my food is ready," Sarah says, blushing.

"Do you speak Italian?" the customer asks, having now forgotten about his order.

"A little," Sarah says.

"Really?" the customer says. "So where are you from? Are you Italian?"

At his table, Gino can hear the interchange and laughs as he delivers the scampi.

Maggie has returned to the podium. Her hair is down and a little wild. She also has a generous dusting of flour across her backside. Kathy notices and brushes it off, prompting a little cheer from the bartender, who has been watching the proceedings with great amusement.

"Need any help with that?" he asks.

In the kitchen, David is taking a minibreak and helping himself to the leftover tiramisu. He eats piggishly, leaning forward so that globs of marscapone cheese and rum-soaked ladyfingers fall onto the floor instead of his jacket. Mario emerges, flushed and sweaty, from the dry storage room, where a burst sack of flour is visible, and berates David.

"Hey, *stronzo, che cazzo fai?*" Mario demands.

"It was just sitting here," David says, his words muffled by the cake. "Why can't I eat it?"

"Fuck you, that's why," says Mario.

"Ooh, baby," David says.

Sarah, Tina, and Gino enter the kitchen together and line up at the bread station. Gino grabs the bread knife first and tells Sarah, "Let me do this for you. How many people?"

"I don't need your help," Sarah says.

"*Per favore, fiorellina.* Don't be mad."

"Little flower?" Mario interrupts. "Why you call her that? Save that for your wife."

"My wife?" Gino says, dropping the bread knife and backing up. "*Che cazzo dice?* Maybe I should save it for somebody else's wife."

"I'm outta here," Sarah says and marches out of the kitchen without her bread.

"And I thought *I* had problems," Tina says to herself.

"Tina, come here, baby," says David. "I've got something for you." He begins feeding Tina bits of tiramisu, which she licks off his fingers with slow exaggerated motions. Disgusted, Mario leaves the kitchen and goes back to his post on the line.

For a very brief moment, the kitchen is all but deserted. The dishwashers carry on behind their cage, but mostly drunk or drugged (requisite conditions for the job they perform) see nothing, hear nothing, and say very little. It is within this pocket of calm that Kathy and Stefano walk into the kitchen from opposite ends, look around, and walk out the back door. Not content to settle for a place as public as the dry storage room or the linen closet (where Tina and Jesus will shortly be frantically kissing and grabbing at each other), Kathy and Stefano climb a ladder that leads to the roof. It's dark, after all, and hell, nobody's going to accidentally walk in *there*. Kathy and Stefano don't last very long on the roof. Later, Kathy will complain to Maggie that Stefano is too quick on the draw. Stefano, in turn, will complain to Vito that Kathy's breasts "hang down like two rotten pears."

As the night lengthens and moonlight replaces sunshine as the source of sparkle on the ocean, the restaurant grows even busier. A seemingly endless parade of parties seeking nourishment streams through the door, across the floor, and over to table after table. There's a raucous birthday party under way in one of the restaurant's private dining rooms. The group is made up entirely of women and the entertainment is a male stripper who has brought his own music and who, for a grand finale, sets his G-string on fire.

"I'm hot tonight!" he exclaims, and the women shriek with laughter and too much white zinfandel. Every time their waiter, Frank, appears at the door with food, water, or wine, the women offer him increasing amounts of money to strip as well. But Frank has five other tables and asks if he can, perhaps, join the party later?

The waiters and waitresses have begun to tire of the constant movement and start bumping into each other with increasing frequency. This leads to several arguments:

"Stop touching me. You've been touching me all night."

"What are you talking about? I don't want to touch you. I'd have better luck touching myself, thank you."

"You're in my space."

"Because you're taking too long putting that order in. What, are you writing a novel or something?"

Gino yells at Sarah that he saw her touch Frank's ass. "What do I want with Frank's ass?" Sarah says.

At her table, Tina prepares to take a wine order. Although she appears to listen intently to her customer's questions, Tina is fixated on the vision of Jesus clearing plates from a table opposite hers. Her eyes become a little glassy as she watches him stack several dishes on one arm.

"So, which one is your favorite?" her customer says. "I've had the cabernet before, but I've never tried this sangiovese."

Jesus meets Tina's gaze and the two exchange a passionate glance.

"The sangiovese is very, very good," Tina says dreamily.

"Wow," the customer responds, "you must really like that wine. We'll have it."

Across the way, Jesus stacks one too many plates on his arm while trying to keep his eyes on Tina and the lot goes crashing to the floor, creating an explosion of broken china and angel hair pasta.

"Job opening!" cries the bartender in the brief silence that follows the crash and all his bar patrons laugh uproariously into their drinks.

At the pantry, Gino is arguing with the pantry girl over a half-melted dish of ice cream. "I can't take this out," he tells her in Italian. "It's disgusting."

"You're too slow," she answers in Spanish. "It's been sitting there for ten minutes. It wasn't melted when I put it up."

"Please, my love, make me another one. Please," he begs in Spanish.

"Forget it," she says and puts up another dish of ice cream for Frank. Very casually, Gino places Frank's ice cream on a liner plate and walks off with it. Frank appears at the pantry moments later and studies the dish of melted ice cream.

"Is this mine?" he asks the pantry girl. "Why's it all melted?"

"*Hijo de puta*, Gino!" the pantry girl shrieks and runs off a stream of curses in rapid Spanish.

"You know what?" Frank says, placing the melted ice cream on a liner plate, "I don't understand a fucking word you're saying, so I'm just going to take this ice cream and fuck off, but if it comes back, don't fucking blame me!"

As Frank delivers his soupy ice cream, telling his table that it's a special Italian blend and that's why it's so soft, Giancarlo walks around the restaurant with a copy of the seating chart in his hand. It is at this time of night that he wields the most power, deciding who will go home and who will stay to close. Several waiters and waitresses make slicing motions with their hands across their necks, imploring to be cut. David wants to go out dancing. Frank is planning to go out with his party of women. Tina begs another busboy to close for Jesus, who says nothing, opting instead to shrug and raise his eyebrows.

"You two," Giancarlo says, pointing to Gino and Sarah, "you close tonight."

"But I've only got two tables left," Sarah whines.

"What's so bad?" says Gino. "We can leave together."

The action at the door slows. Waiters and waitresses begin giving their tables to Sarah and Gino. Sarah inherits an angry couple from Tina's station. They've been waiting to order for several minutes while Tina's been busy trying to arrange her exit with Jesus.

"I'm so sorry about the delay," Sarah says to their pouting faces. "Your waitress is leaving and I'll be taking over now."

"Yeah, terrific," the man says. "Can we just order a bottle of wine already?"

"Sure," Sarah says and hurries to the bar to get their Chianti. The bartender, however, is conspicuously absent from his post.

"Hey," Sarah calls out to the empty bar, "I need a bottle of Chianti *now*." When nobody appears at the bar, Sarah steals a glance at her unhappy table. She can almost see the smoke rising from their ears. She sneaks behind the bar and rummages around in the wines, unable to find the bottle she needs. Now frantic, she heads off to the wine room, hoping that she'll be able to find the bottle in question.

Stumbling into the darkened wine room, she almost trips across the bartender, who is seated in front of the cocktail waitress, who is doing a slow striptease for his pleasure. In the dim light, Sarah can see the outlines of some particularly lovely lingerie.

"Oh no," Sarah sighs.

"Do you mind?" the bartender says, somewhat snappishly.

The cocktail waitress hurriedly buttons herself up.

"I don't believe this," Sarah says. "Can you hand me a bottle of that Antinori, please? I don't have time for this."

"Why are you so pissed?" the bartender says, reaching behind him and grabbing the bottle of Chianti. "It's not like you've never done anything like this yourself."

While he speaks, the cocktail waitress runs from the room. In the flash of light by the doorway, Sarah can see a crimson blush on her cheeks. Gripping the bottle of wine by its neck, Sarah is close behind her.

"Come on, Sarah," the bartender pleads to her retreating back, "it was Victoria's Secret, for god's sake . . . ."

Sarah's couple is fuming by the time she arrives back at the table. "So what did you have to do, press the grapes?" the man asks as she uncorks the wine and pours.

At his table, Gino is whistling. He is waiting on a party of four who are asking him about steak and veal chops. Gino knows that if they order these items, he will be stuck with them for at least an additional hour.

"I'm so sorry," Gino says. "We have only pizza and pasta left."

"Whaddya mean?" his customers ask. "You've run out of steak? How's that possible?"

"Busy night, *ragazzi*," Gino says. "But our pizzas are very good."

"Yeah? Which one do you recommend?"

By the time he's finished with them, Gino has not only convinced his customers to order three pizzas to split between the four of them, he's also talked them out of appetizers and recommended a place down the street for dessert.

Frank rounds up everybody who's left on the floor to go sing happy birthday to his party of wild women, prompting several excuses:

"I can't sing."

"I'm too busy."

"My throat hurts."

But Giancarlo is adamant about the singing. "Everybody goes," he says, "*Vai a cantare*." Everybody trudges over to the private dining room. Frank leads, like some sort of parallel universe Pied Piper, holding a piece of tiramisu with a sunken candle sputtering on top. The song, when it comes, is grating and hideously off-key. "*Tanti auguri a te*," the waitstaff sings. "*Tanti auguri a te. Tanti auguri, carissima, tanti auguri a te*."

The women clap and screech. In the middle of all this sound and fury, Sarah turns to Gino and whispers in his ear, "You won't leave without me, will you?"

Gino finds her hand with his own and lightly runs his fingers across her palm. "*Amore mio*," he says. "Of course not."

As the restaurant begins to clear out, the temperature within drops by several degrees. Gino and Sarah scramble to feed their last few tables so that they, too, can leave. Sarah's Chianti couple is considerably happier after receiving their entrees in record time. Gino's table ravenously slices into three hastily prepared pizzas.

The smell of garlic still hangs in the air, but added to it now are the scents of the beach and night-blooming jasmine wafting in from the open doors. Vito sits down at a vacant table for a late dinner and is joined by the chefs and hostesses. Most of the other cooks are sitting in an enclosed space behind the restaurant, smoking and comparing notes on how the night went. Aside from Sarah and Gino, the remaining staff have begun to move in slow motion.

Tonight there are no last-minute diners. Sarah and Gino finish within minutes of each other and take their paperwork to Vito for his signature. Vito winks at Sarah and tells Gino to get a bottle of champagne from the bar. Gino obliges and brings the bottle to Vito.

"It's for you two," Vito says, winking again. "Go. Have fun."

One by one, the rest of the staff leave. Maggie goes home to her husband, Mario to his knife collection. Stefano and Kathy head to an all-night diner. Vito is the last to leave, after shutting down the restaurant's computer system and turning off the lights.

In the parking lot, four cooks are sitting on their cars drinking beer. The pantry girl and a prep cook dance a merengue to the music echoing from a boom box on the ground. Vito watches as he unlocks his car and starts the engine. Laughing to himself, he backs out of the parking lot and drives home.

True, this scenario seems somewhat unbelievable, yet there is virtually no writer's embellishment in my telling of this tale. And while it was extreme in the quantity and quality of its peccadillos, Baciare was only one of many restaurants that hosted such drama on a nightly basis.

Until I came to work at Baciare, I'd always accepted an underlying sexual current as part and parcel of restaurant work.

After all, part of the thrill of my very first waiting job in the luncheonette was that it was inextricably connected to my first romance. Almost all my future waiting jobs confirmed my belief that food, sex, and the restaurant were a combination as established as peanut butter and jelly. But before Baciare, I never sought to figure out why. Now, after years witnessing, and occasionally participating in, scenes of love and lust between the main course and the dessert, I've formulated a few theories.

To begin with, many of the affairs I've seen conducted in restaurants were of an illicit nature, with at least one of the participants married or otherwise attached. Low self-esteem aside, I have difficulty believing that many men and women seek out relationships destined to be so difficult. I believe, rather, that the attraction restaurant workers so often seem to have for each other stems from the fact that they have similar personalities. As described in detail earlier, servers are a unique breed. They are addicted to a certain element of risk: every night is a bit of a gamble, both monetarily and situationally. They are gregarious: every table is a captive audience, waiting to be entertained, fed, and satisfied. They are creative: the job is literally impossible without the ability to think creatively on one's feet. They are athletic: not *athletes*, of course, but the feeble need not apply. And servers seek stimulation of every kind: the restaurant is a constant kaleidoscope of color, sound, taste, scent, and movement. Put a large group of these types together and add the frantic pace of a busy night, and you're bound to generate a charge or two. But there are other ingredients besides the gathering of kindred spirits that make up the kind of lusty fare so often served in restaurants.

For one, no matter how large the restaurant, servers are literally on top of each other several times a shift. Physical contact is unavoidable when four people in a small space are vying for the use of one computer or reaching for the same bread basket or climbing over each other to grab their drinks from the bar. Being on the short side, I've often been literally overlooked by swiftly moving coworkers and have been bumped, smacked, and pushed. Regardless of whether the contact is accidental or intentional, servers touch constantly and attempting to protect one's personal space soon becomes futile.

In addition to being in close proximity with each other's bodies, servers also freely share their emotions with their coworkers. Because the job is so often tense and stressful, servers, who might be much more reserved and calm outside the restaurant, often vent their anger, frustration, or anxiety at each other. Little things, both negative ("I know you stole that fork from my table, you swine, I hate you, you're evil . . . ") and positive ("Thank you so much for taking the food out to Table Ten, I love you, you're wonderful . . . ") loom large in the space of a frantic moment. In this way, servers expose themselves to each other in a very fundamental way and become, in every sense, quite close.

Then, of course, there is the atmosphere. Heat, movement, food, and drink all mix together to form a heady glow and provide perfect kindling for the flames of ardor. This is an irresistible combination for some, who simply get swept away in a tide of sensuality. To put it less poetically, a little slap and tickle in the middle of a busy shift is just plain exciting. Adding to the edginess of it all is the fact that time is limited (one has to make the most of every second), discovery is a strong possibility, and nobody knows your little secret (actually, everybody knows, but the *illusion* of secrecy is very strong).

It is my belief that this atmosphere is also absorbed and processed by customers in an unconscious way. The racier the behind-the-scenes activity, therefore, the racier the mood at the table. Sarah's customer, for example, probably had no idea that Gino had said, "I want to make love with you," as he walked by her table, but he clearly perceived the tension between the two and it altered his entire mood. Perhaps customers simply feel more comfortable letting go of some of their inhibitions when they sense the currents eddying around them. This was certainly the case at Baciare. For a long time, the restaurant hosted a non-stop party from the back of the house to the front.

Certainly part of the bacchanalian atmosphere of Baciare was due to the Italian element. All of the managers and at least half of the waitstaff actually hailed from various cities in Italy. In fact, one of the bartenders, not an Italian, often complained that all a prospective employee needed to get hired was a baggage tag from Alitalia Airlines. As a result, the primary language inside Baciare was Italian, spoken almost exclusively by the managers and understood by only a select few. (Although some of my non-Italian coworkers stubbornly refused to attempt even a primitive understanding of this language and insisted on mispronouncing menu items, among other things, I took advantage of what I considered a free education. After only a few months at Baciare, I had a better working knowledge of conversational Italian than of the French I'd studied in school for six years.)

While the rigorous authenticity of the Italian experience inside the restaurant very quickly led to the formation of Italian and non-Italian camps within the staff, the customers loved everything about it. Some women literally swooned when their Italian waiter spoke to them in his native tongue. A waiter, in fact, could sling the rudest epithets at these customers and receive not only adoring glances, but very healthy tips. My personal favorite among these was the waiter who, at Christmastime, told his tables, *"Buon Natale, e cadi de la scala!"* and received gushing thanks all around. Would it have mattered if his customers had known he'd told them "Merry Christmas, and fall down the stairs!"? I think not. After all, he spoke the language of love.

The owners and managers of Baciare took full advantage of the ongoing love affair their customers had with all things Italian, including the selection of their own dates from the waiting list. Often as guilty of various indiscretions as their staff, the managers actually encouraged blossoming affairs and followed developments with interest. This free-for-all attitude most certainly contributed to those wild nights on the floor.

But alas, the course of true lust is often a rocky one. Although the atmosphere at Baciare remained at a feverish pitch for quite some time, there were eventually enough explosive events to cool it considerably. Angry husbands and wives started showing up at the restaurant looking to exact revenge on the lovers of their errant spouses. There were tears, threats, and some very ugly scenes. One wife, for example, almost pulled the hair out of a hostess's head after mistaking her for the waitress her husband was sleeping with. In the end, more than one marriage was incinerated in the flames of infidelity.

And unfortunately, sexual desire on the job sometimes leads to sexual harassment. Sadly, many of the waitresses I've worked with over the years, myself included, have accepted a certain amount of sexual harassment as an occupational hazard and have fended off advances, comments, and thinly veiled threats that would constitute an instant lawsuit in any other job. But sexual harassment has traditionally been very difficult to prove. For a waitress, especially, filing a complaint of this nature spells the end of her income. To protect themselves, managers and owners won't fire the waitress but will employ one of the oldest management tricks in the book, which is to schedule the waitress for the worst shifts in the worst stations. Her income will soon be whittled away to virtually nothing, and she will have to quit and move on. Until recently, the attitude about sexual harassment among waitresses I've known was grin and bear it or get another job. Nevertheless, the nineties eventually caught up with Baciare, and after a couple of quiet out-of-court settle-ments, management was forced to rethink its informal "anything goes" philosophy. One manager actually went to the other extreme in his views and threatened to suspend any staff mem-bers who were fooling around with each other anywhere within a five-mile radius of the restaurant.

I worked at Baciare long enough to see an entire turnover of staff, front and back. The tone of the restaurant changed some-what over this period of time. This is to say that, on a given night, one wouldn't necessarily find couples consummating their desires in the linen room, dry storage, *and* the bathroom. Rather, one might only stumble upon the cook and a waitress necking in the stairwell or wait on one couple who refused to order because she was too busy sucking his neck and he was too busy feeling his way under her blouse. So, while it was toned down, there was still plenty of heat at Baciare if one knew where to look. And Baciare, as previously mentioned, was not—is not—an anomaly.

As a final note, I must mention that not content to rely solely on my own experiences in this particular area, I conducted an informal poll of several waiters and waitresses who have worked in restaurants all over the country. I asked these fellow servers if they thought temptation and desire burned just a little brighter in a restaurant, and if they did, could they provide a story or two to back them up? I got more than I bargained for, as every one of these people had several tales to tell. Among these, my favorite came from the very same waiter friend with whom I watched that provocative film so long ago.

"I'd had a great night at my place," he told me. "I'd made something like three hundred dollars in tips. It was very late and I wound up at this all-night pancake house. So, I'm talking to my waitress and she's really cute. I've got all this money and I tell her, 'I'll give you seventy-five dollars right now if you give me the panties you're wearing.' "

My friend paused here to enjoy his memory of the details.

"Well," I asked, "what did she do?"

"She was kind of stuck on the logistics of the thing for a minute," he said. "She asked me how she was going to give them to me in the middle of the restaurant. So I told her, 'Haven't you got to-go boxes here?' "

"And?"

"And she brought 'em out in a to-go box for me and I gave her the money."

"You know," I told my friend, "only someone who had sex on Table Fifty could get away with something like that."

"Yes," he added, "but I actually ended up seeing this girl seriously for about a year after that. It turned into something. You just never know."

Ah, yes. Sex and food. Food and sex. Together, a potent combination. Dinner never tasted so good.

# "hello, i'll be your postfeminist icon this evening"

**Answer:** Several Triple X-rated websites.
**Question:** What comes up when *waitress* is
typed in on an Internet search?

**It's a Saturday afternoon** and I'm standing on line in a
department store coffee shop. A couple stands next to me, pondering the sandwich menu. The line moves slowly and soon
they've made a decision about what they're going to eat. They
glance over at me. A flash of recognition is quickly replaced by
puzzlement in their faces. I know who they are, but they are
completely clueless as to my identity.

"Hello, how are you?" I ask them, smiling.

"Great," the man says, "how are you doing?"

"Terrific," I respond.

"It's funny running into you here," he says. He's fishing,
hoping I'll say something or give some sign of who I am.

"I like this place," I tell him. "They've got great coffee here."

"Yes," he answers. I smile again and look toward the front of
the line. The man's wife leans in close to her husband and whispers desperately, "Where do we know her from?"

I can see him struggling with the dilemma. He has a whole set of feelings set off by seeing me, and I watch them pass across his face one by one. He knows I'm not one of his friends or acquaintances, because if that were the case, he'd surely know my name. But he also senses that he has a peculiarly intimate relationship with me. I know things about him, he thinks. What is it that I know? What is the context in which I belong? For the life of him, he just can't grasp it.

I could help him out. He's correct in assuming I know things about him. I know that he and his wife raise horses. I know where they live. I know his name. I know that his wife will always want to know which specials are good and ask for a detailed description of each one. I know that no matter what the specials are, she will always order the roasted chicken. She will always have her vegetables on the side. I know that he will begin every meal by ordering a bottle of mineral water, one liter, no gas. I know that I am not allowed to bring the mineral water until he asks for it, even though I know he will order it. I know that he likes to finish his meal with a decaffeinated cappuccino and a bowl of strawberries with crème fraîche on the side, but again, I must wait for him to ask for it and pretend that this is the first time he has ordered it this way. I know that he will ask for the check after he finishes the cappuccino and that he will let it sit on the table for ten minutes. After that period of time I will pass by and he will take out his credit card, lay it on the check, and ask me to add one more decaf cappuccino to his bill and bring it along with the receipt for him to sign. I know that his wife will stand up before he does and begin strolling toward the door. He will wait for me to come and pick up the check. And then he will thank me.

Yes, I could make it easier for him. "I am your waitress," I could say. But I don't. I have been waiting on these two for years. They always leave a good tip, and while they are strangely quiet most of the time, they are relatively low maintenance. Recently, they have even started smiling at me once in a while. I must assume, therefore, that I am doing a good job at playing my part. And my part is determined not so much by how well I perform my job but by how close I am to the image of *waitress* that these two have in their minds. I've played it so well, in fact, that they are completely unable to attach an identity to me outside of the restaurant. The relationship is working well. Why ruin it by telling him who I am?

And who am I, exactly? How close is my real identity to that assigned me by this customer or any other who sits down at my table? It is my feeling that these questions factor into every customer-waitress encounter. I am referring now specifically to the waitress and not the waiter for two reasons. The first is simply that as a woman I am limited to a female point of view. The second comes from my belief that there exists in our culture a specific image of the waitress in particular.

This image has morphed somewhat over time yet has retained certain key elements. The waitress is decidedly blue collar but usually street-smart and frequently sexy. She is definitely an independent working girl (or woman); still, she is often quietly glamorous and mysterious. But the waitress also brings food and provides nourishment. She "takes care" of her customers, placing herself in a motherly role. Put sexy *and* motherly together and you've got a powerful package indeed. And although it is only my opinion, I believe that the waitress is as much a postfeminist icon now as she was a prefeminist representation years ago.

Have I gone too far? Assuming for the moment that art imitates life, a quick look at popular culture supports my theory that there is not only a common view of the waitress but an enduring fascination with her. The Internet is full of references to her either in little odes that various authors have penned to her, in sites dedicated to her role, or in the above-mentioned adult websites.

The waitress has also been featured in a variety of commercials and advertisements, in which she has sold paper towels and long-distance phone service, lobbied against cigarette smoking in restaurants, and displayed cosmetics. Songs have been written about her and she has given her title to at least one band, The Waitresses, of the 1980s, who knew "what boys like."

Perhaps the clearest image of the waitress as a popular icon, however, is in Hollywood's version of her through a variety of films and television shows that feature her in a leading role.

The character of the waitress is a popular one, appearing in films from the 1930s on. For the purposes of both clarity and brevity, however, I've chosen a selection from the time period between 1970 and the present, a span I felt would most succinctly reflect the evolution of this particular woman's role.

I had seen all the films and TV shows I'll present here when they first appeared. But in order to get a better sense of how the image of the waitress had changed over time, I watched all of them again within a short space of time. I'd expected to find the films of the nineties reflecting the feminism of the seventies. What I found instead was that while the trappings had changed (and the waitress uniforms had become more comfortable), the view of the woman who was a waitress remained essentially the same.

Before I begin my abbreviated study of the waitress on film, let me offer a disclaimer or two. I make no claim to critical greatness. The plot summaries and subsequent analysis I'll offer here in no way reflect any one film's greater themes or artistic merit. For that I must defer to those who've had considerably more experience. I am, however, a waitress. As such, I can allow myself the liberty of judging how closely these films portray *me*. Ultimately, the heart of my argument is a personal one. That said, let's begin at the beginning.

### Five Easy Pieces (1970)

Jack Nicholson plays Robert Dupeau, a pianist who has run away from his talent and his cultured family to work as an oil rigger in a dusty California town. He lives with his girlfriend Rayette (Karen Black), a waitress and aspiring country singer in burnt orange polyester. Rayette is crude, emotionally dependent, and dumber than a sack of hammers. Dupeau is absolutely faithless and often abusive, but Rayette, sweetly and helplessly in love with him, keeps coming back for more. For his part, Dupeau tells Rayette that if only she would never speak, everything would be fine. When he learns his father is dying, Dupeau drives up to the Pacific Northwest to visit his family, reluctantly taking the now-pregnant Rayette with him.

Even those who have never seen the film know the famous diner scene that follows. Dupeau's memorable interchange with his waitress is one of the most indelible in film history. Trying to order a plain omelette and a side order of toast, Dupeau encounters total resistance from the waitress (Lorna Thayer), who refuses to offer any substitutions on menu items. Ultimately, Dupeau tells the waitress (quite brilliant in heavy mascara, blue eye shadow, and more burnt orange clothing) to hold the chicken in rather a tender place and is summarily tossed out of the diner. He never does get his toast. Ultimately, Dupeau runs away once more, deserting Rayette and all that she represents, without a word.

### Alice Doesn't Live Here Anymore (1974)

Ellen Burstyn won an Academy Award for her portrayal of Alice, a housewife whose abusive husband dies, leaving her and her precocious son to fend for themselves. Alice gets some work as a lounge singer in Phoenix, where she hooks up with a man (Harvey Keitel) who seems all right until he turns into an abusive lunatic. Alice and her son hightail it out of town to Tucson, where she is forced to take work as a waitress (a prospect that completely disgusts her at first) in Mel's Diner. After struggling awhile with her new role, Alice warms to life in the diner and to her coworkers, smart-talking Flo (Diane Ladd) and oddball Vera (Valerie Curtin). Still, she needs a man, and this time Kris Kristofferson plays the customer in shining armor who comes to her rescue. Things start seeming like they're going to work out for Alice as soon as this relationship is on track. By the end of the film, in fact, Alice even defends her job as a waitress to her son, claiming that she has supported both of them on her tips.

### Alice (1976–1985)

This long-running TV sitcom took its premise and characters from *Alice Doesn't Live Here Anymore*. Like the film, the series depicted the blue-collar lives of the characters in and around Mel's Diner. Like the Alice in the film, too, the Alice of the series (Linda Lavin) waits tables while she pursues her dream of making it as a singer. Single parenting, working women, and their relationships were all popular topics over the course of the series' run.

### It's a Living (1985–1989)

A small group of waitresses (Crystal Bernard and Ann Jillian among them) working in a swank restaurant on top of a high-rise were the featured characters of this TV sitcom. Adding to the mix was their neurotic manager, who had a long-running comedic romance with the chef, and a lascivious piano player whose main job was to hit on and be rebuffed by all the waitresses.

### Cheers (1982–1993)

Given the wild popularity and phenomenal run of *Cheers*, a description of the series is probably redundant. I've included it here because of the immense appeal of its characters and its depiction of two very different waitresses: Diane Chambers (Shelley Long), the intellectual whose on-again, off-again romance with barman Sam Malone was followed with avid interest by a huge viewing population, and Carla Tortelli (Rhea Perlman), her much-married, tough-talking foil.

### Frankie and Johnny (1991)

Michelle Pfeiffer plays Frankie, a beaten-down waitress in a New York City restaurant. Al Pacino plays Johnny, the ex-con short-order cook who falls in love with her and tries to win her in this paean to loneliness. Early on, a fellow waitress dies, sick and alone. None of the other waitresses (a familiar mixture of smart talkers and eccentrics) want to end up this way. Frankie, uneducated and with a long history of abusive relationships, can't see much of a way out. She is a tough survivor but destined to live an unfulfilled life. Again, salvation comes in the form of a man. When Johnny breaks through Frankie's tough exterior and reaches her tender core, there is finally a ray of hope.

### Gas Food Lodging (1992)

This film, written and directed by a woman (Allison Anders), features more lonely waitresses looking for love. Brooke Adams plays Nora, a woman who is raising her two teenage daughters alone in a trailer in New Mexico. Nora works as a truck-stop waitress with a somewhat miserable existence. Deserted long ago by the father of her children, Nora has recently given up a long-term relationship with a married man. Her eldest daughter, Trudi (Ione Skye), has problems of her own, having drifted into promiscuity after a brutal rape. Following in her mother's footsteps, Trudi drops out of school and ends up waiting on tables as well, until an unplanned pregnancy forces her to leave town. The younger daughter, Shade (Fairuza Balk), is not yet as jaded as her mother and sister and remains a romantic believer in the power of true love.

## Untamed Heart (1993)

Marisa Tomei plays Caroline, a golden-hearted but unlucky-in-love waitress in Minneapolis. When weird busboy Adam (Christian Slater) saves Caroline from being raped by a couple of ruffians, the two develop a sweet but doomed relationship. Adam, alas, is sick, and his ill health truncates their loving relationship. Like every other waitress on film, Caroline is lonely and searching for love. What makes this film sadder than others, though, is that she actually finds some happiness in love for a while, only to lose it.

## It Could Happen to You (1994)

Based on the true tale of a New York policeman who split his lottery winnings with his favorite Yonkers waitress, who helped pick the numbers, the real story is enough of a fairy tale, but this film takes it one step further. Bridget Fonda plays Yvonne, the waitress, who's been done wrong by her no-good husband (Stanley Tucci). He's charged up her credit cards, forcing her into bankruptcy. Despite a heap of personal trouble, though, she tends to her customers like a ministering angel. Nicolas Cage plays Charlie, the cop with a heart of gold who can't come up with a tip for her after paying for two cups of coffee. He promises Yvonne a half interest in his lottery ticket if the numbers come up, which, of course, they do. Rosie Perez plays Muriel, Charlie's harpy wife, who is as bad as they are good. She wants all the money, and ultimately, she gets it. Again, it's love that saves. Even when Charlie and Yvonne lose their fortune, their newfound love for each other buys them both admission into "happily ever after." (A key point proving that this is obviously fantasy: Yvonne buys the coffee shop when she gets the money, deciding she wants to be a waitress forever. The film gave rise to a question commonly asked of waitresses: "If you won the lottery, would you buy this place?" Buy the place? I'd venture to say that most wouldn't even eat there again.)

### Heavy (1995)

Aptly titled study of the characters who frequent a dive bar in upstate New York. Overweight introvert Victor (Pruitt Taylor Vince) works as a cook with his mother, Dolly (Shelley Winters), who owns the place, and Delores (Deborah Harry), the slutty, chewed-up waitress. Dolly hires lovely Callie (Liv Tyler) as the new waitress and Victor falls for her on the spot. Truly sweet and good-natured, Callie shows Victor attention and affection, prompting him to fantasize about becoming her savior.

### As Good as It Gets (1997)

Jack Nicholson is Melvin Udall, an obsessive-compulsive writer with several chips on his shoulder. Helen Hunt (who won an Oscar for this role) is Carol the waitress, devoted single mother, all-around nice person, and the only one who will put up with Melvin's nasty wisecracks at the table. Melvin can't eat unless Carol serves him, but he soon finds himself needing her for more than breakfast. When he offers his help by arranging medical care for her sick son, the fiercely independent Carol reacts first with wariness and then with gratitude. Ultimately, with the help of Melvin's gay neighbor Simon (Greg Kinnear), the two embark on an unusual journey into romance.

Over almost three decades, the portrayals of waitresses on film are more striking in their similarities than in their differences. What is most surprising to me, however, is that the characters in the early films seem to have not only a stronger sense of self but a more feminist outlook than those in the later films. Again I feel compelled to qualify: I claim no expertise in the area of feminism. Let's not forget that I always thought those Playboy bunny outfits were cute and that I longed to live in Barbara Eden's genie bottle. I've never really worried much about what my role was as a woman in modern society. Whether due to circumstance or the nature of my own personality, however, I've learned that a certain independence of spirit is as necessary as a strong survival instinct to carve an identity as an individual (and as a woman) and not somebody's girlfriend, mother, or wife. It was this kind of aware-ness that I expected to see reflected in film characters of the nineties. Instead, these women/waitresses seemed less liberated emotionally and spiritually than their predecessors.

In my mind, there are only a couple of explanations for this shift in view. The first, that the common conception of women in general has now gone back to some Dark Ages prefeminist notion, I dismiss out of hand. The second explanation seems much more reasonable: that our collective vision of the waitress has, in fact, descended into some murky and decidedly unliber-ated depths. To support this view, it is necessary to present a few specifics of these characterizations.

I'll begin with a quick study of an ever-popular topic: sexual-ity. With very few exceptions, all the waitresses here are intensely sexual beings, bordering, in some cases, on the wanton.

Rayette, in *Five Easy Pieces,* uses her sexuality to hold Dupeau, assuming quite rightly that this is perhaps her only asset. The title character of *Alice Doesn't Live Here Anymore* has no qualms about freely expressing her sexuality, either. Over the course of the film, she's seen in bed with three different men. Waitresses continue to smoulder on screen with *Frankie and Johnny,* which gives Michelle Pfeiffer's Frankie the opportunity to redefine passion in a series of sexy scenes with Al Pacino's Johnny. Nora of *Gas Food Lodging* is imbued with the same easy sexuality. She gives up a long relationship with a married man, resigning herself to loneliness in order to set a good example for her daughters, but she is soon under the covers with a new bedmate, offering him a detailed explanation of what pleasures her. The character of Delores in *Heavy* takes this type of sexual ease to its furthest extreme. Used up, bitter, and denounced as a slut, Delores has had an affair with her boss's husband, a few of her customers, and even attempts to seduce the hapless Victor in one of the film's most uncomfortable scenes.

Even the sweet, fresh waitresses of *Untamed Heart* and *It Could Happen to You* have been around a bit and bring their sexual awareness into their relationships. In the case of *Untamed Heart,* Caroline gently instigates physical contact with the shy, awkward Adam. In *It Could Happen to You,* Yvonne is shocked to learn that Charlie has been with only one woman. When their relationship becomes sexual, it is she who takes the lead.

The character of Carol in *As Good as It Gets,* while arguably more complex than others on this list, is given similar attributes. Although this is the only film presented here that is devoid of an actual sex scene, Carol's sexuality is implicit in her actions and dialogue. After a date early in the film, she is, if not passionate, certainly sexually available, and later she openly laments the lack of physical affection and love in her life.

Finally, there are those sitcom waitresses. The fact that television won't allow nudity or scenes of an explicitly sexual nature matters not when it comes to the portrayal of sexuality in wait-resses. The red-hot passion between Diane and Sam in *Cheers* was one of the series' strongest draws, and Carla's numerous lusty encounters were as much a part of her character as her well-aimed verbal barbs. There's no point in pretending that the waitresses in *Alice* hadn't been around the block a few times. Their relationships (which were as much a part of the series as their pink uniforms) were all of a decidedly sexual nature. As for the waitresses on *It's a Living,* the salient memories for those who watched the show mostly involve what the characters wore (little low-cut dresses) and how they looked (all very attractive). The prominent role of piano player Sonny, who consistently tried to score dates with the waitresses, seemed to serve the sole pur-pose of reminding the audience of their sexual appeal.

Sexuality, however, is merely one in a long list of qualities that these imagined waitresses share. Another common theme is that of loneliness and, by extension, the need to be rescued emotionally. In almost every case, the loneliness and attendant need are caused by the absence of a man—which is somewhat ironic given the fact that all of these characters have endured varying measures of abuse at the hands of the men in their lives. Abuse, in fact, seems an incon-trovertible aspect in the lives of these waitresses. Consider the film version of Alice, for example, first married to an abusive husband, then involved with a psychotic suitor. Still, Alice needs a man in her life and will keep pining for him until the right one comes along to rescue her. An even clearer example is found in *Frankie and Johnny.* The physical abuse that Frankie has taken from her ex-mate is so severe it has left her unable to bear children and terrified of rela-tionships. Her fear causes her to distance herself from men despite overwhelming loneliness, yet it is again a man, Johnny, who ulti-mately provides relief and salvation. In fact, despite verbal abuse, no-good husbands, even rape, these women cannot be whole and cannot find personal fulfillment without a man.

This is not to say that the women portrayed here are not independent. Rather, the opposite is true. Several characters support not only themselves but their children on their tips. They are quite obviously women who work hard and who can take care of themselves physically. Even Rayette of *Five Easy Pieces,* the most emotionally dependent character here, maintains the instincts of a survivor. However, the emotional helplessness present in every one of these waitresses undermines their physical independence and dictates an immutable need to be saved. This notion is perfectly illustrated in *Heavy,* where Victor's fantasies of becoming Callie's savior intrude into his gloomy reality, inspiring him to take steps toward becoming her romantic hero. In turn, Carol's need and vulnerability force Melvin to become a good man for her sake alone in *As Good As It Gets.* It seems clear that all these waitresses really *need* to be rescued. And in almost every case, the right man ends up coming along just in the nick of time.

If these arguments aren't convincing enough to elicit a recognizable profile, let me throw a few more common elements into the mix. With the exception of Diane Chambers in *Cheers* (whose character, I might add, was never a very good waitress), the women in these films are largely uneducated. Those waitress uniforms, according to Hollywood, have very blue collars. This is not to say that the women portrayed here are stupid. In fact, they are all possessed of generous street smarts, are able to tirelessly match wits with any number of smooth-talking customers, always have a quick comeback to any comment, and often have true insight into the human condition. There is not, however, an intellectual in the bunch. Despite her knowledge of his true nature, Rayette is a mental midget compared with Dupeau. Frankie is intimidated by Johnny's superior intellect. Caroline aspires not to advance her education but to complete beauty school. Even Carol, perhaps the most evolved woman in this group, needs spelling help when she writes Melvin a letter.

The inference can be made that if these women were better educated, they would definitely not be working as waitresses. At the very least, they wouldn't be working in *these* places, a collection of greasy-spoon diners, dives, and questionable coffee shops. Of course, *It's a Living* did offer waitresses in the context of a fancy white-tablecloth restaurant, but one has only to look at the series title to ascertain its view of waitressing in general. It is merely a living. This probably explains why there is such a shortage (in least in what my research has turned up) of waitresses in film who have attended or are attending college, who are simultaneously pursuing other careers, or who have any kind of intellectual life involving more than what's written on their order pads. A waitress who is not mired in her job due to limited skills and education doesn't fit the common conception. And although all the waitresses here are looking to get away from their jobs (even in fantasy, nobody wants to consider waitressing a permanent career), their avenue of escape involves the help of a man and not their own resources.

There is one final, singularly important characteristic common to these waitresses. One doesn't need to look too closely to see that they are all possessed of hearts of gold. No matter how tough the exterior, every waitress here has a soft, nurturing center. No matter what blows fate deals them or what states of distress they might find themselves in, they are consistently kind, even motherly toward their customers. Frankie reminds her customers to take their medications. Yvonne nurses the spirit of a customer with AIDS. Callie lavishes attention on social misfit Victor. These are only a few examples. Every film I've mentioned here has at least one scene that exposes the kindness and innate tenderness of these women.

It is this aspect of the waitress that signifies her greatest appeal. For without this quality, the waitress becomes not only useless but annoying. Consider the waitress in that famous diner scene in *Five Easy Pieces*, for example. Uncaring, inflexible, and definitely not nurturing, she is completely unappealing and becomes an object of derision not only for Dupeau but for us as well. We cheer Dupeau as he sweeps the water glasses off the table in disgust. All he wants is some toast, after all. How difficult is that? Perhaps that is why this scene, just one of many brilliant moments in the film, has become such a memorable one. It doesn't matter what decade we're in, it seems, or what changes have occurred in women's roles, offscreen or on. We still need our waitresses to feed us, take care of us, and give of themselves with all the power of their eighteen-karat hearts.

In all honesty, I have never seen myself in any of these characters. And perhaps the majority of the people I've served haven't seen these films. However, it seems possible, even likely, that all of us have been influenced in some way by elements of the common profile I've presented here. Long before I thought to trace a common cultural view of the waitress, and by extension of myself, I experienced examples of this influence in my own life.

Many years ago, my father, who as an ex-waiter and father of four waitress daughters has always been excessively kind to his servers, got into a knotty situation with a waitress in a restaurant that my family often frequented. There was a special that night on pepperoni pizzas. Two large pepperoni pies cost less than two large cheese pies. Since my family is vegetarian, my father ordered the special and asked the waitress to hold the pepperoni. When the check came, my father noticed that the waitress had charged him for the more expensive cheese pizzas. He pointed out to the waitress that she'd charged him incorrectly, but she wasn't having any of it. We'd eaten two large *cheese* pizzas, she claimed, and that was the price. My father laughed a little and then proceeded to try to explain the ridiculousness of the situation to her. Again she couldn't be convinced and offered to get the manager. My father told her that it wasn't necessary, he just wanted her to *understand* what he was trying to say.

At this point, most of my family had filtered out of the restaurant except for me and my sister Maya. We watched as the waitress became first irritated, then flustered, and finally angry. When at last it seemed she was completely unmovable in her stand, my father said to her, "Let me ask you a question. Have you ever seen that movie *Five Easy Pieces?*"

Maya and I fled immediately from the table. We *had* seen the movie and we had no desire to hear him tell the waitress where to hold the pepperoni.

Much more recently, I had the following conversation with a friend I've known since we were both nineteen.

"I've just seen the greatest movie," she said. "You have to see it. There's a character in it who reminded me so much of you. She could *be* you."

"Which movie?" I asked her, immediately intrigued.

"*As Good As It Gets*," she answered.

"And why is the character so much like me?"

"She's a single mom, like you," my friend said. "And she's really devoted to her son—just like you are."

"And?"

"And her kid's sick a lot. He's got asthma, like your son."

"My kid's not sick a lot," I told her.

"Well," my friend said, "she's a *waitress*. You've really got to see it. You'll know what I mean."

The only thing I really understood after seeing the film was that by virtue of the fact that I was a waitress who also happened to be a single mother, I had become, for this friend who had known me almost twenty years, interchangeable with a fictional character with whom I had absolutely nothing in common save for those two features.

The fact that, for my friend, my identity was so closely linked with this concept of *waitress* leads me to believe that it must be an even stronger image for those I wait on—those who don't know me at all. Or do they?

On the face of it, I do seem to share some of those unique waitress qualities. I've been through a few relationships, to be sure. And like most of the waitresses on film, these relationships have started at, near, or around the table. Did I choose and stay in this job because these were the kinds of relationships I wanted, or was the quality of these involvements dictated by my waitress status? That question will most likely continue to be a conundrum. I'd rather try to figure out which came first, the rotisserie chicken or the scrambled egg. I can say, however, that I've never looked to be rescued. I've never had Al Pacino preparing my orders. Instead, I had Leo. And Kris Kristofferson has never sat down at my table and offered his services as savior. Rather, I had Steve of the tossed quarters and bungalow kisses. Nor did Jack Nicholson walk into my restaurant and offer to provide my son with medical care. No, I had Dominic telling me when to potty-train and what to feed my child. A film tells me, "It could happen to you." Quite frankly, I don't think it could.

I am also a single mother and I've supported myself and my child on tips for many years. But rather than feeling forced to work as a waitress to make ends meet, I've mostly felt that this particular job offered me the most free time to spend with a child who was already missing one parent. As for that nurturing, motherly aspect of the waitress, I've no way of gauging whether or not I possess it, save for the reactions of my customers. I've had satisfied customers and customers who really liked me. I've also waited on people who seemed to hate me on sight. I've never had a customer offer me a half interest in a lottery ticket. On the other hand, I've never refused to serve a side order of toast and a plain omelette. And nobody, to date, has ever told me where to hold the chicken.

Most of my success at the table has been determined by how much personal information I've been willing to give out. And by personal information, I mean not only details of how much school I've attended, how many children I have, or whether or not I am married, but also my willingness to take an active interest in the lives of my customers while they are at my table. My ability to take care of my customers in *this* way speaks to my personal ability to nurture, to live up to the predetermined expectation my customer has of me.

This is why, when a woman at my table whispers, "You don't need to worry about me, I've been a waitress before," I know that she is referring to much more than just the job in question. She is implying that she knows *me*, her waitress, on a much deeper level. And this is also why the customers I met in that department store coffee shop had no idea who I was. Outside of the restaurant, I *had* no identity. I was out of my environment, but more important, I was out of character.

I never did explain who I was to that couple. I did, however, wait on them again. The next time I saw them, they gave no indication that they'd run into me anywhere else. When I approached their table, the husband smiled and asked me, "Will you be serving us tonight?"

"Yes," I replied. "I am your waitress."

# still waiting

**When I was hired at Baciare,** I had no idea that it would become my longest stretch in any restaurant. My main goal, at the beginning, was to escape from the chaotic atmosphere of Hoover's and provide myself with a more stable working environment and a steadier income. Baciare satisfied all of those needs so well that I was soon celebrating my first anniversary there, then my second, then a third. This was the first time I'd experienced anything so close to permanence in a waiting job.

Before Baciare, I'd never stayed at any restaurant for very long. The reasons for this were as varied as the restaurants themselves. The nature of the work, as I've stated previously, lends itself to transience, and this was certainly a factor. But sometimes the job itself was seasonal, or the restaurant couldn't support me, or I'd moved. In any case, I'd begun every waitressing job with the feeling that it would be temporary. Like so many of my fellow servers, I never saw waiting as the end, only a means to it.

Because I'd moved around so much before Baciare, I found the stability it provided comforting at first. But as the months stacked up into years, I began feeling uneasy and stuck in my job. Uneasiness was then replaced by dissatisfaction and finally depression. In short, I was experiencing a common waiting malady: burnout.

I've seen many burned-out servers in my day. Although they manifest in several different ways, the signs of burnout are quite visible, especially to fellow servers and managers. Usually the victim of burnout has simply been waiting on tables for too long or possibly has overstayed his welcome at a particular restaurant. Once well into burnout, there is little the waiter can do to alleviate his condition. Good tips don't help and neither do vacations. As long as that uniform is hanging in the closet waiting to be donned for the next shift, the waiter will continue to sizzle, crisp, and fry.

Servers burn out for similar reasons. As I did, many find themselves suddenly wondering where all that time went and why they are still working a job that was meant to be only a temporary source of income. Some develop a general intolerance for management and start griping about unfair treatment. Often these complaints are warranted, but as the server grows more and more dissatisfied, everything becomes a personal affront. One waiter I worked with, for example, complained that he was deliberately being seated with low-tipping parties. When the manager asked this waiter which customers, in his opinion, were guaranteed low tippers, the waiter came up with the following list: old people, young people, couples with children, groups of women, people celebrating birthdays, and families. "And," the waiter added with a straight face, "they're all in my section!"

Other waiters and waitresses grow tired of the servile aspect of the job and find themselves unable to cope with customer demands and complaints. It is common to hear a server suffering from this weariness say, "I hate people," several times a shift. One fellow waiter in the end stages of burnout phrased it in a particularly visual way. "I'm so sick of watching people eat," he said. "I can't stand to see them chew anymore, to see the food in their mouths, to watch them swallow. When I look out there, all I can see is an ocean of open mouths stuffed with food going up and down, up and down."

The attitude of the burned-out server is the first casualty. And attitude, of course, is everything. Having a bad one more or less guarantees a lousy tip, and the waiter's complaints about his customers become self-fulfilling prophecies. One waiter I worked with, for example, refused to spend any extra time at a table when his customers ordered white zinfandel. This was the order of the unsophisticated diner, he claimed, and these people would obviously leave an unsophisticated tip. Why should he bother, he said; they were only going to run him around for nothing. "White zinfandel!" he spat. "Why don't they just bring in a bucket of wine coolers?" Naturally, this waiter's customers picked up on his tart attitude and, feeling offended although they couldn't pinpoint why, tipped him badly. "See?" he would say, waving the 8 to 10 percent tip in front of him. "I told you!"

Occasionally, however, it's not just the attitude of the burned-out waiter that sours. Some servers begin exacting revenge in small but meaningful ways. The waiter who couldn't stand watching people chew, for example, actually began torturing his customers. He refused to bring water to the table, even after the customers requested it several times. He would avoid the table, watching from a distance as the customers stared despairingly into their empty glasses and craned their necks looking for him. He took a perverse delight in waiting for his customers to become so parched they were almost screaming with thirst. "Why shouldn't they suffer?" he said.

Of course, this waiter was pretty far gone by the time he began pulling these stunts. Others feel compelled to try to protect their income while pursuing their vendettas against humanity. In these cases, tampering with leftovers before they are packaged to go is a particular favorite. Many times, I've seen these plates of food picked at, poked at, and dropped "accidentally" before making it into a takeout container.

Similarly, there is the practice of splitting dishes. It was policy at Baciare that no plates were to be split by the cooks. Mixing dishes up, the theory went, destroyed the integrity of the food and its presentation. Should the guest desire to split his food with others, the policy stated, the waiter should perform the split at the table. In theory, this was a good policy. It allowed the waiter to show off a little and "bond" with his customers while he made their meal more leisurely and enjoyable. However, the split policy was incompatible with another, more pressing policy, which was to pack as many tables into the restaurant as possible and turn those tables over at the speed of light. Basically, the restaurant sought to impose fine dining standards on a fast-food schedule. This put stress on the servers, which filtered, inevitably, to the customers. Many customers also rebelled outright at the notion that splits could not be done by the chef and insisted that the food not come out to the table before it had been divided. This was always a perfect opportunity for the burned-out server to release a little frustration. Thus, salads, fish, even pasta got split in the kitchen by hand. I'm speaking quite literally here—as the waiter would reach into the plate with his fingers and throw equal parts of the food onto two or more plates. Sometimes, if he felt there was enough to go around, the waiter would help himself to a small portion of the meal.

"So what?" the rationale went. "They're not going to care what I do for them. They'll probably just stiff me anyway."

There are still other passive-aggressive ways for a waitress to get back at the customers she feels are persecuting her. Revenge, they say, is a dish best served cold. Or, perhaps, scaldingly hot—which is how soup is served when a customer rudely demands a reheat. This customer will invariably receive a fresh bowl of soup that has been heated to a temperature of several hundred degrees with the express purpose of burning the skin right off his tongue.

"Is the soup warm enough for you, sir?" the waitress will say sweetly. "Because if it isn't, I can have the kitchen heat it a little more."

And then there's the coffee. There is a general rule of thumb for every restaurant I've worked in: the more a customer protests the need for decaf, the likelier the possibility that he will receive regular. This is the line that really seals it: "Is that decaf? Because I'm going to take your phone number and if it's not decaf I'm going to call you in the middle of the night when I can't sleep." (If only I had a dollar for every time I've heard this original line, I would be a wealthy woman indeed.)

The honest answer? No, it's probably not decaf. At Baciare, the busboys were responsible for brewing the coffee and keeping equal supplies of both regular and decaf available. It never worked out this way. Often, when I grabbed a pot off the burner and asked the busboy, "Is this regular or decaf?" he'd respond, "Yes." This was an area that really separated the burnouts from those with a considerably fresher attitude. The burned-out waitress assured her customer that the coffee was 100 percent decaf, or regular, or a mixture of both if need be. The fresher waitress told her customers that if ingesting caffeine was truly hazardous to their health, ordering coffee entailed a certain amount of risk.

I've included these examples in the interest of fair reporting. While not regular occurrences, these things do happen. Chances are that anyone who dines out regularly has encountered a burned-out waiter or waitress at some point and has suffered the consequences, knowingly or unknowingly. Chances are even greater, though, that the server has encountered some very challenging customers and has simply lost the ability to cope. I will say this: I have never seen waiters or waitresses punish a customer who treated them decently or respectfully or who acknowledged, even in the smallest of ways, the service they were receiving. It really does pay to be nice to your server.

Truthfully, I never sabotaged any of my customers even at the most charred point of my own burnout. What happened to me was that I stopped taking an interest in my customers, started complaining about my lot in life, and developed a generally negative aura. I stopped smiling at the table and really resented it when anybody pointed out my lack of warmth. If I felt my customers were treating me like an idiot ("Can you remember my order without writing it down? You're not going to forget that I want no dressing/extra dressing/light sauce/easy garlic/no oil, are you?"), I started using big words at the table, like *abstemious* and *misnomer*. This never went over very well, I must say. "What was that word you used before?" a customer once asked me as he scrawled in a 10 percent tip on his credit card receipt. "You'd better tell me again so I can write it down, 'cause I'm definitely lookin' to get an education from my waitress when I go out to dinner."

Inevitably, some sarcasm came sneaking through in my dialogue at the table. I knew it would come to no good. I slipped badly just once.

"How's the duck tonight?" my customer asked.

"Dead," I told him.

I don't know which one of us was more shocked at my response.

It would have been possible to limp along this way for years more, watching the gradual erosion of my attitude and sense of self-worth, had it not been for the passing of those inexorable reminders of time gone by—the holidays.

Spending the holidays at the table is a bittersweet fact of every server's working life. Bitter because the holidays are often referred to as "amateur hours," times when people who don't dine out any other time of year come to the table with impossible demands and expectations for a special experience. And sweet because the very fact that so many people are dining out almost guarantees a big payday for the server. Each holiday has its own unique flavor in a restaurant, and there is much to be learned about human nature in general just by watching the way people act on each one of these days.

Allow me to elaborate.

I'll begin with Valentine's Day. There is so little love in evidence on this day of lovers it's enough to inspire cynicism in the most romantic of hearts. Rather, couples trudge out to lunch and dinner with a sense of duty to some false ideal of what they think they should be feeling for each other. If this sounds too jaded, consider the following scenarios. Several times, I've seen married men bring their mistresses to lunch on Valentine's Day. (How do I know that the woman is a mistress and not a wife or girlfriend? Please, rest assured that your waitress knows these things.) These lunches involve champagne, sumptuous desserts, and gifts of lingerie. (The mistress always gets lingerie for Valentine's Day. The wife, on the other hand, usually gets jewelry.) I've seen the very same men bring their wives in for dinner on the same day in the same restaurant.

If this isn't enough to harden the heart, there are always the couples who choose Valentine's Day to argue viciously over dinner. On any given Valentine's Day (and by my calculations, I've worked at least a dozen), I would find at least half the couples in my section fighting with each other. Naturally this makes taking an order very difficult, but what's worse is that there is no way these couples are going to enjoy themselves. And no matter what the nature of the argument, it always ends up being the waitress's fault.

The couples in deep-freeze mode are the most challenging. These couples exchange not a word with each other throughout their meal yet manage to direct vitriolic darts at their waitress every time she comes to the table.

Then there are the couples who select Valentine's Day to propose. This is a powder keg of a situation. What if she says no? (I'd love to include a tale or two of a woman proposing here, but I've never seen one.) I've served engagement rings in champagne glasses and on top of desserts and had to stand by to make sure that the unsuspecting recipient didn't end up swallowing two months of her date's salary. I have to say that this little scene never plays the way it does in the movies. Unfortunately, the rest of the scenery doesn't fade into a soft-focus glow leaving the happy couple in a spotlight of love. Rather, there is noise, embarrassment, and, sometimes, disappointment. I'll never forget the deer-in-headlights look of the woman who received her diamond ring in a glass of Dom Pérignon. She became pale, nervous, and a little desperate. When her would-be fiancé went to the rest room, she pulled me aside and whispered frantically, "He wants me to *marry* him. What am I going to do?"

Servers, as I mentioned before, are under tremendous pressure to facilitate the perfect experience on Valentine's Day. If the evening doesn't go as planned for the customer, the server is often held responsible. And because the rest of humanity also has a reservation for dinner on this night, servers are also under pressure to turn over their tables as quickly as possible. This is sometimes a monumental task, considering that most couples want to linger over their heart-shaped dishes for as long as possible. Most of the servers I've worked with don't mind working Valentine's Day. Usually they've seen enough to adopt the same cynical attitude I've outlined here. And in the absence of true love as defined by this holiday, nothing provides comfort like a large amount of cold cash.

The same comfort does not extend to Mother's Day, the mother of all restaurant holidays, a day feared, reviled, and hated by servers everywhere. Waiters and waitresses prepare for Mother's Day like soldiers preparing for war. For weeks before this particular Sunday in May, servers attempt to find ruses to avoid working it. Their cars break down, they are deathly ill, they have to fly home and have already bought plane tickets, they are so sorry, but they just can't work it. Before I had Blaze, I found working Mother's Day difficult. After I became a mother, however, I found it absolutely loathsome. "Why do I have to work?" I'd ask my managers, "I'm the only mother in this restaurant. Don't I deserve a break?" The answer was a resounding no in every instance. At Baciare, in fact, management posted a note in the kitchen in early April stating, "Everybody works Mother's Day whether it's your shift or not. No excuses will be tolerated." Every restaurant I've worked in has counted Mother's Day as its single busiest day of the year, with a guaranteed nonstop flow of business from opening to closing. So why do servers dislike working it so much?

Let me count the reasons.

**M** is for the menu, difficult to make, impossible to serve. There is just no way any kitchen can simultaneously prepare one hundred orders of eggs at a time. Brunch items are the most delicate of restaurant dishes and the easiest ones to ruin. Anyone who has received stodgy oatmeal, cold omelettes, or burned toast will attest to this. On Mother's Day, every restaurant must suddenly transform itself into a breakfast joint whether it excels in this area or not. And over the last few years, breakfast has become a complicated affair indeed. Eggs have to be cholesterol free, pancakes made with whole grains, orange juice squeezed fresh to order. But it's Mother's Day, and the customer is the only man of woman born—nobody else in the restaurant has a mother—and he wants his cholesterol-free omelette with a side of extra-crispy bacon, hot and fresh, and he wants it *now*. At Baciare, more cooks quit on Mother's Day than at any other time of the year.

**O** is for the obnoxious attitude of the dining sons and daughters. Many diners seem to revert to childhood patterns of behavior on Mother's Day. This is to say that they are demanding, petulant, and whiny. Since they can't direct these behaviors at their mothers, although they'd clearly like to, the server is once again the target.

**T** is for the terrible tips. Undoubtedly the agony of Mother's Day would be considerably lessened were it to result in some extra money. But inevitably, one works much harder than usual and makes much less. Very few people actually want to be there at all on Mother's Day and they certainly don't want to tip. It's purgatory, no doubt about it.

**H** is for the hatred families feel for each other and the hatred that develops in all the staff members witnessing it. Tolstoy might have revised his opinion about all unhappy families being unique had he ever worked Mother's Day in a restaurant. I've heard the same arguments many times over, witnessed the same recriminations, and felt the same tension from families that were quite obviously miserable about being together. I've even heard a few mothers say that they hated this day since it only served to remind them of the mistake they'd made in giving birth!

**E** is for the energy it takes to get through a Mother's Day shift, which is more than the human body is capable of sustaining. One Mother's Day, I worked a five-table section that had four complete turns. That adds up to twenty tables, all of which were seated with four or five people—close to a hundred diners and their mothers, all looking to me to provide them with the perfect day. It doesn't matter how fresh you are when you begin the shift, by the end of it you're feeling beaten emotionally and physically.

E is also for the effort management puts into making the server's life as miserable as possible during said shift. That familiar battle cry "I want to see the manager!" rings louder than ever on this day, forcing all managers to start Mother's Day in crisis mode. Of course, there is often good reason. Over the course of years, I've seen a few disasters. One mother was hit squarely in the head with a chair that a waitress was hurriedly moving in order to accommodate a large party. Another mother wiped out on an olive oil slick near her table and landed on her tailbone. Yet another woman received an added bonus in her organic salad: a scorpion. While the manager juggles these potential lawsuits in his head, one thought occurs to him over and over again: fire all the servers as soon as the shift is over.

**R** is for ruing the day you began working as a server, because if there is ever a day that will make you do this (and also contribute to your general feelings of misanthropy and hopelessness), Mother's Day is it. However, since this is *Mother's* Day we're talking about, let me not end on a totally negative note. There have been saving graces along the way. I have waited on some happy families and I have received some good tips. One year, I waited on two women and their daughters who wrote me a lengthy note on their check stating that I was the kindest, most attentive waitress they'd ever had the pleasure of meeting and that I had absolutely made their Mother's Day. They would always remember what a wonderful morning they'd had. They even went so far as to include me in their family photos of the day.

The holidays between May and October aren't nearly as strenuous as Mother's Day but do have their moments. Father's Day and graduations come close together in June, spurring at least one crazy weekend, which servers like to call "Dads and Grads." The same sorts of uncomfortable family get-togethers are in evidence here but with only a fraction of the stress caused by Mother's Day. Then there is Independence Day on July 4. This is usually a slow day in a restaurant, as it is one of the very few holidays that dictates people stay home and barbecue instead of dining out. Of course, I worked in a town that hosted tourists from all over the world, many of whom were as clueless about American independence as they were about how much to tip. These tourists often showed up on July 4 and wondered what the fuss was all about. Baciare, being staunchly Italian in its approach to everything, consistently refused to acknowledge any distinctly American holidays (although one Italian waiter did express a desire to see "the fireplace." Of course, this was the same waiter who believed that Superman lived in Minneapolis). This served to make July 4 a rather depressing day to work all around. Often, a group of waiters could be found standing outside, straining to see evidence of any fireworks, complaining about their own personal lack of independence.

Halloween, while not technically a holiday, is certainly worth mentioning because of the bizarre behaviors it inspires. It's long been a theory of mine that adults use Halloween as a convenient excuse to dress up in ways that reflect how they really feel about themselves on a less-than-conscious level. Thus, it was always amusing for me to see which waiters chose to don costumes on Halloween and which chose to remain in uniform. At Baciare, the Italians never wore costumes (there is no Halloween in Italy) but loved to see their coworkers in full regalia. As for the customers, it's been my experience that they generally don't share the strangely festive atmosphere. After working in costume just once and receiving exasperated sighs from my tables, I decided it simply wasn't for me. Some customers get extremely offended. A waiter I worked with dressed himself up as a Hassidic Jew one year (for reasons only he was privy to). A couple who ate at the restaurant regularly complained bitterly to the manager about his costume, claiming all kinds of indignities and stating that they would never patronize the restaurant again. The waiter was forced to resume working in his backup costume, which was that of a waiter. Another year, a fellow waiter dressed himself as a woman, complete with high heels, miniskirt, and bustier. Although he flounced around the restaurant in delight for the first hour or two of his shift, his mood turned ugly indeed when he started getting goosed, stroked, and whistled at every time he entered the kitchen. When the waiter complained that he was going to file a claim of sexual harassment, the manager looked at him perplexed and said, "You're kidding, right?"

I have been lucky enough to avoid working in any restaurant that will open on Thanksgiving, but I have worked as many Christmas Eves as Valentine's Days. Christmas Eve is an interesting shift to work. Generally, this is one of the few days of the year when the customer feels truly philanthropic toward his server. The religion of the customer matters not, it seems. For some reason—the ghosts of Christmas Past looming, perhaps—the customer feels sorry that the server has to work instead of being home with his or her family and becomes not only generous but ingratiating. I've enjoyed working Christmas Eve for this reason. And I admit I have been guilty of manipulating the situation when I saw the opportunity. Toward the end of the meal, I'd wish the customer a happy holiday and mention how anxious I was to get home to my boy (not a lie, after all). This would almost always garner me another five, ten, even twenty dollars.

The last stop on the calender is New Year's Eve. In terms of making money, this is the best night of the year to work. The cash is flowing, the atmosphere festive, the champagne abundant. This is not to say that it's not a difficult shift to work. It's always very busy, for one thing. For another, most patrons get progressively drunker as the night wears on and start becoming a little more difficult to deal with. Most, however, seek to invite their server into the party atmosphere (it's a new year for everybody, after all) and tip very well. I have made hundreds every New Year's Eve I've worked. One year, trying to cash out amid the streamers, balloons, popping champagne corks, and flying confetti, I found I had actually made too much money to count. I had to take my cash into the back room and lay it out in piles according to denomination. I'd made half my rent in one night.

There is always a spectacular party in the restaurant after the customers clear out, as well. Baciare always pulled out all the stops on New Year's Eve, busting out champagne for all the staff, playing danceable music from the sound system, and allowing for at least two hours of unbridled gaiety.

Despite the obvious advantages of working New Year's Eve, however, it was this very shift that did me in. No holiday has the same finality as New Year's Eve. Every time I worked one, I realized that I had passed still another year within the confines of a restaurant and that, in all likelihood, next New Year's Eve would find me in exactly the same place. New Year's Eve 1993 found me at the height of burned-out misery. I looked at the gold, silver, and black balloons adorning every corner of the restaurant and felt like weeping. I was approaching five years at Baciare. It was high time, I reckoned, to take stock of my life. What had I actually been *doing* all this time? What markers stood out over the passage of these years? In my review, I started with the most basic of concepts: stability.

Since starting at Baciare, my life had become more grounded than ever before and at least some parts of my future had become clearer. Those parts involved my son. My plan, however loosely shaped, was to offer him the most secure environment possible. This involved a certain amount of routine as well as some kind of financial stability. I made much more money at Baciare than I'd ever earned in a restaurant before. That in itself was enough of a draw to keep me there long after I began to tire of waiting tables.

In addition, Baciare provided affordable health insurance, a real anomaly in the restaurant business. Most restaurants rightly assume that they will have considerable staff turnover. In addition, most servers technically work only part-time. There is therefore little reason for a restaurant to spend money on health insurance for servers. The fact that Baciare offered a health plan was a large part of the reason I went to work there. Less than a year after starting at Baciare, in fact, I was faced with an unexpected need for surgery and a brief hospitalization—all of which was covered by this insurance. Had it not been, I would probably still be in debt today.

In addition to the obvious financial considerations, Baciare was an exciting place to work for quite a while. There were a hundred little human dramas unfolding on and off the floor every day. The restaurant was large enough to require a large staff, among which certain players came in and out, leaving enough of the original hires to create a sense of family. It was an ultimately dysfunctional family, to be sure, but it was family nevertheless. Besides this, Baciare's customers were certainly the most varied, colorful, and entertaining of any I'd seen before. People from a broad spectrum of society came to eat at this restaurant, bringing with them all kinds of stories and providing all kinds of experiences. There was the couple who wrote sitcom scripts, for example. These two never ate with silverware, preferring to use their (presumably cleaner) hands, and they demanded at least four baskets of bread at every meal. Then there was the family that used dinnertime as a means of torturing their son over his table manners. I watched this boy grow from childhood to adolescence in a vale of tears. There was the family that hailed from New York and had logged many summers in bungalow colonies. They remembered the terrible comedians and bad jokes that made up the acts in places like Maxman's. Every time this family came in, we waxed nostalgic about the old days. There was Deepak Chopra, a regular diner, and his not-so-regular guests: George Harrison one time, Olivia Newton-John another. During the America's Cup one year, the entire Italian team came in for pizza, bruschetta, and Pellegrino.

Slowly but inexorably Baciare became both my job and my social life. This may not seem that strange, since many people, no matter what the job, have a certain amount of social interaction there. But for me, it was a little different. When I went to work, I was also "going out." In a way, I was able to carve a new identity for myself every night. My customers didn't know that I had a child or a college education. As far as they were concerned, I could be anyone. I made some friendships among my coworkers as well. Some nights were more like scheduled get-togethers than work for all of us. I never had to go anywhere to meet people; they came to me.

At the same time, I was able to spend my days with Blaze, watching and participating in every stage of his development. Because my family was so close, I never had to put him in day care like so many other single mothers, and I didn't have to worry about meeting exorbitant child care costs.

It was the best of all worlds, really. In a way, I became very spoiled. But although I didn't realize it at the time, I was traveling a slippery slope. Ultimately, it couldn't last.

Up to a certain point, time had tended to move very slowly for me. Almost imperceptibly, things took a fast-forward trend after a couple of years at Baciare. I'm certainly not alone in my realization that life moves along much faster as you get older. But I was a little slower than most in arriving at that realization.

At first I noticed the little things. For example, I started collecting regulars. I saw some couples marry, conceive, and give birth. Then I saw the children grow. Kids I'd known as embryos were now ordering their dinners from me. I saw other couples court, marry, divorce, and come in with new partners. Then there were the couples more advanced in years who lost partners over the course of time. Learning how to offer condolences while waiting on a surviving spouse was a brand-new lesson for me.

Many customers started remembering me. I'd greet a new table, only to find that they'd been in a year before and had liked me so much that they'd requested my section again this time. "How's your boy?" they'd ask. "He must be getting big." To my look of shock they'd say, "You *are* the one with the kid, right?"

I started to lose a certain amount of the anonymity that table service had previously afforded me. This was a little difficult. Part of the draw of waitressing (for me, at least) was that every new table was a new adventure. They knew little about me, but on the other hand, I knew nothing of them. The information they provided me with was new. I'd always thought that once I had a section full of regulars, I'd been in a place too long. I was on my way to becoming a "lifer," one of those waitresses so effectively portrayed in film and television who knows exactly how you like your potatoes, what foods you're allergic to, how many kids you have, where you grew up. . . . In other words, a waitress who had no life other than the one she was living right at the table.

This notion stood out in sharp relief every time an ex-waiter came in for dinner, looking to show off his new career, and said, "Hey, I can't believe *you're* still here." As the years rolled along, these kinds of scenes became increasingly frequent. The most striking example was that of Daniel, a tall, rusty-haired busboy. I watched him graduate from busboy to food runner and then to bartender. He finished college while working at Baciare and then quit. The next time he came in, he was employed as a marine biologist. The time after that, he came in with his fiancée. Then he came in with the wife and in-laws. Finally, he arrived with his new baby son.

I could probably have ignored all of this for much longer than I did. So, too, could I ignore the passing of several of my birthdays. Playing the "how old do you think I am" game worked for a while with this one. Since my Dining Room days, customers had inquired as to my age. Actually, it was usually couched in a more politically correct way. For example, "Are you sure you're old enough to be serving liquor?" or "When you get to be my age, honey, you'll understand" (and this from people who *were* my age). So I started a little routine, asking the customers to guess my age and assuring them that they could be totally honest and I wouldn't be the least bit offended. Consistently, they guessed much lower than my actual age. I had the most fun when a couple bet each other on the number. The women always won, as they always went with a higher number. This game, where I always ended up being younger than I was, made it much easier for me to believe that time was not actually moving at all. If I looked twenty-one or twenty-two to my customers, then perhaps I could fool myself into believing that I hadn't gone for years without thinking of moving on to another line of work.

Blaze's birthdays were another story altogether. There is nothing that delineates the passing of time so distinctly as one's own child. "How's the baby?" people would ask and I'd be forced to admit that he wasn't a baby at all, but a toddler and then a little boy. Quite suddenly, it seemed, I was over thirty and my "baby" was in school. He had his own personality, his own particular needs, and he had a whole social structure made up of school, peers, and teachers that was completely independent of me.

When he began school, I found myself with several hours of free time during the day, something I hadn't experienced for six years. In the glaring light of all these hours, it didn't take long to reach the conclusion that I was doing nothing productive with my own life. And for the first time in almost a decade, I started thinking about marketable skills and how I didn't have a single one.

It was even more depressing to measure myself against my peer group. I'd reestablished contact with a few friends from my college days who were scattered along the West Coast and knew that most of them had been spending the years following graduation establishing careers. A few of them were doing quite well. Many of them had bought houses. Almost all of them had married, but none of them would even think about having children for several years. There was not a waiter or waitress among them.

Not only did I not own my own home, but the concept of having enough money to buy one was just this side of impossible. And because of Blaze, moving to a more affordable housing area was now out of the question. I was following the path of so many parents before me and living in an area that was out of my financial league because of the school district. Very early on, Blaze had demonstrated some special needs, and I was convinced that aside from private school, which was completely unaffordable, his particular elementary school was the only option.

I didn't see marriage as much of a possibility, either. My last relationship, which had fallen apart just as Blaze was starting school, had ended in such a total emotional disaster that it left unerasable scars. In my early thirties, far from old, far from finished, I came to the conclusion that relationships were just something I couldn't "do." Although it would be a few years before this notion changed from fatalistic to comfortably factual, I accepted the fact that I'd made a mess of every involvement. Every one had ended in some sort of wild emotional roller coaster, leaving me to pick through whatever damaged pieces of my psyche were left. I couldn't figure out whether this was due to character flaws (mine or theirs), unrealistic expectations, or just plain bad luck. Whatever the reason, the end result was the same. As it was, Blaze had only one parent. It was clearly my responsibility to ensure that this parent didn't fall apart and become emotionally unavailable over some man. Those days were definitely over.

And what of my career, such as it was? It had been ten years since I'd taken a "temporary" job waiting tables in the Dining Room. I was a fledgling writer, after all, and had needed the time, space, and life experiences to add to my store. Since Blaze's birth, I hadn't written a thing. I'd even given up writing in a journal, a practice I'd faithfully followed since the age of eleven. A writer who didn't write. Was there anything more pathetic than this? There were excuses, of course. I reviewed and rejected all of them: All my creative energy went into Blaze. I was busy sorting out some relationship or other. I was struggling to keep my head above water financially. What it all came down to, ultimately, was that I'd hardly put any effort into what, prior to having Blaze, had been most important to me.

Finally, there was the question of the job. Waiting tables had supported me nicely for a long time. So long, in fact, that I'd made no attempt to do anything else. Little piles of cash can be seductive indeed. Why think about switching jobs when you could consistently count on at least a hundred dollars a night and occasionally come home with over two hundred after six hours of work? And of course, what it took to get those little piles of cash was usually interesting enough to make it worthwhile.

Over time, however, there were some permanent shifts in this landscape. Business, which had been uncontrollably busy in the restaurant's early days, began to level off due to a gradual lack of novelty and a rise in competition. Then the seasons became wildly divided in the amount of income they would provide. Spring and summer were still very busy, but the winters became a bit grim. Every time it rained, the patio had to be closed, eliminating a third of the seating and at least four waiters. Fights started breaking out over who was called off the most, and disputes with management over matters of fairness became commonplace. Some of us looked to the weather as anxiously as farmers praying for their crops. Was it too cold, too wet, too windy? If so, we risked being told to stay home or, worse, came all the way in to work only to be given a table or two on the frigid patio, where we would wait on parka-wearing customers who complained about the weather and refused to tip. After a couple of these tables, we would be sent home without enough money to cover the gas it took to get there. What made the latter scenario so bitter was that management would contend that the unfortunate waiter or waitress who had come in to work in the tundra had received the benefit of a shift. Next time it rained, that waiter would stay home.

"But I didn't make any money!" the impoverished waiter would cry.

"That's not my problem," the manager would say. "You came in, didn't you? You had a section, didn't you?"

Various sections of the restaurant started receiving their own unofficial names. The patio, for example, was divided into the North Pole and the South Pole, the north end being decidedly cooler and windier. A section near the door became the Wind Tunnel. The group of tables next to the hostess podium was the Runway because it was so empty one could land a plane in it.

Winter conversations between waiters began assuming familiar patterns:

"Where are you tonight?"

"I'm in the North Pole again. This time I'm going to ask the chef to prepare a bucket of raw fish for me because the only tables I'll have are going to be full of penguins. Where are you?"

"Not much better. I'm in the Runway."

"Well, you're inside, aren't you? What are you complaining about?"

"Why shouldn't I be inside? I drive thirty miles to get here every day."

"So what, you think that means I don't have to pay *my* rent? You never get called off, come to think of it."

"Talk to the manager if you've got a problem. I'm not listening to your shit."

"Fuck you."

"Fuck *you*, asshole."

The salaried management's response to stressed-out waiters complaining that they couldn't make ends meet was less than comforting. "Do we complain when you make hundreds of dollars in the summer?" they would say. "This is a tourist town, business is slower in winter." My personal favorite was this one: "If you don't like it, you can always find another job."

With the exception of a few busy holidays, the months between November and March became more of a gamble. If it turned out to be a particularly rainy or cold winter, I'd end up losing more than just a few shifts. The lottery aspect of waiting tables began to lose much of its luster for me.

To make matters worse, the restaurant's owners decided that they were spending too much money on health benefits for their staff. Up to that point, anyone who worked over twenty-two hours a week was eligible. By switching the hourly requirement to twenty-seven, the owners were able to eliminate much of the waitstaff's eligibility. Management helped by shaving hours off the schedules of several waiters. Shortly thereafter, my health insurance was canceled.

Individually, the lack of health insurance, slow winters, and the nagging feeling of going nowhere fast were manageable, even possible to ignore. Together, though, they started creating twinges of anxiety and despair. I started feeling that something had to change but felt powerless to effect or even identify that change.

Finally, on New Year's Eve, I decided that enough was enough. I had to stop moping about my fate and take some control over it. I made a promise to myself that I would put forth my best effort to be out of the restaurant business altogether by this time next year.

By that point, I had already taken some tentative steps away from total dependence on waitressing. Using contacts I had made in the restaurant, I had begun doing some freelance writing and editing work. I unearthed the novel I'd written so long ago and started making some revisions. An attorney friend who dined in my section regularly offered me some part-time work doing billing and laying out his monthly newsletter. The irony inherent in using the restaurant to find a way out of it wasn't lost on me.

By the middle of 1994, I was frantically busy. I was in the middle of a long assignment ghostwriting an autobiography, working part-time for my attorney friend, and still working full-time at the restaurant. Individually, the only job that would be able to sustain me financially was the one in the restaurant. It was impossible to let go.

Freelance work, I quickly discovered, is catch-as-catch-can— especially for someone as new to it as I was. The client who was writing his autobiography became frustrated at the slow pace of publishing and abruptly canned his project. I wasn't having much luck generating interest in my own novel, either. And although my attorney friend was very generous, he had only limited work for me. Winter was approaching and I was back at square one.

At last, in July of 1995, somewhat later than the deadline I'd given myself, I hung up my apron forever. I tossed out all my black rubber-soled shoes and put my wine opener away in the cutlery drawer. I was finished. No more Saturday nights watching real people eat dinner while I served them. (Such was the transformation of the perceptions I'd had at twenty-two. I had gone to the table to become a real person and wound up serving that real person instead.) No more wondering whether or not I'd make my rent if it was a wet winter. I had been offered a real job with a real salary. Again the offer came through a person I'd waited on, and in this case the job was in the area of publishing. I'd hit paydirt, I thought.

My last night at the restaurant was curiously low key. In my hours of rage at the cruelty of humanity, I'd always believed I'd make a grand exit from the floor. I'd tell every annoying customer exactly how I felt and let every boneheaded manager have a piece of my mind. I might, if the circumstances were right, indulge in a fantasy common among longtime waiters and waitresses: I'd walk right out the door in the middle of a busy shift without a single word. My last night was nothing like this. Although I'd spent six and a half years in the same restaurant, nobody in management saw fit to give me any kind of send-off. My coworkers were envious. My customers were all extremely friendly and generous and some regulars wished me well and told me they would miss me. The only act of resistance I pulled was to tell my manager that I wouldn't work the closing shift, hardly the tirade I'd imagined. When I punched out for the last time, I felt strangely deflated.

There were so many aspects of my new job that I loved. I was paid to read and evaluate manuscripts, I met published authors I admired, and I was surrounded by people whose love of litera- ture had brought them all together. What's more, I was building a career. Of course, when I added it up, which I tried not to do, I was actually making less than I did working half the hours in the restaurant. And I no longer had time to do any of my own writ- ing. I took work home with me and thought about it all the time. For the first time, I enrolled Blaze in after-school day care on the days when Maya was unable to pick him up. And as for Blaze, I saw him for about three frantic hours at the end of the day before he went to bed and on weekends. Waiting tables had kept me in good physical shape. After a few months in an office, my body started looking as if it belonged to a different person—one who didn't move very often. But despite my new sedentary lifestyle, I was exhausted most of the time. I reckoned that these were necessary sacrifices to be made in the name of going some- where, doing something productive. What I chose not to think about was why sacrifices had to be made at all.

For all of these reasons, plus a few assorted others, I began a slow descent into deep unhappiness. This malaise was only exac- erbated by the notion that somehow I had failed. Theoretically, this was supposed to be a time of great personal advancement. There was therefore no reason to be feeling so unhappy other than that of a defective character. Why else would I sit at my desk and watch the waiters walking by on their way to work lunch in the restaurant below the office and feel a deep sense of envy? A few hours later, I'd watch the same waiters leaving work, their pockets full of cash, the whole day and night ahead of them, free to do exactly as they pleased. "I'm so glad I'm not doing *that* anymore," I'd tell myself and then force myself to believe it. I was doing something with my education, I told myself, shaping a future for myself in the world.

Occasionally, to reinforce these notions, I'd stop by Baciare for a coffee and a chat with my old coworkers. They'd mill about me, asking how I was doing, inquiring about Blaze. They asked about my new job and tried to hide their boredom when I described it. The bartender said I looked great in "civilian clothing." The chef told me that business had been great lately. "Don't you miss us?" he asked.

"Oh sure," I laughed, telling myself no, no, I don't miss it, not at all. How could I? Why would I?

I could have gone on like this indefinitely and perhaps turned into a very bitter, unfulfilled person who blamed the very work she had fought to get for her own misery. Because, in the end, there were no sparkling revelations. I had lost my ability to see the forest for the trees. Ultimately, it was Blaze who came to my (and his own) rescue.

While I had spent the previous months preoccupied with myself and my work, Blaze had entered his own drift into unhappiness and away from me. He had been having problems at school, both socially and academically, and had reacted by retreating further and further into a little world he was building around himself. It had been easy to whitewash over his difficulties; I never saw his teachers and I certainly didn't have time to observe him in class. It was a rough patch, I assumed. He'd done well enough the year before and he was bound to snap out of it. But one afternoon, as I sat at my desk pondering my future, Blaze simply took off from school instead of heading over to the child care center to wait for Maya to pick him up. Although an alert child care worker had spotted him and reeled him in before anything tragic happened, I got the fright of my life. My son himself had very little in the way of explanation for his actions. While he was unable to verbalize it, though, his message was quite clear: I was not paying attention, and he needed much more of my time than I'd been giving him.

I was lucky to have my priorities so carefully and completely delineated for me in this way. Blaze was still quite young and I hadn't been "away" for long enough to lose touch entirely with what was going on in his world. In a way, though, the luckiest part of the whole debacle was that I realized, once more, that the one unequivocal responsibility I had was to my child. I didn't always know if the decisions I made were the right ones, nor could I predict the future. I did know, however, that nobody could do it for me. I had to be there. I wanted to be there. This time around, there was no sacrifice at all. The decision to quit my job, therefore, was easy. The actual quitting was not quite as smooth.

My boss understood my need to spend more time with Blaze. She didn't understand why I had to leave her employ to do so. What was I going to do? she wanted to know. Where would I work? When I told her that I would probably go back to waiting on tables (I'd only met her in the first place because I'd served her lunch years before), she was horrified. I was so talented, she maintained. Did I want to spend the rest of my life as a *waitress*? What a waste.

This was nothing I hadn't thought myself many times before. This time, however, my feelings about it were much different. Waiting on tables would not be an indication of failure. Rather, it would be a way to avoid failing at the most important task I had. I couldn't afford to take time off from raising Blaze. There would be no second chances here. If I screwed it up, there would be no way of going back to "fix" it later. I had known this when Blaze was just an infant, but somehow I'd managed to let it slip right out of sight.

My wine opener came back out of the cutlery drawer. I went shopping for sturdy shoes. In short order, I got myself a job at another Italian restaurant. On my first shift, I cleared a hundred dollars in four hours. I was back.

It took leaving the restaurant business to realize how much free time I'd had while I was in it. If nothing else, my time away had taught me how to utilize those hours effectively. Because the actual time spent working outside my house was so abbreviated now, I was able to volunteer at Blaze's school every day. I was able to witness firsthand what was really happening inside his classroom and directly address the problems he was having. Blaze, for one, was very happy about the change and seemed nothing less than incredibly relieved that I was spending so much time with him. Ultimately, I spent so much time at the school over the next year that the director of special education offered me a paying job as a special education aide.

Despite the full-time waiting job and volunteer time at the school, however, I still had time to write. In fact, I began to write more than I ever had before. Several freelance jobs came my way, nicely supplementing my income. I finally retired my dead horse of a novel and wrote another. When I finished that one, I started a third. Now, when I went to work at the restaurant, I saw it as a break from the "real" work I was doing at home. As a bonus, I returned home with a handful of cash. Finally, it seemed, I was doing not only what I should be doing, but what I wanted to do.

But before I drift too far into a warm fuzzy wallow here, let me interject that waiting still held the same frustrations and minor annoyances as before. It was still a challenge to deal with rude customers and uncaring managers. It was still easy to lapse into negativity after a series of trying tables and poor tips. And, perhaps more than ever, I felt my age. Previously, I'd been either the same age or younger than my coworkers. Now, in my mid-thirties, I was a senior member on the floor. Most of my managers were younger than I and boasted fewer years inside a restaurant. I still had many nights when I could see the dawning of the new millennium and feel depressed at the thought that I might be serving champagne to partygoers at the end of the twentieth century. And what would happen, I thought, if my writing (which was now on the front burner, right next to Blaze) never translated into a living? How likely would it be that I'd be able to find a job other than waitressing at forty? Forty-five?

These questions surfaced, panicked me for an hour or two, and receded several times a week. But if nothing else, my year away from the restaurant had given me the ability to focus on the tasks at hand and avoid spinning out into a future I had much less control over. I realized, too, that it's not always necessary to know how things are going to turn out. And perhaps the most valuable lesson I'd learned was that the act of waiting itself is an active one. That period of time between the anticipation and the beginning of life's events is when everything really happens—the time when actual *living* occurs. I'd spent so much time worrying about the outcome of my life that I'd forgotten how to live it. I'd also come to know that not everything was fraught with a vast and complicated meaning. Sometimes it was only about timing the order just right, recommending a particularly good dessert, or making a friend out of a stranger at my table. I began to see not only the simplicity of these acts but also their beauty.

They say that good things come to those who wait. Finally, after almost two decades of waiting, I had arrived at a real understanding of that aphorism.

Call me a late bloomer.

# epilogue

**I'm one of those people** who always wants to know what happens in the end. It's difficult for me to read a book (particularly a good one) without flipping to the last page and sneaking a peek. I find it difficult to wait for the end even when the read is compelling. And then, when it's over, I want to know what happened after *that*. Of course, one of the main ironies of waiting, in all of its senses, is that, if you are a "waiter" (as in, one who waits), you can never really know what happens in the very end. After all, you will always find something else to be waiting for, some other end to reach or conclusion to draw. Even if the world explodes on the last page, there is always the possibility that something can happen to start everything going all over again.

So I find it particularly ironic that I am now in the unique position of skipping beyond the covers of *Waiting* and writing my *own* ending. Although there's a curious sense of finality in the act of writing this epilogue, it also seems quite fitting. *Waiting* certainly marked the end of a long life phase for me while linking it to the beginning of another. But before I investigate what looms over the next horizon, let me back up for a moment and go to the beginning of this particular end: what happened after *Waiting*.

When I began writing *Waiting*, I had several very different jobs. I was working as an instructional aide in a preschool program for severely handicapped children during the day and I was waiting on tables a couple of nights a week. My freelance editing business was operating in fits and starts as well. I'd have a month or two with no work and then be deluged with deadlines. And of course there was my son, Blaze, a full-time job in himself, but a rewarding one. As usual, my waitressing job proved to be the most lucrative, even with an abbreviated schedule at the restaurant.

I got some characteristically amusing reactions when I informed my restaurant coworkers that I was writing a book about the job and that it was going to be published. The chef, for example, responded this way:

"What do you mean, book? You are writing a book about what?"

"About this," I said, making a sweeping gesture across the restaurant. "About this job. About my life as a waitress."

"What?" the chef asked again. "Are you serious?" He smiled and wiped the edge of a splattered plate with a kitchen rag. "You are kidding, right?"

"No, I'm not kidding," I told him and took my order from the line. The chef paused for a beat or two and scratched his head.

"What are you going to say about *me*?" he asked and smiled again.

After expressing a similar sense of disbelief, my fellow waiter Franco said, "I want my cut, eh?"

"What cut?" I asked him. "Why should you get a cut of anything?"

"You write about me, no? I want my cut."

"Please," I said, shoving him aside so that I could put an order into the computer, "why would I want to write about *you*?"

"Eh? Come on, look at me." He grinned broadly, revealing a mouth full of nicotine-stained teeth, and straightened his raggedy tie in a mock gesture of vanity.

"My point, exactly," I said.

My managers were somewhat nonplussed with the idea that I was writing a book. They wavered between mild paranoia about what I might say and befuddled amusement that anyone would be interested enough about restaurant life to publish a book about it. (Of course, none of my managers actually *read* books so this wasn't an entirely surprising reaction. In fact, several of them were barely literate in both Italian and English, which explained the inadvertently hilarious items on the "nightly specials" sheet. We often had "pork lion," for example, and "veal lever." My personal favorites, however, were the "stripped sea bass" and "ravioli staffed with salmon.")

I realized that my status as resident restaurant writer wasn't exactly an elevated one when I signed my cashout one night and told my manager jokingly, "You might want to save that signature, you know, it might be worth something soon."

"Don't worry," he said, "I'll have plenty more of these before that happens."

My fellow servers were rather more excited about the book and began offering me all kinds of information about their past experiences on an almost hourly basis. There were some doozies in these tales. One server once had a manager who'd set himself on fire in the middle of the dining room. Another had waited on a party whose host hurled curses at the server for twenty minutes until another member of the group politely pointed out that the host had Tourette's syndrome. Still another server had waited on an elderly, querulous Beverly Hills matron who had passed out at the table. Since she was out cold when the paramedics loaded her onto a stretcher, they asked the server if he knew about how old the woman was. "In her seventies," I think, the server said, at which point the woman shot up from the stretcher and shouted, "Excuse me! I am sixty-five and don't you forget it!"

Although I loved all of these stories, I knew I would never be able to write about them. I knew that I was not an objective expert on restaurants, servers, or waiting, but after twenty years in the business, I was certainly an expert on my own experiences with all of the above. And it was only my *own* experiences that I could write about with any kind of authenticity. Somewhere in there, I hoped, I would strike a common chord.

Shortly thereafter, I started becoming overwhelmed with memories of the previous two decades every time I went to work at the restaurant. Since I couldn't really think about waitressing while I worked at the school or while I edited manuscripts, my waiting shifts became, in a sense, writing shifts. I found myself jotting down notes when I should have been folding napkins and drifting into reveries about my first experiences at the table when I was actually *at* the table of a patron who wanted service now and not twenty years ago. I was preoccupied and for good reason. There weren't actually enough hours in my day to keep all my jobs, spend time with my son, *and* complete the book I'd been waiting so long to write.

So, once again, I decided to leave the restaurant. This time, however, I did so assuming that, sooner or later, I'd be back. I looked at it more as a sabbatical this time and less as an escape from a trap I'd gotten myself entangled in. I had no illusions that I was going off to become some kind of literary star. In fact, my time floating in and around the book business had shown me that authors who became rich and famous from their writing were rare birds indeed. The concept of making a living from my writing alone was one I still couldn't wrap my mind around.

My last shift was lacking in any kind of fanfare. It was such a nonevent that I had to remind my manager to prepare my separation papers at the end of the shift so that I could receive my last paycheck. Nobody was particularly sad to see me go, although some were extremely envious. (There is always that whiff of parole in the air when a fellow server "gets out.") Perhaps they thought I'd be back soon. Had they given voice to that thought, I wouldn't have disagreed with them. The rate of recidivism in servers is pretty high, after all.

What actually struck me about that last shift, though, was not leaving at the end of it but arriving for work some five hours earlier. I had come up in the service elevator like I usually did and tarried behind the restaurant in the few minutes before my shift began. Back there with me were a couple of cooks sitting on overturned milk cartons, smoking and inspecting their splattered aprons. There was a busboy eating the staff meal with his hands (all the forks were still dirty because the dishwashers were on a break) and the bartender, also smoking, stocking liquor for the night ahead from the outside storage unit. I buttoned my shirt collar and straightened my tie. These were the same motions I'd been going through for twenty years and I did them without thinking. After I donned the jacket I worked in, I checked my pockets for the night's essentials: lipstick, wine opener, order pad, pen, mints, and a dollar's worth of loose change. I was joined by another waiter who, after an hour on shift, was already taking a cigarette break.

"What's it like in there?" I asked him.

"Slow," he said, shrugging. "Nothing yet. The book looks good, though. Should be a busy night."

"It's my last night," I told him.

"Oh yeah?" he answered. "Cool."

"I'm working with you tonight, *chapparita*," the busboy said through mouthfuls of chicken and gestured toward me with a greasy finger. "We're making good money."

"Okay," I told him. "Fine with me." I applied the night's first coat of lipstick using the blade on my wine opener as a mirror and checked my watch. The waiter stamped out his cigarette on the ground, exhaled the last of the smoke in his lungs, and followed me into the kitchen.

I punched my time card and all five of my senses sharpened to the immediate assault. Behind the rumbling sound of the dishwasher I could hear knives hitting meat and marble. A radio was tuned to the Allman Brothers' "Whipping Post" and the souschef was singing along loudly and off-key. There was water running and waiters screaming for silverware. The air crackled with curses in four different languages. I smelled coffee, steaming vegetables, and garlic. A busboy rushed past me with an armful of fresh bread and dusted me with a fine layer of flour. As I was brushing the white crumbs from my black pants, a sweating waitress came into view. It was only five o'clock, I noted, and already she had splotches of coffee and red wine on her jacket. Not a good sign.

"Oh, good, you're here," she said, slightly out of breath. "Can you take table forty-two? They were seated a while ago but I haven't been able to get to them because I've been slammed, but they're in your station anyway. They need bread. And they look like they're ready to order. And they're probably a little pissed because nobody's been there yet but it's not my fault." She disappeared in a whirl of bread, butter, and olive oil.

I sliced bread for table forty-two and felt a familiar surge of adrenaline through my body. In moments, I'd be out onstage again, performing my own show. Although I had a clue about how I'd be greeted by table forty-two, I had no idea what the rest of the night would bring. After twenty years, the anticipation of going out to that uncertain audience still caused a butterfly flit. There wasn't anything in the world quite like that moment of expectation, I realized. Every night, at least for one moment, I got to be sixteen again, with everything fresh and the promise of excitement just outside the swinging doors. As I prepared the bread basket for my first table, I knew I would miss that moment for as long as I was off the floor. It was a little epiphany but an important one, nonetheless. One can't really ask for more at the beginning of a dinner shift with a station already full and at least one table in a bad mood.

I finished work on *Waiting* shortly after that last shift, but the book wasn't published for a year after that. In the interim, I had plenty of time to work myself into a full-scale panic over the kind of reception it would receive. After all, there's nothing like anticipation to fuel paranoia. Once again, it was authenticity that I worried about. I didn't expect that any reader would have had the exact same experiences as I since *Waiting* is essentially a memoir, but I hoped that those experiences would echo those of the reader. In addition, I really wanted other servers to be able to relate to what I had written about restaurants and a life spent waiting.

As soon as it was published, *Waiting* proved to be an entirely entertaining experience with a dash of the absurd thrown in for good measure. Just before the book was released, I taped a segment for the game show *To Tell the Truth*. For those not in the know, this is a game where a celebrity panel questions three people, one who is telling the truth about her/himself and two impostors who are lying as effectively as possible. As my two impostors attempted to absorb my personality during the course of the day, we watched a parade come and go in sets of three. As well as we three waitresses who had written a book, there were three women who lived with a horse and three naked cowboys who sang country music. There were three plus-size models in lingerie, three female boxers, and three policemen who played in a rock band. In the spirit of the game, nobody would admit to who was real and who was an impostor. As Debra #1, Debra #3, and I were riding the elevator down to the studio, we were accosted by three medieval knights in full regalia.

"Ah, you waitresses," one of them sneered convincingly, "you never claim any of your tips."

"Yes, we do," said Debra #1 who was, in reality, a housewife who had never waited tables. "We claim all of our tips."

"Get out of here," the knight said, "you know you don't claim tips."

"And I suppose medieval knights *do*?" I said.

"You said it!" cried Debra #3, a comedienne who had actually waited tables. "What do these riffraff know?"

Soon after this, I taped a short segment for another television show. The interview was held in a restaurant and the reporter, who had not read *Waiting*, kept badgering me to admit that all waitresses spit in their customers' food. When I wouldn't, the reporter sighed heavily and, off camera, asked me to get him a fresh glass of lime soda. "This one has little black spots floating in it," he said disgustedly, gesturing at his glass. As I approached the kitchen to refill his glass, a waitress leaned over to me and whispered, "*This* is exactly the kind of person who gets his food spit on regularly."

I heard from very few of my old coworkers when *Waiting* finally hit bookstore shelves, but those who did write to me seemed to like the book very much. I heard from my friend who'd had sex on table fifty and who had once asked his waitress to place her panties in a to-go container. "I read the 'Food and Sex' chapter first," he wrote. "Boy, did that ever bring back memories. This book has to be more fun to read for those of us who were there. It makes me realize how many friends I've left behind over the years."

Shortly after this, I received an e-mail from a waitress I'd worked with who'd gone through both her pregnancies at the table. "Thank you for writing about what I've been trying to do with my family and with waiting all these years," she said.

A waiter I'd worked with for years and complained to end-lessly about the kickback-taking hostess Angela, who never seated tables in my section but filled those of the waiters around me, wrote me a letter and said, "The book was really funny. I wish you had thrown some bile Angela's way. After all, she probably cost you about five thousand per year." He was in a position to tell. Most of my loss was his gain!

By far the biggest response to *Waiting*, however, came from people I had never worked with and never met but who felt immediately familiar with me, my family, and, especially, the restaurants I wrote about in the book. Some servers wrote to me saying they were sure of the identities of the restaurants I mentioned and named a few of their best guesses. I did a guest spot on a local radio show and one of the producers told me breathlessly, "That thing with the spoons . . . I thought my restaurant was the only place that never served spoons with coffee!"

Many of the interviews I did for *Waiting* in both print and radio began with the interviewer stating that he or she had waited on tables for a number of years. All remembered the experience vividly and a few of the interviews turned into chat sessions where we shared war stories and laughed about the foibles of human nature. And when I made appearances for book signings and readings, all of those who attended were either servers themselves, had waited tables at one time or another, or had relatives who waited on tables. One gentleman asked me to sign three copies of *Waiting*, one for each of his waitress daughters. Another purchased copies for all of the waitstaff at the restaurant where he was the manager. And a third asked Maya and Blaze (who I considered my entourage and who came with me to as many engagements as possible) to sign his copy of *Waiting* as well.

There were a couple of responses from waitresses that I found quite humbling. One Seattle waitress wrote to me and told me that she had been burned out and completely sick of her job until she read *Waiting*. "I did not know how badly I needed a fresh perspective until I read your book," she wrote. "You helped me to remember that although I may not have a 'real job' I certainly have a *real life*." I met the second waitress at a book signing in New York City. "I bought a copy of your book," she said, "and all the waitresses I work with bought a copy, too. It's our bible."

Everything about the response I received to *Waiting* and the tour and interviews I did to promote it was fun, intriguing, and rewarding. It was like working a particularly profitable and pleasant shift with a huge staff of interesting and intelligent people. I heard a whole new batch of stories that could have easily happened at some of the places I'd worked: For example, a man who asked where the television was located because he'd read in a dining guide that the restaurant offered "game in season"—and a woman who ordered "the corkage" (the fee the restaurant charges to open wine the customer brings in) complete with French pronunciation, mind you, because it seemed like the most reasonably priced item on the menu.

What pleased me the most about the response I received, though, was that both servers and nonservers alike could *relate* to my experiences. Indeed, there was a commonality to those experiences that even I hadn't seen the full scope of when I wrote *Waiting*. When I read the letters and e-mails, and shared stories with people at signings, I felt that I *had* managed, at least in some way, to write authentically about those twenty years at the table. For that, I was not just happy but grateful.

Of course, there have been detractors as well (Nothing's ever perfect, is it?). I tried not to take the criticism I received too much to heart, especially when it was based on a "I didn't like it and I don't like her" kind of feeling. After countless appearances at tables where, no matter what I did, I simply could not please my customers, I had developed a slightly thicker skin. At least, I realized that sometimes it's just about chemistry. There will never be a way of pleasing everybody. There was one criticism, however, that I feel compelled to answer. There were a few comments stating that I seemed defensive and negative about the profession of table service in *Waiting* and that I felt the need to justify my years as a waitress. In one sense, this is true. I still believe that, despite the large numbers of men and women who make their living in this profession and despite the proliferation of restaurants of every kind in all parts of the country, waiting tables does not have the aura of respectability found in other jobs—even those within the restaurant itself. Perhaps this is because the job is considered unskilled—something that anybody can do—unlike, for example, the profession of chef.

While I was writing this book, in fact, and in the months following its publication, I noticed that chefs were becoming a new breed of celebrity on the landscape. Various chefs have become iconic figures for a large slice of the public, filling out a territory once occupied by very few. Chefs now have their own TV shows, bestselling books, and films about their lives. Their restaurants have become destinations on vacations, and the language and style of cooking has become its own cottage kitchen culture. Is this a profession to aspire to? Yes, indeed. But one would be hard-pressed to uncover a celebrity waitress in this revered kitchen culture. Indeed, I don't believe we'll ever see the day that we choose to travel to a restaurant because of the national reputation of its servers. I don't disagree that chefs have a job that requires both skill and talent, yet I do believe that the job of server (at least if the job is done well) requires quite a high level of skill as well. The fact that I've rarely seen this acknowledged in any meaningful way over my years at the table may account for some defensiveness.

As to the charge of negativity, I have to plead innocence. Despite its many difficult moments, waitressing has served me very well indeed. I could never have spent twenty years in a job I hated. The flexibility and kaleidoscopic range of experiences I found waiting tables allowed me the time and the material with which to write. More important, it allowed me to live comfortably while raising a child as a single parent. Really, could I have asked for much more than this? Should it turn out that I can't make a living from my writing alone, waiting tables is one of very few jobs I would consider taking. And this brings me back to the real end of this story.

I have not returned to the table since the publication of *Waiting*. This is not necessarily because I haven't wanted to but because I haven't yet had to. Other writing assignments have come since I completed the book and I've been able to support myself as a writer at least for the time being. I can speculate endlessly about the future but time has taught me that this is an amateurish exercise at best. Recently, my father (a real restaurateur at heart) began developing a concept for another new restaurant. I am quite sure that, as we have in the past, my entire family will in some form or another be involved in this project. ("What about Blaze?" my father asks. "Surely he'll be needing a job soon.") Whether I end up at the soda fountain again or scratching out notes on an order pad, I can rest assured that, in some fashion, I will be waiting. I've learned that there really isn't a true end to waiting. There is only the beginning of what comes next.